Everything in its Place Reviews

"Everything in its Place" is a document of personal and external achievement. It is an interesting blend of plain English explanation of hard science, personal anecdotes, experimentation and spiritual information. It is a remarkably appealing and inspirational document.
— **David Sands**

Highly informative insight into the mysteries of the self-healing powers of the mind. A personal, intuitive, and enlightening account of dealing with various mental health issues.
— **Vivian Waring** (author *When Tears Ran Dry*)

Through the development of a technique that allows individuals to easily access the contents of their subconscious minds and identify negative programmes they have created for themselves, Beverley has identified something very important. Demonstrating over and over again with case studies that provide compelling reading, she describes changes that occur when people identify and address the negative programmes they have created for themselves as children. The strategy she describes has been shown to transform peoples' experience of life from academic misfit, sporting incompetent and social outcast to encompass academic excellence, adoption of leadership roles and positive relationships with themselves and their peers. Fascinating reading, her work provides the basis for further investigation.

— **Neil Bennell** O.B.E.

"Everything in its Place" is well presented and insightful leaving the reader with many considerations with regard to where we are and where we could be headed. It balances both intellectual and esoteric themes with aplomb and is by far my most interesting read of the year.

— **Kerry Sweet**

Beverley has written a very well researched guide to achieving a more positive life. Everything In It's Place is filled with real life stories of individuals who have been struggling to find their way, and have put the principles outlined in this book into practice in their own lives and have found help and answers. Common sense, listening, and the ability to get to the heart of the matter, have helped many people who have come into contact with Beverley and reading this well written book may give you some answers too. Definitely worth reading and can only help the reader seeking more clarity in life;"

— **Alison Lewis**, author of *Missing* and *Seasons of Life*

Beverley is a Master Story Teller! *Everything In It's Place* is filled with timeless wisdom and helps the Reader to transform their life from victim to victor. Through her work with the Stress Defusion technique and her conversations with the Elohim, Beverley guides you as a Pilgrim on life's rich journey. Similar to Michael Singer's "The Surrender Experiment" Beverley will have you following your guidance and trusting that you are heading in the right direction through the Matrix. What an amazing journey this inspiring and competent lady has had.

— **Karen Perttula**

Final Days of Judgement Reviews

The idea that our thoughts create our reality is at the heart of *Final Days of Judgement.*

Here, Beverley, an educator, sustainable farmer and spiritual channeller. explains in simple proc how fear based thinking causes many of our personal and social upheavals.

Buckley suggests that if you act from a position of trepidation, you build the house of your endeavours on sand. Any slight movement can cause your world to collapse. Bust, she argues, those disasters may be a blessing in disguise. " Pain and suffering are wonderful teachers", she writes. Our mistakes can actually be a bridge to psychological and spiritual renewal.

Using seasoned wisdom and personal anecdotes - including stories of past lives and messages she obtained through the Elohim, or spirit guides - Buckley explores the Twelve Laws of the Universe: divinely inspired tools and gifts that can help us live with more clarity. These laws include abundance, synchronicity, duty and attraction, among others.

Buckley's argument is essentially this: the Universe is conscious and works for us and not against us. We conspire against ourselves when limiting beliefs prevent us from seeing how life flows effortlessly. Activating these 12 Laws will move you to a high level of consciousness.

Buckley's message is astute and rousing but for a few quibbles. The title *Final Days of Judgement*, though provocative, is misleading. The message here is much more uplifting and encompassing. While Buckley is a delightful writer, some] times she introduces ideas without enough set up, such as the book's beginning which lists the Laws of the Universe right out of the gate. Without more background about the book's purpose, this feels jarring and disorienting.

Overall, Buckley delivers and effective read. Fans of Jerry and Esther Hicks and *A Course of Miracles* will likely enjoy this book that argues there is a new, golden age in store for us if our minds are in the right place.

— BlueInk Review (August 2016)

Progressive and philosophical audiences will be enthralled by Buckley's unconventionality and ingenuity.

Beverley Buckley's *Final Days of Judgement* is an intriguing spiritual exploration of the origins and future of the universe, make by its passionate outpourings of ideas on what is wrong with the world and when - and how - all will become right.

The book's leading assertion is that soon, individual lives and individual pain, fear and anger will be eradicated, and the universe will return to its original state, where love is everything and everything is love. Buckley also argues that people are slowly becoming aware of this shift and are changing their lifestyles accordingly, from adopting habits like eating local and organic food, to realising that money does not equal true success.

Incorporating aspects of Eastern spirituality, Christianity, physics and environmentalism, the book is a remarkably modern and global perspective.

Whilst the doomsday title gives a dark and intimidating first impression, Buckley's brand of spirituality, though it is certainly non-traditional is more about compassion and awareness than it is about the end of the world. While it firmly predicts an overhaul as the world as we know it, the book also emphasises that the new order hinges on the absence of judgement, a notion that is the exact opposite of most end-of-the-world discourses.

Though many schools of thought are taken into account, the book often has a stream of consciousness style than it has an academic one, The interjection of supposedly channelled messages from the Elohim, god-like figures said to give Buckley's prophecy-like information about the future of the Universe, makes the book more accessible to those unfamiliar with quantum physics or chakras, but also lends it a somewhat offbeat flavour.

— **Foreword Reviews, Clarion Review (Paige van de Winkle)**

"Once the lessons are learnt, there is no need to repeat the experiences that have allowed us to learn that which we needed to learn."

Describing her own awakening and attunement to a new concept, the author of this book shares her enlightening revelations about the future of the planet and how it will affect humanity. Using wisdom that she channeled from the Elohim, the council that will guide the earth's new transition, she was given twelve laws, twelve degrees of freedom, and the message that each person has twelve core issues they need to resolve. Using her method of Stress Defusion to help both herself and others, she prepared people to move beyond fear and greed-based motivations as the increasing vibrational frequency will bring people with it out of the third dimension and into the fifth. As this transition continues to occur both in the world and its people, Buckley shares what she has learned personally and through the Elohim's law to lead others towards harmony.

With the exception of the introductory chapters that lay the foundation for the learning in this book and the conclusion that shows how to move forward after taking everything in each chapter in this book concerns one of the twelve laws. From the rules of attraction to our flawed thinking on how balance is achieved to discovering our purpose for life and existence, there is an integration of both what we an do now to improve and what we can look forward to as humanity ascends. That combination of present and future allows readers to put a plan in place immediately while working towards a long-term improvement. Providing new ideas and a message

of empowerment and ability to its readers, this is a great read for those that feel like they're stuck, in a rut, or incapable of creating change in their lives
— **Book Review by Michael Radon, US Review of Books**

Everything in Its Place

How and why we create the patterns of our lives

BEVERLEY BUCKLEY

If you would like to order copies of
Everything in its Place or wish to contact the author,
send an email to Bev.growinghealthy@gmail.com

Published in Australia by Sid Harta Publishers Pty Ltd,
ABN: 46 119 415 842
23 Stirling Crescent, Glen Waverley, Victoria 3150 Australia
Telephone: +61 3 9560 9920, Facsimile: +61 3 9545 1742
E-mail: author@sidharta.com.au

First published in Australia 2020
This edition published 2020
Copyright © Beverley Buckley 2020
Cover design, typesetting: WorkingType (www.workingtype.com.au)

The right of Beverley Buckley to be identified as the Author of the Work has been asserted in accordance with the Copyright, Designs and Patents Act 1988.

The Author of this book accepts all responsibility for the contents and absolves any other person or persons involved in its production from any responsibility or liability where the contents are concerned.

All rights reserved. No part of this publication may be reproduced, stored in a retrieval system, or transmitted, in any form or by any means without the prior written permission of the publisher, nor be otherwise circulated in any form of binding or cover other than that in which it is published and without a similar condition being imposed on the subsequent purchaser.

Buckley, Beverley
Everything in Its Place: How and why we create the patterns of our lives
ISBN: 978-1-925707-11-3
pp430

About the author

Being born female into a middle class suburban Sydney household in the 1930's meant being raised in the manner befitting a future wife and mother. Good deportment, correct speech and obedience were encouraged. Academic achievement and preparation for a lifelong career were discouraged because "a woman's role was in the home".

Life went pretty much according to the plan established for Beverley as a child, except for the fact that she earned a scholarship to Sydney University. Against the wishes of her parents, she completed a Bachelor of Arts degree, after which she drifted into the world of advertising and public relations. Later, married, with three young children she became a teacher, something she had vowed she would never do.

An upbringing like the one described was unlikely preparation for what was to follow. Having fulfilled the job description of wife and mother, and seen her three children launched into successful careers, Beverley chose to pursue the goal of finding out why some children had learning difficulties and what, if anything, could be done to help them overcome those difficulties. What she discovered was far different from what she expected. Her investigation into learning difficulties led her down a rabbit hole into a world that hitherto she did not know existed. *Everything in its Place* is the story of what Beverley discovered.

To the Elohim, my thanks and gratitude. Without the support, guidance, encouragement and direction provided by these non-material entities, it is unlikely that I would have had the courage, resilience or fortitude to follow the extraordinary journey that has been my life.

Contents

Preface		1
Introduction		3
Chapter 1	Helen's Story	21
Chapter 2	We Create our Reality	33
Chapter 3	Preparation	51
Chapter 4	Learning Difficulties Investigated	59
Chapter 5	Stress: Origins and Responses	79
Chapter 6	Eyes: Filing Clerks of the Mind	101
Chapter 7	Decisions, memories, values, attitudes and beliefs	121
Chapter 8	Strategies for handling negative decisions	133
Chapter 9	Identifying the Patterns of our Lives	159
Chapter 10	Energy	177
Chapter 11	Energy of the Body	189
Chapter 12	Emotions	203
Chapter 13	The Brain	221
Chapter 14	Identifying Issues	241
Chapter 15	Mind/Body Connection	273
Chapter 16	Energy and Health	287
Chapter 17	Past Lives	307
Chapter 18	Ending Separation	325
Chapter 19	Fake News	345
Chapter 20	Every Experience is for a Purpose	357
Chapter 21	Ancient History	371
Chapter 22	Holographic Patterns	391
Chapter 23	The Plan	409
Chapter 24	In the Beginning	419

Preface

When people ask me whether 'Everything in Its Place' is a personal memoir, my answer is that it is, but only in so far as the information contained in the book has been shaped by my life's journey.

Others question whether the book is about the development and scientific explanation of the Stress Defusion process that I developed. This process allowed me access to the contents of the subconscious minds of hundreds of people. Again, their suggestion is partly correct, because the Stress Defusion process was vital in allowing me to understand the importance of stress, the importance of emotions and the ability of individuals to create their reality. But Stress Defusion was simply the mechanism I used to access information that allowed me to see the patterns of peoples' lives and understand the process by which they create their lives to be as they are.

Some have suggested that many of the references are very old and should be updated and my answer has been that these were the sources I used to understand what I was seeing. This was the information available at the time I was developing the Stress Defusion process.

The most correct answer to what the book is about is that it is about the conclusions I reached through having the opportunity to delve deeply into peoples' subconscious minds:

conclusions related to the purpose for Earth's existence and the purpose for human life on this planet. It is about the patterns of peoples' lives, and how those patterns were created. From sharing their experiences, my hope is that you will see the connections and the patterns in your own life.

My conclusions came from applying holographic principles relating to individual life patterns to the whole of Earth's experience; over time, as far back as I, and others, through their journeys into past life memories, ventured. My investigation led me in a direction I had no intention of going to a conclusion I didn't expect: a conclusion that will, I suspect, surprise many. It certainly surprised me.

The book's information is, of necessity, compartmentalised. The coming together of the various strands didn't happen in an orderly fashion in real life. Each tiny piece of information was presented randomly and my job was to piece them all together in order to understand the much bigger picture — and to be able to explain it.

Introduction

As an adult, my life has been full of challenges and varied experiences: a stark contrast to my memories of childhood, which I remember as being intellectually and socially sterile. As an adult, I became interested in investigating esoteric ideas and for a period I regularly attended what would best be described as New Age workshops and seminars. This meant that I was confronted by a variety of ideas that expanded what had been up to that time very limited thinking and I connected with people from backgrounds very different from my own. Lee was one of these people.

Lee was an American. When I met her, she had just arrived from Alaska and had been in Australia for about two hours. I asked her what she planned to do and she replied that she had come to Australia to facilitate workshops that would help people identify their life purpose. She had no plans as to where she would stay and asked if I could suggest somewhere.

I was not in the habit of inviting strangers to live with my husband and me, but on this occasion, I did. That is how Lee's first workshop came to be held in our house and why my husband and I became participants.

Lee's workshop was about Purpose. It was not something I had thought much about. I believed that the things I did were of value to others, but, until that time, I had not considered the notion that there was an overriding reason as to why I was here on Earth. Lee thought differently. She believed that everyone had specific things to learn in each lifetime and that this was each person's 'life purpose'. Having this new knowledge or skill would equip them to contribute something of value to the world. She referred to this as a person's 'higher purpose'.

Lee planned to run a workshop the following weekend and, if I agreed, it would be held in our living room. She told me there would be twelve people attending. The workshop would last for about three hours and would consist of a talk about the participants' purpose and higher purpose, and would be followed by two meditation sessions. After the meditation sessions, those attending would know his or her purpose and higher purpose and would be able to write this down.

At 2 p.m. the following Saturday afternoon, there were 13 people, including Lee, my husband and myself sitting in our lounge room. Lee spoke for an hour or more, explaining her understanding of life purpose and higher purpose. She asked us all to close our eyes for a meditation and suggested that we ask to be given information relating to our life purpose. She told us that after the meditation we would have that information and at the completion of the first meditation we all wrote the information we had accessed about our life purpose and shared what we had written with everyone present.

I didn't understand much of what I wrote. It alluded to unfamiliar ideas. Part of the message that I had received and written down told me that my purpose was 'to remember the encoded knowledge'. I didn't know what this was. The message that came to me was that I needed to be open to all information that was relevant to changes in the Earth's vibrational shift, and to seek information available from the 'highest source'. I wasn't aware that a vibrational shift was happening on Earth, let alone who or what the 'highest source' was. Logic aside, the message felt true. It spoke to me at a far deeper level than that of my rational understanding.

During the second meditation session Lee instructed everyone to access information relating to their higher purpose. Again, everything happened as Lee said it would and, when instructed, everyone wrote down the information he or she had accessed.

Part of the information I received this time was that I would 'help people remember and understand that they have the power to heal themselves using the Atlantean crystal healing knowledge so that they could be whatever they choose to be'. Additionally, my purpose was to 'communicate the truth to those who seek to know the truth, so that they can rejoice that everything is happening the way it is meant to happen'.

As with the information I had received about my life purpose, I had absolutely no idea what this was about. I knew nothing of Atlantis, let alone Atlantean crystal healing or what truths I needed to communicate. I didn't know that anything special was happening or why people needed to be reassured that it was happening in the way it was meant to happen and I certainly had no better handle on 'the truth' than those around me.

The manner in which I had received this information was

surreal. I accepted it, although I didn't understand its significance. It simply felt true. I put my newfound knowledge aside and forgot about it; grateful because it helped me to understand why things had happened in the way they had in terms of my career path. I had always wondered why I could not rationally explain the variety of jobs I had chosen. For maximum financial reward, it would have been sensible to build on past successes, but I didn't do that. Once I gained familiarity in a particular field, I embarked on something new and often quite different from anything I had done before. In doing this, I had to start each job as a novice, rather than building on what I already knew. Once I gained a level of proficiency, I changed direction. By doing this, I was always being challenged by something new and needed to develop different skills from those I already had.

§

I often wondered whether my constant search for new challenges was in response to what I remembered as unrelieved boredom as a child. The highlight of the week was to go to the cinema on Saturday afternoons and watch *Tarzan* or *Bing Crosby*. This was before the days of television. Outings as a family were rare, with the exception of a week's annual holiday in a hotel or boarding house somewhere a couple of hours' drive from Sydney. As an adult I had no time to be bored as I combined being a wife and mother of three small children, with full-time work.

As a result of my choice of jobs I developed communication skills that I had totally lacked as a child because in my upbringing I was to be 'seen and not heard'. After graduating from university, my first job was as an advertising copywriter. I developed communication skills by working in public relations in England where I toured the country speaking to journalists, radio presenters and television show hosts. I went on to work as a teacher, in sales, and as the promoter of an Australia-wide educational program. When I met Lee, I was involved in developing a series of personal development training programs.

Following the life purpose workshop, I completed the training programs that I was working on. The people who attended the courses loved them and I was asked to develop an additional program to train trainers in the techniques I had incorporated into the original suite of seven programs. After completing that, I took on the role as presenter of the Train the Trainer program every month.

As well as developing the adult training programs, I was also testing a learning-to-learn program that I had developed for teenagers who wished to improve their results at school. These were also very popular and I was getting great feedback from the teenagers who attended.

Years earlier, I had determined that I wanted to identify the cause of learning difficulties and help children who had problems. About a year after attending Lee's workshop, I awoke one morning with a sense of absolute knowing that it was now time to start this project. Although it seemed that I had put aside my life purpose statement, it had awoken something within me at the deepest level of consciousness and this needed to be translated into concrete action. This hadn't happened immediately, because the projects I was working on formed part of the preparation that I needed to complete before I could even think about starting to investigate how to resolve children's learning difficulties.

I decided that the best course of action was to put the education strategies and techniques that I had tested in my adult and teenager training programs into practice within a school environment. Only by doing this would I be able to find out whether these strategies could be used to help children with reading and learning problems. In order to do this, I needed to find a school principal willing to try a different approach to this problem.

Accepting the challenge to identify the cause of reading and learning difficulties had consequences far beyond my initial expectation. It enabled me to access knowledge that, years later, I realised I had worked with in many previous lifetimes. Somehow, by researching and applying a range of educational and healing technologies, I brought knowledge of the Atlantean crystal healing process to conscious awareness. I called it Stress Defusion. This wasn't my original intention, which was simply to apply what I had already implemented successfully, within a more challenging environment. What developed was something very different.

Stress Defusion was not something that I learned from others, although experts in a variety of disciplines had introduced me to ideas that I needed to understand in preparation before I could 'remember' the Stress Defusion process.

Several years prior to returning to a secondary school environment with the intention of helping children who had learning difficulties, I had written the description of my higher purpose. What I wrote included the idea that my higher purpose involved re-awakening in others the knowledge that they have the power to heal themselves. At the time of Lee's workshop, Stress Defusion wasn't even a faint light on the horizon, but it was to develop into a technique to empower people to heal themselves. It is a process involving teaching people how to access information that they already have available to them so they can understand how and why they have created problems in their lives. I am not a shamanic healer. I cannot heal anyone, but I can teach others how to heal themselves.

§

Everything in its Place tells the story of how the Stress Defusion process was developed and describes how people have changed their lives by working with the process. By reading stories of some of these people, you will identify with them and know that you too can heal. When you understand that this is possible, the means will be provided for you to do as these people have done: release emotional baggage, let go of judgments and change your life. You need to do this before you can work with your higher purpose.

As I was developing Stress Defusion, I had the opportunity

to follow and document the academic progress of many of the secondary school girls I worked with once they had overcome their reading and learning problems. In the years that followed, I worked with many other children and teenagers. I never advertised what I was doing but people came because they had heard others speak of their own experiences.

The majority of children were brought to see me by their parents because they were struggling academically. For most, this was because they had problems with reading or learning generally. Additionally, some suffered from chronic illness such as asthma. Many had problems associated with being accepted by their peers. Their parents were worried about them and were looking for help.

Adults came for a variety of reasons. A few, like the children, had literacy problems. Years after I first met her, I discovered that Lee was illiterate and needed to employ a professional reader. The fact that it took such a long time for her to share this secret indicates the stigma attached to the problem of illiteracy. Fortunately, once she was able to confide in me that she had this problem, it was quickly rectified. Many adults share this problem but are reluctant to acknowledge it.

Some adults I worked with had life histories involving extreme trauma. Others had a variety of problems associated with day-to-day living. I have included accounts of what happened during and after sessions with some of these clients. Many I only saw once or twice. A minority spent months working through their problems. Some were happy to share their experiences but in doing so, I have respected their privacy.

I now know that Stress Defusion is a healing modality that I have worked with over many lifetimes. I used it in Atlantis, but its origin goes beyond that. I actually came into this lifetime with the unconscious knowledge of how it works, but it took a lot of research and learning to bring that knowledge to conscious memory. Initially, research was done to find ways to help my son, who was brain damaged at birth. Later, as a consequence of interest in the process of learning I studied a variety of different strategies designed to enhance learning. I believe that this was necessary before I could access the 'knowing' that had lain dormant. Later still, I searched for information that would help me understand how the changes I saw in people who worked with the Stress Defusion process could actually happen. Initially, I found it difficult to believe what I was seeing and even more difficult to explain it: the changes that I witnessed were totally inexplicable in terms of accepted teaching practice or Western medicine.

§

At Lee's workshop, in response to my request for information relating to my higher purpose, I wrote that I should seek knowledge from 'the highest source'. 'Channelling' is the term used for accessing information provided by tapping into what can be called 'universal knowledge'. Many people do this and there are several quite well-known books available, which explain the process in detail and provide accounts of information accessed in this way. One of the best known is *Conversations with God* written by Neale Donald Walsch[1] which was on the New York Best Sellers List for 137 weeks.

I didn't start receiving knowledge from the 'highest source' immediately after Lee's workshop. I needed time to become a clear channel so that the information I received would not be contaminated by my own negative programs. This was why the Stress Defusion process needed to be developed first. Stress Defusion helped me clear my own emotional blockages so that I could access information of high frequency. It took about five years to do this, which was when I found myself waking at 3 am every morning. I felt a strong need get up and go upstairs to my study, pick up a pen and start writing. It was as if I was a stenographer and was taking dictation, but I was not aware of the words until they were actually on paper. No thought was involved. I just wrote with absolutely no idea what word would follow the word just written. I wrote as fast as I could. As I became accustomed to what was happening, I used my computer. At the beginning of each sentence I had no idea what ideas would be incorporated. The words and ideas flowed through me without conscious thought. After an hour or so I would return to my bed and sleep until morning.

I was always surprised that, the following day, I had absolutely no recollection of what I had written during the previous night. Some of the information didn't make sense at the time, but now it does. Some of it was statement of fact that I could

---

[1] *Conversations with God* by Neale Donald Walsch Published 1995. Available free on the Internet. Made into a movie in 2006

accept. Most of what I wrote seemed practical even though it dealt with ideas that I had never previously thought about. On occasion, I was told to do something, or I was reassured about the things that were happening in my life at that time.

When I asked where the information was coming from, I was told that it came from the *Elohim*. When I received this information, I didn't know who or what the *Elohim* was. They told me that they are a group of higher beings whose role is to oversee Earth's shift to a higher vibrational energy frequency. When I asked why I was being used as a channel, they confirmed that my role in this lifetime is to seek knowledge from a 'higher source'. The Elohim was the 'higher source'. When I questioned the process, I was told:

Thoughts are picked up from the universal consciousness because of the energy radar, which is our transmitting frequency. Depending on the frequency of the broadcast signal, we pick up sound, words and pictures in much the same way television picks up sound, words and pictures. We arrange these according to existing pre-programs that we have written for ourselves.

When I asked about the changes in learning capability that I had witnessed in the children I had worked with by teaching them how to look within to access memories and emotions, the answer I received was:

When you learn to look inside as well as outside you find the meaning of life and by facilitating the power of thought from a place that is not contaminated by fear, amazing things happen. In children there is immediate change in their *ability to learn.* It increases ten-fold and what in the past has been a chore, now becomes a joy, a journey of exploration. Their physical complaints and illnesses vanish. Their athletic prowess improves. They can run, skip, throw, swim with co-ordination and strength — easily and without hours of training. Friendless children suddenly find themselves at the centre of their peers, who are suddenly attracted to them without knowing why. More importantly, their lives start to have meaning — real, deep, inner meaning which results from an awareness of the job they have chosen to do on Earth. When they are allowed to follow this path in the way they decide, even when the means they choose lie outside 'normal' practice, it will allow them to take their place as rightful leaders in this lost society, so that they too can light the torch so that people can understand.*

My observations of the children and teenagers that I worked with up until that time, confirmed this and the improvements that were immediately obvious, became more and more impressive as the years passed. Children who were unable to read or spell at the age of nine or ten went on to graduate from University and hold high-powered positions.

Over a period of several weeks, I was given detailed instructions as to how to structure a program so that I could teach groups of people the Stress Defusion process. To my amusement, I was given a marketing strategy for the program. I was told that I would train twelve people at a time and that I needed to identify twelve possible participants, write to them and invite them to do the training program. The twelve who participated in each program weren't necessarily going to be the twelve who had been invited, but my positive intent that the training would take place was sufficient to attract the people who needed to attend.

When I told my husband that I had channelled this information and that the Elohim had told me how to market the new training program, he laughed uproariously. His comment was that the Elohim obviously didn't understand how marketing worked in Sydney in 1995. He was convinced that it was impossible to get 100% acceptance. He was wrong. Each time it felt right to work with another group, I sent out twelve letters, and twelve people came. When the numbers fell away, as they did after a few years, I stopped running the programs.

§

I was surprised to be told by the Elohim that I would be moving from Sydney and that I would experience a completely different lifestyle from anything I had previously known. They gave me plenty of advance warning. My new location was described to me as a riddle. I had to find it by following my intuition. It took me about a year to identify the property that I would move to, but far longer to convince my husband that we were to purchase this place and move, but eventually this happened.

I was also given 'instructions' to fully document everything that had happened over the preceding six or seven years and describe what I had observed and what I had learned.

It appeared that this was the starting point for a book that I was to write at some time in the future. The book's title was to be *Everything in Its Place*. The documentation was to be completed before I left Sydney because, I was told, I would be too busy after that. When I completed this task, I put the manuscript aside. I didn't know then that this work would not be completed for a further twenty-five years.

I moved from Sydney on the exact day that had been divulged. I found the location that fitted the information I had been given and my husband and I purchased the property. Then my life changed dramatically, as had been foretold. At the time I didn't understand why I needed to be at this new location. All I knew was that it was a place of extraordinary beauty, peace and abundance and I immediately felt at home.

It took two decades of working intimately with the land to realise how important it was for me to be in a place where I could truly appreciate the significance of living in a way that was fully connected with nature. It was only by really getting in touch with it that I was able to appreciate the following message about the importance of the land:

In the beginning the Earth was a place of exquisite beauty. You have evidence of this if you care to look. Now much of it is ugly. It is scarred by man's intervention and greed. Vast areas have been turned into desert, laid to waste by inappropriate farming or other forms of overuse. All this is carried out with the aim of acquiring monetary wealth. In seeking wealth, mankind has destroyed the means through which wealth is available.

The Earth is not something that can be abused thoughtlessly forever without suffering the consequences. As part of the universe it is subject to the Laws of the Universe. It is in a position where it strives all the time to maintain balance. Balance is being restored constantly. As the despoiling of the land occurs, man must leave. Left alone, the land regenerates.

Man is creating blocks within these natural systems by the overuse of water, air, soil, vegetation and minerals. As despoilers, the human race is destroying the very vehicle that it needs to support itself.

People too, by their undue regard for their own systems, are creating situations in which their own body functions, all of which are dependent on each other, are disrupted. By putting undue load on these systems, through living habits which do not allow the body systems to operate as they are intended, they create problems for themselves. The holographic principle always applies.

The very activities that assist man to regain what is optimal for life also assist the Earth to regain how it was in the beginning.

I combined running workshops and seminars and helping clients resolve their problems with growing and selling fruit and vegetables, and by doing so I gained knowledge that allowed me to understand the complexity of the systems that support mankind's well-being. More importantly, I realised that my purpose for doing this was to see what happened when I lived and worked in accordance with the spiritual laws of the universe. These laws were explained to me as part of the information that I had channelled while I was still in Sydney. Only by applying the laws, and living and working to the best of my ability in accordance with them, could I fully understand them and be able to explain them. It was only when I realised that this was the primary purpose for moving to the country, that the move from Sydney made sense. I also needed to do this to understand that for Earth to shift to a higher vibration, people need to heal. Healing requires energy and I needed to learn about energy. Working with the land taught me about energy. It taught me about balance. It taught me about inter-relationships. The work was physically demanding so I gained fitness. It proved to be more intellectually stimulating than anything I had done before and I gained confidence by taking on a challenge that required physical stamina and strength at an age when most are thinking only of retirement.

§

The information that I was given through channelling provided the basis for many of my subsequent decisions. It was, and continues to be, highly significant.

The Elohim told me that those who have used Stress Defusion (or, more accurately, Atlantean crystal healing) in previous lifetimes just need to be reminded of it and they too will know how to work with it. I don't know whether this is true or not but I trust that it is. I do know it is true for children because on many occasions, I have watched them use the process confidently without any need for guidance. They seem to know what to do once it is explained to them.

Over a period of more than thirty years, I have worked with many people, teaching them how to heal themselves. The changes I have witnessed are profound. I continue to do this work.

I channelled much information from the Elohim. I believe that the information relating to the spiritual laws of the universe is of such great importance that I have spent more than twenty years of my life in order to validate the laws by living and working to the best of my ability in accordance with them. What I discovered by doing this is described in my first book *Final Days of Judgement* which was published in 2016.

The information I brought through from the *Elohim* remains as significant today as it was back then, perhaps even more so. In the interim period scientists have confirmed much of what I was told almost thirty years ago. The world has changed as I was told it would change. Events have happened as I was told they would. The shift that was foretold has been taking place and the information that I accessed so long ago remains relevant and necessary in order to help mankind understand how and why things are happening as they are. The imperative to help things become what they need to be is more crucial than ever, if mankind is to continue to exist on Earth.

A significant aspect of my higher purpose is to teach the power of thought to create reality because:

Once that is understood all else will follow.

Everything in Its Place provides the information needed to understand that, by our thinking, we are the creators of our own reality, and that it is time for us to create with conscious intention.

My journey has been extraordinary, but now everything is in its place. It is time for me to complete the challenge that this lifetime was intended to provide: to help people understand that they have the power to heal themselves. Within this book are the tools and the understanding to facilitate this. *Everything in Its Place* is my gift to you.

Chapter 1
Helen's Story

I don't know who was more surprised. Helen had taken the book I handed to her and read the opened page. Less than an hour earlier she had not been able to read. A week before that she wouldn't have even tried, but now she was reading fluently. Because of the apparent severity of Helen's disabilities and her initial reluctance to have anything to do with me, I had expected it was going to take much longer than two half-hour sessions for such a breakthrough to have occurred.

'What did you just read about?' I asked, and she gave me a brief summary. 'How do you feel about having done that?'

'Good,' she mumbled. It was clear that she was overcome by what had just happened and wasn't sure what to make of it. Even her uncertainty indicated a change of sorts. On two previous occasions when I had tried to communicate with her, all I had seen was a blank stare and hooded eyes; not vacant, but totally disconnected as if she was guarding herself against contact with someone she didn't trust. Only a week earlier she hadn't been prepared to answer any of my questions, or offer any information at all. Following the first session I had with her something had changed. She came up to me and spoke to me in the corridor. Her brief response to my question when that happened represented almost as big a breakthrough as the fact that she could now read.

My immediate reaction was that Helen's ability to read was so extraordinary that she needed to tell someone about it, to reinforce the change that had occurred. I was afraid that otherwise she would discount that it had happened and go back to how things were.

I asked her if there was anyone she would like to tell.

'My sister.'

'Let's go and find her then, so you can read to her.'

Helen's sister was in a senior year at the school. On our way out of the library we passed the librarian. I told her that Helen could read, and then asked Helen whether or not she would like to read to Mrs Mitchell.

I wasn't hopeful that Helen would be prepared to do this. As far as I was aware, she hadn't spoken to a teacher in the six months since she had come into Year 7. Asking her to read to the librarian was asking a lot. To my utter astonishment, she replied 'Yes, Miss,' and proceeded to read the same book that she had read to me a few minutes earlier.

Mrs Mitchell blinked a few times, swallowed and tried to look as if what had happened was an everyday occurrence. 'Well done, Helen. Now you'll be able to borrow books and read them at home.'

On the way to the office, where someone would be able to tell us where we would find Helen's sister, we encountered the principal coming out of his office. I told him that Helen could read and asked him if he would like her to read to him.

'Wonderful. Will you do that for me Helen?' His eyebrows rose questioningly as he looked at me, but it wasn't the right time for explanations.

The principal was possibly the only member of the school's teaching staff who understood what I was attempting to do and was fully supportive of the program that I had introduced. He knew Helen's background and he would have realised that if Helen could actually read, this was a demonstration that what I was doing was achieving exceptionally positive results.

Helen read to him. She also read to the women in the front office, the teacher who was on her way to the staff room and finally, when the bell rang, we found Helen's sister and Helen read to her, too.

Since the beginning of the year, when Helen had started at the high school, her story had been told over and over again. All the teachers knew that Helen couldn't, or wouldn't, do anything a teacher asked her to do in class. She wouldn't obey even the simplest instruction; she would neither talk nor answer any questions. Suddenly that had changed. It was not only the fact that Helen was reading that was so amazing but also the fact that she was answering questions and talking to teachers.

In the weeks that followed, not everyone was happy. The change in Helen's behaviour was quite dramatic but not entirely welcomed. Her presence in the classroom could no longer be ignored. She soon became candid in her reactions to anything that she found amusing or boring. She was also unselfconscious when it came to telling everyone what she thought, or how she felt. Having repeated a year in primary school, she was older and larger than all the other Year 7 girls and without inhibitions Helen was not easy to ignore. Her emotional and social development had apparently been frozen since her first day of school and she was now behaving like an oversized five-year-old.

When I returned to the staffroom, I recalled the sequence of events that had preceded this dramatic change. By the time I worked with Helen, I had been at the high school for a couple of years. The school principal had invited me to work at the school because I had convinced him that I might be able to help the girls who had difficulty with reading. I was hopeful that a variety of successful strategies that I had used previously could be adapted for a school situation. They didn't work. What did work, however, was something totally different and completely unexpected. It proved to be highly effective, but it wasn't something that was standard in terms of commonly accepted teaching techniques. This was the strategy that I had used with Helen.

After hearing about Helen's difficulties when she first arrived in Year 7 and wanting to observe her to ascertain whether or not I might be able to help her, I had attempted to help Helen understand what she needed to do in a mathematics class. She refused to talk to me or accept the help I offered. I tried to show her how to draw a straight line using a ruler, but she refused to pick up a pencil. Unable to help her do this simple task, I gave up in defeat.

A few months later, I overheard a conversation in the staffroom between two teachers who clearly knew Helen's family.

They were discussing the fact that Helen had been developmentally normal until she started school.

I learned that eight years previously, on her first day in kindergarten, the teacher asked her for her name but Helen refused to tell her. I did not know whether this was because she might not have been able to understand English, due to her Greek background, or if she didn't want to be at the school and had decided to be difficult. I was told that the teacher kept asking Helen for her name and the question was repeatedly met with a total lack of response. Eventually, in frustration, the teacher sent Helen to the back of the room where she was told to stay until she was ready to cooperate.

In the weeks that followed, Helen did not speak to anyone, not even family members. She was so traumatised by what had happened on her first day in kindergarten that at home, she reverted to behaviours more typical of a toddler but, as time passed, she resumed normal behaviour within the family. In kindergarten, and in the years that followed while she was at primary school, she continued to sit and do nothing, as she had been told to do on that first day when she was sent to sit at the back of the class.

I had no idea of the accuracy of this story and how much had been exaggerated but that was inconsequential. I had a starting point and some understanding of what had happened to cause Helen to refuse to talk to anyone at school. This information was sufficient to give me hope that I could help her because, after hearing her story, I knew that Helen wasn't brain damaged or mentally incompetent.

I decided to invite a member of Helen's family as my interpreter to communicate with Helen because she refused to talk to a teacher. With approval from the school I phoned Helen's parents and they agreed that a family member would come to the school to take on this role. A few days later Helen, her big sister and I went to the little upstairs room in the library where I worked in private with individual students. Helen was prepared to follow instructions so long as they came from her sister. I showed Helen's sister the exercises that would provide me with information about Helen's level of brain separation and she then demonstrated the exercises to Helen. It was a funny situation. Helen's sister and I both knew Helen understood exactly what was required of her, but we had to play by Helen's rules in order to get her to co-operate.

First, I presented Helen with some 'brain gym' exercises, which were diagnostic tools frequently used by kinesiologists at that time. These included cross-crawling, which involved using opposite legs and arms at the same time. A second exercise involved moving the arms to make an infinity sign across the body. These exercises provided me with the information I needed to confirm that Helen had separated left and right brain function.

I massaged the back of her legs to release the tension that I suspected she would be holding in the backs of her legs. Severe leg muscle soreness was something I had identified as a common problem for many of the girls I had worked with previously. While her sister continued to tell Helen what I needed her to do, I checked Helen's peripheral vision by asking her to follow my hand with her eyes as I checked to see whether she could follow the movement. By doing this I discovered that she had a restricted visual field. Helen was unable to look up. She displayed evidence of a classic case of tunnel vision, which occurs when a person does not want to remember events from the past.

The work that we did on that first session was quite superficial and I didn't expect much progress to be made. However, I did ask her sister if she would work with Helen to continue doing the arm exercises she had done during the session.

A few days later, I met Helen in the corridor and I was very surprised when she came up to me and said, 'Look, Miss, I can do those exercises you showed me. I've been practising'. She proceeded to show me how well she could do the arm exercises. The fact that she had come up to me and talked to me was an indication that something had changed.

'Does this mean you will see me again?' I asked.

'Yes, Miss.'

'Do we need your sister to come too?'

'No, Miss.'

During the second session I worked with Helen's eyes getting her to access those parts of her peripheral vision that she had shut off. I hoped that this process would allow memories of the event that had caused her problem to surface and this seemed to be what happened. Helen didn't share with me what she remembered. She didn't need to but because of what happened subsequently, I assumed that she had re-visited her traumatic first day at school and this had been sufficient to allow her to remember the events of that day. If I was correct in my assumption, she had also recalled the decisions that had controlled her school experience from that point on. Remembering was all that she needed to do.

A few weeks after Helen's breakthrough, one of the children I was working with asked me if I knew that Helen could read.

'Yes,' I replied. 'Why do you ask?'

'I don't think any of the other teachers in the school know. They still treat Helen as if she can't learn anything. Helen isn't stupid, Miss,' the girl confided. 'She's really good at drawing but she can't do maths. We're teaching her.'

'Who is teaching her?' I asked.

'Well, you see Miss, Helen is one of our group now. We all have lunch together and we are teaching her.' I was thrilled to hear this. Until I worked with Helen, she had no friends and her sister was the only person she spoke to in the school.

Several months later I saw Helen. She was one of a large gaggle of girls running along the corridor, yelling and shouting to one another. Running along the corridor was forbidden so I called them to slow down. Helen emerged from the midst of the group and came over to me. She had good news to share. 'Miss, I've been allowed to go into the algebra class. I can do algebra. It's easy.' Algebra was for students who had reached a level of mathematical understanding that would allow them to succeed. It seemed that the girls had taught her well.

In the time that I had been working with the techniques I used with Helen, I had begun to realise that when decisions are made that have a high level of emotional energy attached to them, they act as a program for the brain. I suspected that Helen had set some very powerful programs into operation when she was sent to the back of the classroom on her first day of school. Whilst I don't know what decision Helen made when the kindergarten teacher asked her what her name was, it is likely that it was something like: 'I'm never going to do what the teacher wants me to do.' From that moment on this became Helen's reality. Change could only occur when she had the opportunity to remember the event at the origin of the behaviour pattern she had developed and realise the consequences of the decision she had made.

§

The school principal and I both realised that the strategy I was using to help the students with reading and learning difficulties was outside the range of mainstream remedial teaching methods. When I accepted the principal's invitation to develop a program to help the girls who had literacy problems, my intention had not been to introduce radical alternative practices and methods. I had planned to adapt strategies that I had successfully implemented previously. They didn't work. In my attempt to find alternative solutions I stumbled on something that changed the girls' ability to read and learn more effectively than anything I had ever witnessed before. With the headmaster's approval, I had an opportunity to test it and see whether the immediate benefits were permanent. I was not surprised that the teaching staff found it difficult to comprehend what I was working with. I found it difficult to comprehend even though it was something I was working with every day. I wasn't able to explain why the girls were suddenly switching on their ability to read and learn. I didn't know why, I just knew that it was happening.

The day that I stopped Helen from running in the corridor was the last time I saw her. I had resigned the previous week after an episode with the head English teacher which made me realise that, despite the evidence I was accumulating, the teaching staff had not recognised the fact that the strategy I was using was actually working. Somehow, even the amazing turnaround in Helen's attitude and learning abilities had gone unnoticed, let alone what had happened with many of the other students.

I was hoping to bring the improvement in reading ability that I had witnessed in many of the students to the teachers' attention when I joined a staffroom discussion about one of the girls.

'She's surly, and she doesn't co-operate. She's got no ability at all. How can I teach someone English if they can't even read?' The teacher was referring to one of the girls that I had been working with, and I knew for a fact that, for the past two weeks, but only for the past two weeks, she had been able to read.

'I think you will find that she can read,' I had said. 'Would you like me to get her so that she can read to you?'

'Yes. OK. If you like,' he replied, without enthusiasm.

Her name was Amal, and I sent a message asking her to

come to the staffroom. When she arrived, I asked her to show everyone how well she could read. I knew she was very proud of what she had achieved and was very happy to demonstrate her newfound skill. In a similar way that Helen had read to the librarian and the school principal almost a year earlier, Amal took the book that I handed her and read a passage fluently, without hesitation or stumbling. I thanked her and sent her back to class.

'Well done Amal,' said the English teacher, as the girl left the room. Returning to his desk I heard him muttering, 'Well she might be able to read, but she doesn't understand a word of it.'

If he, or any of the other members of staff, had realised the significance of what was happening, or shown any interest in how these changes had come about, I might have continued working at the school. As it was, I decided that it was time to leave.

I had worked with over 200 students and seen many of them improve their reading ability and later improve their overall academic performance. I had watched as their academic performance levels improved over a period of time. I decided that it was time to see what would happen when I applied the techniques that I had been using with the girls to help people who had more than just reading problems.

Chapter 2
We Create our Reality

I have told Helen's story to illustrate something that was for me, inexplicable in terms of my understanding at that time. Helen was one out of many students who did something that I thought was impossible. I knew that it wasn't normal for someone who couldn't read, to suddenly be able to do so. But this was what occurred.

Over and over again, as I worked with more and more people, things happened that just should not have happened. I knew that it wasn't possible for someone to heal chronic physical problems without some form of physical intervention. I also knew it wasn't possible for someone who was totally inflexible to suddenly regain flexibility. But these were the sorts of things that I was seeing, and I didn't know why. I had to keep doing what I was doing in order to convince myself that what I was experiencing was actually true. Every time I worked with a student, I would caution myself with the thought: 'Don't expect another miracle. This time the process might not work.'

Over a period of almost three years I worked with as many as 200 students in the high school and, whilst the results were different for each student, some remarkable things occurred and I had the opportunity to watch the impact of these changes over an extended time period. This is what it took before I could actually accept that what I was seeing was true. I wasn't imagining it. The changes I saw were real and they were permanent.

Before I could fully understand what I was seeing, I needed some sort of theoretical explanation that made sense. The one I came up with was that we program the physical and mental constructs we call our body and our mind by our thoughts and emotions. In essence, we are the creators of our own reality. I understood that this conclusion had enormous implications and it was not one I reached without a lot of thought but it was the only one that fitted all the stories that clients shared with me, and the changes I had seen. It seemed to be the only rational explanation that made sense.

I asked myself the questions 'Can thought have this much power? Can this be possible?'

Over time I came to the conclusion that the answer was definitely yes. And it was confirmed by my clients, including Andrew, who came into my life to demonstrate how powerful just one emotionally charged thought or decision can be. I worked with Andrew for a period of over three years:

Andrew was the nephew of one of my clients. She brought me a photo of him and asked if I thought I might be able to help him. She explained that he had severe learning difficulties and people found it very difficult to understand him because of his speech impediment. The photograph interested me. It showed a boy with a lopsided face. The left side was normal. It was the face of quite a good-looking boy. The right side looked as if had been made of melted wax.

Everything drooped. Andrew's right eye was at least two centimetres lower than his left eye. His mouth, on the right side headed sharply down. The right side of his face appeared to have no muscle tone so his mouth was constantly open. Andrew's right arm was spindly and fell loosely by his side and his shoulder on that side was weak and undeveloped. He favoured his right side so his stance was lopsided. What the photograph didn't show was that Andrew dragged one leg as he moved — ungainly and uncoordinated.

I suspected that his lopsided face indicated a split brain where neither side was communicating with the other. I don't think I realised initially that the right side of his face and body were paralysed. My thinking was that if I could help him re-establish the connection between the left and right hemispheres of his brain, it might help him overcome his learning difficulties. I had no expectation beyond this, and I was certainly not convinced that I could help make this connection happen.

As soon as I met him I knew that I had not been told the full story about his problems. Had I known, I don't think I would ever have considered that I might be able to help him. The extent of his disabilities was obvious when he arrived. His hands were scarred and misshapen because he gnawed them whenever he became irritated. He was often irritated by the challenges that life presented him. He drooled constantly because he was unable to close his mouth. His speech was unintelligible but he didn't seem to understand this. He spoke a lot and became very frustrated when he was not understood.

Where was I to start?

Because of the difficulties he had been coping with all his life, there was a lot of work needed just to release the energy that the frustrations of his day-to-day life were causing. I explained to Andrew that my plan was to work with his peripheral vision and get rid of blocked energy. Since I was not able to understand Andrew's garbled speech, I made no attempt to ask him what he was experiencing or thinking. I worked with him as if he were a small child, identifying the areas of energy blockage and facilitating its release. This was all we did for an hour or so each day for three days.

On the third day, something miraculous happened. Andrew's facial distortion suddenly corrected. His eyes aligned. He was able to close his mouth and his speech clarity instantly improved. I was able to understand him when he spoke. I didn't know precisely what had happened, but I welcomed the change because it showed that something significant had occurred and his paralysis was partially or wholly gone.

I suggested he telephone his mother, who was in Canada, and it was an extraordinarily emotional phone call. She could understand her son for the first time in his life.

As he left that day, I watched Andrew skip across the road to where his father and older brother were waiting for him, patiently sitting on a stone wall in the sun. He was excited about what had happened, as were his father and brother. A few days later I received a note from his grandmother with whom Andrew was staying during his visit to Australia. She thanked me and told me how happy that she was that she *could actually understand her grandson. Andrew returned to his home in Canada the following week.*

I didn't see Andrew for nearly a year after that, but he kept in touch. With speech clarity no longer such a problem, Andrew regularly phoned me to report on progress. He was learning a musical instrument and was a member of the school band. He had joined YMCA and was playing sport to help develop muscles that had atrophied because of the paralysis. He was also making progress at school.

When Andrew and his father returned to Australia from Canada the following Christmas, we resumed our work and this time Andrew made a significant discovery. Surprisingly for me, and for him, he went back to the time immediately prior to his birth. He told me that he felt as if he was in the birth canal and was experiencing excruciating pain. He was stuck. He made a decision to shut off the pain. The effect of this decision was to immediately paralyse the right side of his body. This was how he was born. Paralysed down one side.

'How could I have done that to myself?' he sobbed. 'I didn't know it was going to be so difficult. I had no idea what it would be like to have people think me an imbecile. I didn't know how hard it would be to have people avoid me because I looked so hideous. I didn't know what it would be like to live in a world where no one could understand me and to know that what they could see wasn't the real me. It's been so hard.' And he sobbed and sobbed and as he did so, he released all the pent-up anguish and despair that had been such a feature of his life up till that time.

'Why did you make that decision, Andrew?'

'It was either that, or die. I knew I couldn't die. I had to be born because I have an important job to do on Earth. I knew then what it was, but I can't remember any more. But I had absolutely no idea how hard it was going to be. Nobody could have any idea of how hard it has been to be dependent and useless.' And he continued sobbing.

'Perhaps what you have had to experience has been some of the preparation you need in order to do what you have come to Earth to do,' I suggested. 'Few people know, as you know, what it is like to be trapped in a body that doesn't work properly and have people treat you as if you can't understand. And you have the ability to communicate that. Your dad has sent me examples of your writing. You are wonderfully talented. Perhaps what you have experienced has been part of a higher plan?'

We discussed these ideas at length and Andrew agreed that perhaps there was some truth in what I was suggesting to him.

Six months later, Andrew graduated from high school and gained entry to college. The improvements he had made in his life had been spectacular over a relatively short period of time. He had worked to strengthen his body. He had developed a passionate interest in music and was playing a musical instrument. This should have been the happy ending that I wanted for him, but that wasn't to be.

After spending almost his entire life without the expectation that he carry-out the tasks of a physically and mentally normal person, Andrew found the challenges of college life to be very daunting. He panicked. When his mother, who was separated from Andrew's father and had always been his full-time carer, suggested that he wasn't yet ready for college and that he should return to school where he was safe, he chose to do this.

'I'm bored. I'm unhappy. I made a mistake. I'm a failure because I wasn't brave enough to keep going.' Andrew realised that he had made the wrong decision. He phoned me regularly to tell me how unhappy he was.

Even worse, unbeknownst to him, his mother had applied to the Court to have him classified as a dependent minor so that she could continue to receive financial assistance from his father after he turned 18. Andrew was not interviewed as part of the court hearing. His medical and school records provided all the evidence needed for him to be classified as permanently mentally and physically disabled.

Enraged, his father arranged for Andrew to attend a music academy in Australia and flew him out from Canada to enrol. To my amusement, the young man who had been classified by the court as totally dependent mentally and physically disabled flew to Australia on his own, stopping a few days in Tokyo for some sightseeing. He was excited by the idea of studying music but again, he didn't have the mental stamina to face the challenge. After a few weeks, he returned to Canada.

At this point, I chose to cut all ties with Andrew. He planned to return to his mother because, as he explained *the situation to me, 'She needs me. She looked after me when I wasn't able to look after myself and I can't just leave her.'* I felt that returning to the care of his mother was going to be difficult for him in the same way that returning to high school had been difficult, but it was what he needed to do until he gained the emotional maturity and strength to let go the security his mother represented. I also suspected he was going to regret his decision as he had regretted the decision to pull out of college. I thought that whilst he had already overcome very significant challenges, even more lay ahead and he needed to handle these for himself.

It is many years since I worked with Andrew but my memories of him are vivid. My favourite memory is of him standing in front of a group of about 15 people, describing his experiences. In his right hand, he held a mug of hot coffee. He wasn't even consciously aware of the significance of the coffee mug. Three years earlier his arm had been paralysed. Two years earlier he held a pencil with that hand and wrote his name for the first time. That he could talk coherently to a group of strangers, totally relaxed and confident, was all but unbelievable but it is what happened.

I always thought of Andrew as my gift. He introduced me to many things I hadn't thought of previously. He taught me not to take people at face value: underneath a distorted facade may lie extraordinary talent. He taught me that decisions could be made prior to birth that have a major impact. He taught me the power of thought to make profound choices in response to critical situations; choices that have unintended repercussions. He taught me how people, with apparently loving intentions, can be guilty of letting their own fears override their concern for even those they love most.

Most of all, my experience with Andrew taught me that no one asks, 'Why?' No one from the school that Andrew had attended all his life, asked why he was suddenly able to speak, use his right hand, play a musical instrument, learn effectively, or earn a place in college. They just accepted the new Andrew. His doctors didn't ask why he was no longer paralysed, and, quite possibly, had they done so they wouldn't have believed the answer they were given. The courts assumed that such changes were not possible and accepted what they were told, whilst Andrew was not given the opportunity to demonstrate that he was no longer disabled.

So, what mental process do we work through to create the programs that design our life path? With Andrew, it was easy to identify. One life-threatening traumatic event was sufficient. For most, I believe it involves many incidents, which typically occur in a normal childhood, to which we react negatively. I think about it this way:

If, as a child, I decide that I can't get it right, when I've just done something that others have judged to be wrong or bad or because I can't do something that I expect to be able to do, this thought becomes an instruction to my brain. My brain then determines ways to change the thought (decision) into concrete reality.

When I become really proficient at *not getting it right*, others confirm this for me and I am told that I'm stupid. I am criticised with phrases such as, 'Don't you know how to do anything right?' or, 'Anyone would think that you don't have any brains at all.' Comments like this make me feel bad. Then I compound the problem by thinking of myself as a failure for *not getting it right* where in fact, I have been very successful in doing what I decided to do. I do *not getting it right* superbly well.

The purpose of the decision I have made has been to avoid the pain of having to accept that I have made a mistake or that I am in some way inadequate. I take one instance and, over time, I generalise it to include all possible eventualities. I negate myself and negate the feelings of shame, guilt, sadness and fear that I felt in that pivotal moment.

As with computers, my computer-like brain didn't identify the intention behind the decision I made as a child. Regardless of my intention, my brain took my decision literally and the decision became a program that I followed every time I tackled a new task. I reinforced my negative self-image from the poor results I got from each of these experiences.

§

The process seems simple, too simple perhaps. Could this explanation actually be a description of what happens every time someone makes an emotionally charged negative decision? Could such things as illiteracy, poor eyesight and inflexibility simply be unintended side effects of a self-programming process? Could this explain why some peoples' lives are lacking in love and support or illustrate spectacular failure?

I had inadvertently identified a way to locate negative programs that we store in our subconscious. Having done this, I had no idea how or why identifying and processing the thoughts surrounding the decision was having the effects that I was seeing.

Decades later I have much greater clarity. I believe that my research has been into what I think of as the negative aspect of the tool of creation. My investigation over many decades involved looking at example after example of negative situations in peoples' lives, which have been created by emotionally-charged decisions. Additionally, I inadvertently identified a process that allows a person to identify how, when and why they have used the process to create negative situations. Even more significantly, I developed a strategy to facilitate the undoing of decisions that were made at some earlier time.

§

This process does not only apply to creating negative life situations. The same process can be used to create benefits in our lives when applied positively. However, I don't think that using the process positively is quite as simple as the explanation I have just given makes it out to be.

Wanting something, when we have already decided we cannot have it, creates stress. We cannot create what we want when we are stressed.

Attracting positive life situations involves working in a personal environment of total, unconditional love, which is what remains when we eliminate all judgement. To attain such a state is easier said than done because it means accepting absolutely everything without judgement. It means accepting violence, hate, greed. It means accepting the most heinous acts of callousness and viciousness that man inflicts on his fellow man. It means accepting everyone: the drunken bum in the gutter, the rapist, the arsonist, the abused child, and also their abuser. This is not something that is easily achieved.

We also need to determine if what we *want* to create in our life, is what we *need* in terms of our soul's journey. We might *want* to have lots of power and influence, but not yet have the integrity to operate for the highest good of all. The process won't work until we have total integrity, and often more learning is required in order to attain that degree of integrity.

Therefore, before we can move into a state where we will be able to apply this process appropriately, and for positive benefits, we first have to undo the programs that we have created up until this point: the programs that stop us from attaining a state of unconditional love.

Many people are reluctant to do this. Our resistance is enhanced by our lack of preparedness to face the truth about ourselves. This is explained, in part, by our unwillingness to re-feel the emotions that were appropriate to the original traumatic situation or event that triggered the process of negative creation.

For many of us, a more normal strategy is to shut down emotionally and/or hide from what has happened. The intention behind this type of strategy is to allow us to neither feel nor remember. What we try to keep hidden, actually causes us to re-experience similar situations over and over again, and from each such situation, we learn.

To change the patterns we have created for ourselves, we need to go back and re-experience, in our minds, the event or events that set off a series of unanticipated and unwelcome consequences. We have to feel the emotions that were appropriate in the original situation as if we are in the same space as we were then. This is not a matter of remembering but of being totally involved, being in the 'now' of a past event.

We can process negative decisions and memories more easily when we accept that the event happened in order for us to learn something important. Remembering what happened and accepting that, at the time, the anger/fear/hurt/ or sadness that was felt was an appropriate response, means we can let go judgement of what happened. The most important step in the process is to feel the emotions that were not felt the first time around.

When we judged ourselves for feeling as we did and judged others for making us feel that way, the judgement came in the form of a decision: 'I'm stupid' or 'the world is not safe'. In all likelihood, this decision would have resulted from a situation where the decision was a valid response. Over time, what was true for one situation became generalised, to cover any situation where it might have been true.

Provided we *really* mean it, we can say to ourselves:
'I am now willing to feel the emotions that I refused to feel

when I made the decision that I wasn't safe. I made a decision about myself, others and the world that were appropriate at the time, but this decision does not apply in my life right now and I am willing to let it go.'

This is all that is needed to release the emotional energy that has built around the event and, even more significantly, to cancel the decision that was created by that event so that it no longer has the power to control our lives. When the circumstances of our lives improve, we know that the process has been successful. It is that simple.

For many people, going back and reliving their worst nightmare is something that they refuse to do because of the fear that it will be extremely upsetting. Clients have told me that even though they have remembered past events with a high level of intensity, there is, at the same time, an awareness that the memories are from a *safe space*, which provides a level of objectivity. This awareness reduces the apparent danger of revisiting traumatic past memories. For others, it is impossible to go back because they have filed the memories away so deeply within their subconscious that they don't even know that they exist. In such cases, they require deeper work to identify memories and the related decisions that they made.

§

The design of the strategy I have described involves the unintentional fusing of events, decisions and strong negative emotions in one package and hiding the package in our subconscious. Emotion is the glue that holds our decisions in place and when decisions are held in place by very powerful negative emotions such as terror, humiliation, shame or rage, they are hard to shift. Allowing access to stored emotional memories seems quite threatening. Once we recognise that the emotions we felt at the time of the original traumatic incident were valid and absolutely authentic, they lose their power because we can feel the emotions objectively. Accepting this idea gives us the freedom to go back into the emotional state that accompanied the original traumatic incident and releasing it.

The following personal story might help to illustrate how this can happen:

A few years ago, I was standing in a courtyard in The Rocks, one of the old areas of Sydney near Circular Quay, on the harbour. In the courtyard stood an old, hand-operated wooden wool press. I hadn't seen one of those for many years but I recognised it instantly. It was the same type of wool press that stood in my uncle's shearing shed. I spent many hours in that shed as a very small child when, during World War II, I was sent away to the country. The reason for this was due to miniature Japanese submarines entering Sydney Harbour and torpedoing a couple of boats. At the time, my family lived a short distance from the harbour so they were worried about what might happen. For a year I lived on the farm with my aunt, uncle and their teenage children.

Seeing the wool press in Circular Quay I walked over to it and was immediately immersed in feelings of absolute panic and terror. 'Interesting reaction,' *I thought.* 'What is this all about?' *I stood beside the wool press for a while, allowing these emotions to pulse through me. Some hours later, I recalled the events, which explained why the wool press elicited such a powerful reaction.*

On the farm, my cousins loved to torment and tease me. Terrifying a small child was great fun and I had always had conscious memories of them hanging me high over the wheat bins by my legs and threatening to drop me, and of them threatening to shoot me and skin me in the same way they skinned the rabbits that were in plague proportions. I had forgotten about one of their torment strategies until this day when I had stood near the wool press. They often threatened to wrap me in a wool fleece, put me in the bale that was being prepared for pressing, press me into the bale and send me off to be sold. One day they actually did what they had threatened to do. I suffocated. When they got me out, I wasn't breathing so they put me into the freezing sheep trough, to shock me into breathing again.

Seeing the wool press was a trigger that elicited a very strong reaction. Even as a small child, I must have realised that telling on the boys would have led to even more torment. Because I was unable to tell anyone what had happened, I suppressed the memories. Re-experiencing the emotions I had shut down at the time, allowed the memory to come into conscious awareness. Once this happened I was able to process the event and understand it as a stupid prank that could have had disastrous consequences.

As I mentioned earlier, for many people their main concern is to never remember horrific experiences in their lives. The perfection of the design is such that this isn't likely to happen. Each time we find ourselves in a situation that vaguely resembles a previous event that was traumatic, we hook into the emotional storeroom that we have buried inside and emotion starts bubbling to the surface. Not understanding what is happening, we try and suppress the emotions. The Stress Defusion process, the process I used with Helen and Andrew, works to bring forgotten memories to conscious awareness and allows emotions to be felt. This is enough to break the cycle. It isn't the only process that does this. There are many including meditation, kinesiology, reiki, crystal therapy, colour therapy, and counselling. Massage and different forms of bodywork are also effective for some.

The main point of difference between the Stress Defusion process and other therapies is that it facilitates unlocking of memories held in the subconscious, allowing them to come to conscious awareness — memories of this lifetime, and for many, memories of past lifetimes.

Before delving into what I learned from people who told me about their amazing experiences, I will go back to where my journey began.

Chapter 3
Preparation

Long ago, I reached the conclusion that many of the important decisions people make during their lives come about as a consequence of events that they would prefer to not have experienced. Whilst they might judge such events as being really bad, the events may actually be highly significant in terms of providing the motivation needed to follow a life path that they would never have otherwise followed. By responding to unwelcome situations or events, they are led in a direction that allows them to achieve what I think of as their life purpose.

My belief is that our life purpose is achieved when we learn whatever it is that we designed this lifetime to teach us — something we haven't understood in the course of our soul's journey. This is the preparation needed before it is possible to work with our higher purpose.

The *Elohim* clarified for me the need for preparation in this channelled message:

The length of time for preparation depends to a large extent on the magnitude of the task we have to perform. The bigger the task, the more we have to remember. Preparation allows us to identify our own learning. It may also be required for us to clear the blocks for those around us who have agreed to work with us to fulfil the obligations we have contracted to perform.

Preparation builds depth and breadth of experience. What may appear at the time to be random wanderings, do have a purpose when seen from the larger perspective. Like pieces of a puzzle, they fit together when we see the whole picture. It is from this tying together of seemingly unrelated people, understanding, knowledge and an appreciation of what happens when we work according to beliefs that do not support our higher purpose, that we gain full understanding.

§

The work I did in preparation for what was to become my life's journey was motivated by what I thought at the time as a very unfortunate set of circumstances. My son was brain damaged at birth because of a condition known as *hydrocephalus*, which is an excessive accumulation of cerebrospinal fluid that causes harmful pressure on the brain.

I don't know whether *hydrocephalus* was the cause of all the problems that occurred in the early years of my son's life, but the combination of severe food intolerances, hyperactivity and learning difficulties meant that living with this child presented a constant series of challenges.

Trying to find answers, I spent hours reading and eventually came across some studies that suggested a connection between food allergies and hyperactivity. When my son was born, the idea of different foods creating problems was not readily accepted. After living with a screaming, sickly baby for six months, I substituted cow's milk with a soy product and the screaming stopped immediately. With nothing to lose, I changed the family diet by eliminating all sugar, food colouring, food additives and anything processed. Dairy products, with the exception of cream and butter, had already been eliminated from my son's diet because of his allergic reaction. With these changes, my son's hyperactivity decreased to such an extent that we were able to link his irrational, hyperactive outbursts to foods that he had eaten which were on the 'prohibited list'.

Once the hyperactivity problem was more or less under control, I was able to think about his learning difficulties. At the age of seven he was unable to read. Numbers were a total mystery and he had developed his own phonetic written language. It consisted of a stream of consciousness with scant regard for standard spelling, sentence structure or punctuation. I still remember the first sentence he wrote: 'Wunts a ponatom ther wus radts'. It didn't have one word spelt correctly. When I asked him what he had written, he read his sentence to me: 'Once upon a time, there was rabbits.' Realising that the educational opportunities we wanted to provide our son were going to take considerable financial resources, I chose to complete a Diploma of Education course and become a teacher. This decision turned out, in retrospect, to be very significant.

Studying for my Diploma of Education, I clearly remember a 'light bulb' moment during a lecture on cognitive development. The impact of this was to set off a chain of events that had amazing consequences.

The lecturer was talking about the work of Dr Wilder Penfield, a Canadian neurosurgeon whose primary research area was epilepsy. With the aim of identifying the location of problems that were causing epilepsy, Dr Penfield used electrical probes in the brain while his patients were conscious. This process led to some fascinating discoveries. Some patients re-experienced events that they recognised as having occurred earlier in their lives and even previous lives.

Recall included not only the pictures, but also sounds and associated emotions as if the events were occurring in the present, rather than as memories of something that had happened in the past. Dr Penfield concluded that stimulation of the brain provided proof of the physical basis of memory. Fascinated not just by the physical workings of the brain, which he subsequently mapped,[2] he went on to investigate how brain function influences the mind and the personality.[3]

Dr Penfield's conclusion was that past experiences are stored as memories in our subconscious. He went on to identify which parts of the brain correspond with different mental and physical functions and he discovered that when mental functions are destroyed by brain damage early in life, these functions are taken over by different parts of the brain by the age of about twelve years. This was the conclusion that interested me.

If his findings were accurate, then it followed that the damaged parts of my son's brain were the parts used for such things as reading and mathematics. It was useless for my son to try and learn these things because he just didn't have the

---

[2] https://www.vox.com/ ... and ... /wilder-penfield-brain-surgery-epilspsy-google-doodle

[3] https://can-acn.org/wilder-penfield

mental capability to do that. This didn't mean that he would never have that capability. If the brain functions that had been destroyed at birth were re-established in some other part of the brain by the time he was twelve, then his brain would be capable of learning these skills when he reached that age, not when the teacher and the education system decided.

My introduction to the work of Dr Penfield, back in 1972, and my subsequent reading about brain structure and function made me realise that there was no easy explanation for learning and behaviour problems. My thinking and reading suggested that children may be judged to be of low intelligence for reasons other than their genetic inheritance, which had caused them to be born this way. Poor diet could be just as much to blame as genetic background because the brain needs energy to work properly, and a poor diet leads to low energy levels. Lack of a wide range of experiences could also account for low intellectual capability because incoming information is most quickly absorbed when it can be associated with a brain file of similar information that has already been established.

During the cognitive development lecture, the lecturer emphasised the fact that whilst brain function could be restored over time, problems relating to poor self-image could not be rectified so easily. According to books that I read later, belief in one's ability to learn and achieve was a very important factor in determining learning outcomes[4].

---

4   *The Power of Positive Thinking*, Norman Vincent Peale. Published 1952

The challenge for me became one of finding something that my son could become good at so that he could build on that to give him a sense of personal value. Over the next few months, he tried art, music and drama classes in an effort to find something he was interested in. Then, one day, he jumped into the deep end of a harbour-side swimming pool. At the time he couldn't swim but that was the thing he became very good at. Within a few months, as a result of joining a squad that was trained by the then Australian Olympic coach, he became the school junior swimming champion. A few months later he was also the school's athletics champion.

Nothing much changed in the classroom. Regular swimming training meant my son was often tired, so his behaviour became less disruptive. His concentration improved because of his involvement in a very demanding swimming squad. He learned that effort and persistence were needed if he was to do anything well. His co-ordination improved. Most importantly, his self-confidence grew.

My son learned to read when he turned eleven. Subsequent testing showed that he had gone from a reading age of five years to a reading age of fourteen years in less than six months. This seemed to verify that Dr Penfield was correct about different parts of the brain taking over the functions of damaged areas, provided the damage occurred at an early age. Four years later, my son was among the A grade scholars at an exclusive boys' college. At the end of high school, he was offered places at 9 different universities and colleges. He chose to study agriculture at what was then called

Hawkesbury Agricultural College, and he was one of only a handful of students accepted to the degree course straight from school.

As the mother of a son who learned very little during the first six years of school, I was told by his teachers that it was unreasonable for me to expect that he would ever achieve academic excellence. Until I came across the work that was being done by Dr Penfield, I agreed with them. Once I understood that the problem that was creating his inability to learn was not permanent, I looked for solutions. The solutions were not for his reading problems. I accepted that he was unable to read and I made no effort to help him read or to do mathematics until he turned eleven. The problem concerned the labels he had learned to give himself and those that had been given to him by others. These came about because he was unable to do what other children could do. That was actually far more of a concern than his inability to learn. It was finding ways to minimise the effect of those labels that provided the greatest challenge and I solved them by:

- Building self-esteem by concentrating on things that provided a sense of achievement, rather than concentrating on problem areas.
- Encouraging physical activity before academic achievement.
- Providing a wide range of creative activities to facilitate and integrate right and left brain processes including music, art and drama.
- Working within an environment of practical experience,

variety, challenge, independence, self-reliance and adventure.

- Regularly pushing him out of his comfort zone, where he could rely on past learned behaviours. By being constantly challenged, he developed the habit of finding out how to solve new problems. This meant that he was not overly concerned when he didn't know how to do something straight away.

Whilst I followed a game plan for working with my son and dealing with his learning difficulties that was very different from the more conventional strategy, his was a relatively small achievement compared with what was to follow. However, through following Dr Penfield's line of thought and working with my son accordingly, I discovered a framework of thought that was to become the foundation for a challenge I set for myself: identifying the cause of learning difficulties and finding a way to overcome those difficulties. My son's success prepared me to step even further outside conventional thinking than I had already done. It provided the incentive to look for solutions to problems that others regarded as insurmountable. It gave me a level of confidence that allowed me to step outside the box of conventional thinking.

Chapter 4
Learning Difficulties Investigated

The day my son graduated from university in 1987 I made a very profound decision. I set myself a goal: to find the reason why some children could not read or learn no matter how much they wanted to, or how much effort was put into helping them. This was a long-range goal. I had a lot of work to do before I would be ready to start looking for answers.

I had succeeded, beyond my wildest expectations, in helping my son to overcome the problem of being unable to achieve academically as a young boy. His problem was caused by brain damage at birth and I had found the information I needed, which made it possible to develop a plan to help him.

Many children have learning problems similar to my son's. Unlike my son, their learning disabilities are not usually traced back to brain damage. Within the education fraternity, problems like this are explained in terms of either genetic inheritance or environmental deprivation. Whilst these explanations are partially correct, they did not satisfy me in terms of providing the whole answer. Initially, I thought that something more was needed in order to explain why some children could learn easily and others could not. Identifying the reason for learning problems and discovering a way to help children with these problems was the goal that motivated me for more than a decade. It provided the motivation for a journey that led to me to discover one of the main reasons why learning difficulties occur, and eventually to find a solution to the problem. It led me to discover lots more besides.

§

During the years between my son starting school and his graduation from university, I stayed involved in some form of education. For ten years I taught economics and geography to senior students at a prestigious girls' school. After an experiment in sustainable farming, which was designed to test my son's determination to study agriculture, I returned to city life and became CEO of an organisation that helped teenagers develop an understanding of how business works. From this came confirmation that the most effective form of learning comes from doing rather than learning about. I moved from this into sales, working with a company that had developed a very powerful individualised learning program, which helped students perfect their mathematics skills.

In addition to working full-time during this period, I studied a variety of alternative methodologies including kinesiology, accelerated learning and neurolinguistic programming (NLP). At the time, the ideas introduced within these disciplines were causing changes in thinking about how learning occurs and how the mind and body are inter-connected. I went on to apply what I had learned when I developed different training programs. Later, I studied counselling.

A positive aspect of these studies was that I was connecting with a variety of extraordinary individuals whose thinking was definitely outside the box in terms of most people's experiences at that time: motivational speakers Tony Robbins and Robert Kiwosaki were two of them. I studied under NLP practitioners Stephanie Burns and Marvin Oka as well as Colin Rose, the acknowledged expert in Accelerated Learning theory at the time. Jacob Liberman, an interesting optometrist who didn't believe that glasses fixed the problem of poor eyesight, and author of the book *Light, Medicine of the Future*, taught me a lot about vision.

Meeting and spending time with these people, as well as others who were interested in the knowledge that I was being introduced to, in a variety of learning situations, provided a kaleidoscope of new experiences, different skills, new ways of thinking and different ways of living. For me, it was an extraordinary period of rapid growth and change.

Around this time, I read the book *Unlimited Power* by Tony Robbins in which he says: 'You don't have to be an expert before you do something. You become the expert by doing it.' This piece of advice really caught my attention. For some time, I had been thinking that it would be wonderful to develop introductory programs for adults using the techniques that I found had worked extremely well and which were used by the experts I had studied under. The courses I had experienced were amazing, but often threatening because on many occasions they required participants to step far outside their personal comfort zones. On occasion I doubted my ability to do what was asked of me. Board breaking and fire-walking were just two from a large range of experiences that were used to illustrate the power of the human mind when it is harnessed and focused. I was comfortable accepting the challenge of congruently aligning thought and action in order to be able to crack a board with my bare hand, because this didn't seem to put me in a life-threatening situation. The idea of using fire walking as a demonstration of congruent thought and action was so terrifying that I refused the opportunity to experience this when it was offered as proof of the principles that were being introduced; a refusal I have regretted ever since. It was by seeing what was possible, over and over again, that I gained an understanding of what people are capable of achieving when they are able to override their self-imposed limitations.

I thought that it would be a great idea to design softer and less threatening workshop programs as an exploration of some of the techniques and strategies to which I had been exposed and which had taught me so much. Taking Tony Robbin's advice on board, I decided that if I didn't try to develop a series of programs and present them, I would regret it. I targeted what was, at that time, Australia's largest and most successful computer training company and was successful in persuading the managing director that it would be a good idea to expand their range of programs into the area of personal development. By doing this, I applied the techniques I had learned and saw how well they worked.

What I learned, and successfully put into practice during this period, gave me the confidence to test whether or not what

I knew, and had applied successfully, could be used to help children with learning difficulties within a classroom situation. I felt ready to work on the goal that I had set almost a decade earlier. I didn't have any doubts at all that the program that I intended to introduce would be effective.

§

The principal of the school I approached recognised me from his personal experience with a teenagers' business program, called Young Achievement. Students from his previous school had benefitted significantly from participation in this program while I was CEO of the organisation that promoted it. His knowledge of my work with this program provided the credibility that I needed. It did not take much to persuade him that I might be successful in developing a program to help the girls who were coming into the school with poor reading skills.

After outlining my experience, and explaining my intentions, the headmaster told me, 'Nothing we have tried so far has ever made any difference, so there is nothing to lose.' We made a plan that I would take the poorest achievers from the group that would be entering the school the following year. I would be the home teacher for this group and would be with them for most of the school week. Different teachers would take them for mathematics and science.

The agreement I reached with the principal was that I would do my best to find a way to help the students at the school who had reading and learning difficulties. He did not ask me how I planned to do that. Just as well. I didn't have a definite plan. My intention was simply to apply all the strategies I had used previously in the hope that some would make a difference. I had the freedom to try whatever strategies I thought might be useful and the opportunity to see what sort of difference they made.

At this point, I hadn't channelled information from the *Elohim* relating to intelligence and capabilities, however, I had developed a strong belief that somehow our education system, and society in general, was labelling children in ways that were detrimental to their development. I had personally witnessed and experienced what happened when those labels were temporarily suspended under situations of trance. I thought that if I could change the labels that the children carried and if I could build their confidence in themselves, they would benefit. The problem, at that stage, was that I didn't know how deep the labels went or how they originated.

Later, the *Elohim* confirmed some of my beliefs in human capability.

Acceptance that everyone has capabilities far beyond what we accept as the norm will cause these abilities to be developed and expanded. What is now exceptional will become the norm. Our true potential can be far more readily attainable if we are just prepared to let go of judgement and beliefs as to what is normal and expand our acceptance beyond what we now accept. Being open to opportunities is the key.

Everyone has a special talent or gift, which they are

provided with, which enables them to make a contribution to mankind. This gift might be the ability to care for animals, or take care of children. It might be designing clothes or growing vegetables. If they follow a life which enables them to use the gift, they are content.

All gifts are equally special. None is more important than another.

Children know what their gift is. They get talked out of it by well-meaning parents, teachers and friends. Their life purpose will best be achieved when they use the special gift.

I had taken on a big challenge but I felt confident that I had the answers. The group I was given initially consisted of twelve students whose reading level ranged from Year 2 to Year 5. The majority of them were 3-4 years behind the expected level for their age. The emphasis of what I was attempting focused on their reading skills.

I felt that it was necessary to provide alternative strategies to the traditional chalk and talk approach. They hadn't worked. My innovation was to use a variety of teaching strategies. I developed graded reading material supported by audio tapes to reduce stress in the initial reading activities. I introduced phonics. Because of the small size of the class it was possible to develop individualised work programs so that the students could work at their own pace and at their own level. Group work was encouraged. I applied accelerated learning principles, ensuring that I presented work using visual, auditory and kinaesthetic input in ways that were similar to the techniques that I had used successfully in the corporate training world and with the motivated teenagers that I had worked with previously.

The girls in my class were not an easy group. Generally, their concentration levels were poor. Giving them a task that required them to read created a situation of high tension. Sometimes the whole classroom erupted into chaos for no apparent reason, as they projected their feelings of frustration and inadequacy onto each other, and also onto me. When things got out of hand, I took them outside so that they could shout at each other and at me and not interfere with what was going on in other classrooms. Some weeks we spent a lot of time outside.

I had high expectations of the girls, but didn't pressure them to do anything more than they were capable of achieving. They quite enjoyed the relaxation sessions where they lay on the floor and listened to soothing music. They loved the meditation sessions that we had regularly. They also did 'brain gym' exercises. After some lessons they went outside and ran around on the oval. It was a small group so they were able to talk to each other and work in pairs. Most were motivated and wanted to succeed, so they willingly tried each new task I designed for them. The highlight of each week was going to the library to work on the computers, which were a great novelty in a school environment at that time. Computers were non-threatening and provided instant feedback. There were simple games designed to improve comprehension, grammar and vocabulary and the girls quickly learned how to work with these. This was a very special privilege that few of the other students in the school were able to enjoy.

Unfortunately, being selected to go into a class for poor achievers was bad for self-esteem. The children were teased and this didn't help the situation. The confidence that I had when I started at the school that I would find a solution to the girls' reading problems diminished rapidly over the next two school terms. Nothing I tried made a significant difference.

Did they improve academically? No. Could they read any better than they could when they arrived at the school? No. Did I have any idea why they weren't responding? No.

Towards the end of the second term I was ready to admit defeat. I didn't have any more bright ideas to try. In my mind, my experiment was a failure. I was at a point where I was ready to give up and, in a state of despair, I shut down my conscious mind and rational thinking and allowed my unconscious mind to come up with the solution: a combination of kinesiology exercises, eye exercises and massage. I went into the classroom the next day with something different to try.

There are several different brain gym exercises but I used only one of the processes: stimulation of the kidney meridian acupressure points. I had introduced brain gym at the beginning of the year and the girls were accustomed to doing the various exercises designed to integrate the left and right hemispheres of the brain. In addition to this exercise, I adapted an idea I had been introduced to by the optometrist, Jacob Liberman, by tracing an infinity sign and asking her to follow my hand with her eyes.

Within this sequence I combined techniques from different disciplines. What I didn't realise at the time was that it was the eye movements that were critical in terms of the changes that occurred. That understanding came much later.

I took one of the students aside and got her to do this combination of exercises. After the session, which lasted less than half an hour, she returned to her desk and resumed the activity she had been working on. A few seconds later she looked up with an expression of absolute amazement and said: 'Miss, I can read'.

And she could. It wasn't the slow, stilted reading I expected, rather a fluent, confident flow of words. Even more outstanding was the fact that she actually understood what she was reading. This was the real difference. Previously she had, through years of tuition and practice, learned to decipher words and be able to sound them out. The words, however, had little or no meaning.

This result made me cautiously optimistic.

I thought it possible that the technique I had used with one student might work for all of them so I repeated the process with all the girls. Then I sat back and watched what happened. Some of the girls improved their reading ability dramatically and immediately.

I was excited but I had seen this sort of thing happen before. I even knew how to get people into a trance-like condition so that they could attain reading speeds that were nothing short of miraculous. In trance, the limits set by the expectations of the conscious mind are eliminated, and the extraordinary abilities of the unfettered subconscious come to the fore. This condition is not permanent however, and people soon revert to their normal level of expertise when the trance condition no longer operates. Trance induction is the basis for the effectiveness of neurolinguistic programming, using language, which puts people into a temporary trance-like condition so that they are susceptible to suggestion.

What I saw was different. Rather than the effects dissipating over a period of a few hours or a few days, the improvement was permanent and provided the base line for improvement in a variety of areas over time. The process worked with almost half the group and these girls started making immediate and quantum leaps in terms of their concentration. They were now able to work on their own. Week by week the list of books they were reading grew longer and longer. I set them more and more complex tasks.

While this was happening, the gap between those who had made the change and those who hadn't, grew larger. Tension in the classroom grew. Fighting broke out and I watched as one group demanded more and more assistance as they shot ahead, and the others retired to their corners, or belligerently undermined my efforts.

Late in Term 2, a situation developed where five out of my twelve students had improved between 2 and 4 years in reading ability in a period of less than a couple of weeks as a result of the Stress Defusion process. Two others, Erica and Maria, were making good progress because I had realised that the cause of their reading difficulties was not related to brain shut down. By observation and talking to them I had discovered the origins of their reading problems and once identified, the solutions were obvious.

Erica was thirteen. Her reading standard was that of a nine-year-old and Erica lacked self-confidence in all aspects of her schoolwork. In primary school, Erica had attended remedial reading programs for several years. For her, change came when she was able to question the logic of her thinking in relation to her inability to read. Her reading problem, she had decided, was because she was just like her mother. Her mother couldn't read, so in Erica's mind, it was obvious that she wouldn't be able to read either. We talked about this and I explained that her mother grew up in Holland during the war and it was possible that during the war she hadn't been able to go to school or have the opportunity to learn to read. Then she had migrated to Australia and had to learn a new language. It wasn't hard to understand why her mother couldn't read, but the reasons didn't apply to Erica. Looking at her situation logically put a whole new slant on Erica's thinking. Changing her belief at a conscious level was the only key needed to unlock Erica's reading ability. The realisation that she didn't have to be like her mother in terms of her reading skills had an immediate effect. From that moment, Erica became a fluent reader. From then on, it was nothing for her to read several books in a week. A few weeks after our conversation I tested her to check how much she had improved her reading skills. I discovered that Erica was reading at a level of skill typical of a fourteen-year-old. Since nothing had been done in the intervening weeks to teach Erica reading, it was quite apparent that she knew all she needed to know to be able to read quite competently, but had somehow blocked this ability.

Twelve months later Erica received her half-yearly report in Grade 8. She had A grade passes in two subjects and B grade passes in six others. This meant that within a year Erica had gone from almost the bottom of a group of 120 girls, to within the top 20%.

§

Maria's problem was different and was an example of a miscommunication.

Maria had come into the high school with the reading ability of a six-year-old. Like many of the students in the school she spoke Greek in the family home and she was unable to speak English fluently when she was five years old when she first went to school.

As the youngest in a large family, Maria was extremely self-reliant and resourceful. She gradually learned English and her teacher, hoping to make Maria less self-conscious about her difficulties with spelling and writing, told Maria to 'Just write how it sounds.' At the age of 13, Maria was recommended for a school for the mentally retarded.

I watched Maria for several months and noticed that she spent most of her school days absolutely silent, making sure that no-one noticed that she wasn't coping. One of the things I found strange was that Maria's writing was well formed. She could copy anything written on the board correctly. She couldn't read it, however. Another conflicting piece of evidence I had was that in this first year at high school, Maria had learned how to read music. This was not something one would expect from a person of low intellectual capability.

Maria made some progress when I started teaching her simple phonetics rules and when she gained a little confidence, I encouraged her to start writing. By analysing her writing, I recognised a few larger words, and realised that, far from being intellectually backward, she was extremely resourceful and creative. She had invented her own spelling system and was quite proficient in using it. The problem was that Maria's written language bore no resemblance to standard English because the spelling conventions used in English were not the ones Maria was using. For Maria, written English was a foreign language.

Taking her first teacher's instruction to 'write it as it sounds' as a six-year-old, meant that her writing phonetically replicated her own Anglo-Greek speech patterns combined with western Sydney pronunciation. By the time Maria had learned English and was starting to read, none of the books were written in the language that Maria had perfected. Once it became possible to identify the rules that Maria had developed for herself in relation to spelling, it became easy to understand what she had written.

Understanding what she had done meant I could help her, but first I had to get her to understand that she was clever and creative and that she had invented her own language. Now she had to unlearn the written language she had used for many years and learn the one that everyone else was using.

Maria was the only one of the Year 7 girls that I actually helped learn to read and spell. From her story I learned that it is so easy *to label people, and once given a label, that label affects the way others perceive them. Maria was 'intellectually disabled' according to the bureaucratic education department and by her teachers, and consequently, she had adopted that label.*

§

I knew why Maria and Erica had problems and I was able to help them. I had no idea why the other girls were unable to read and understand what they were reading. Without understating how or why, I had seen that the unexpected intervention tool that I was using worked far more effectively than I would ever have imagined, but only for some of them. I didn't question the girls to discover possible reasons for their reading difficulties. The process worked without me knowing how their problems had originated. Maria and Erica were the only ones whose stories I knew. Because they told me something about themselves, I was able to work out what had gone wrong.

Repeating the Stress Defusion process I had used a few weeks earlier, a couple more of the girls opened whatever switch had been turned off, and were able to read and learn.

Now I had something totally unexpected to think about. I had seen what had happened but couldn't explain it. I doubted that anyone who hadn't seen the shift in reading ability that happened instantaneously would believe it to be possible. Even I found it difficult to comprehend. I needed a demonstration that something unexpected and quite profound had occurred to convince myself that what I was seeing was actually real.

§

About this time a friend mentioned that his eleven-year old son was reading *The Power of One* by Bryce Courtenay and seemed to be enjoying it. The next day I phoned the school's book supplier and ordered twelve copies of *The Power of One*. This was to be my demonstration. I planned to give the girls a copy of the book and suggest that they read it.

Staffroom comments when the books arrived ranged from total disbelief to amusement at this evidence of my dismissal of conventional wisdom. As one member of staff commented: 'How can you expect girls in the lowest level Year 7 class with the poorest reading standard in the school to read a 650 page book when I wouldn't even ask my Year 12 girls to read a book of that standard?'

The next day I took the girls out into the sunshine and read the first chapter of the book. It was funny watching their reactions. Some of them just drifted off. Others sat totally enthralled by the story. They were horrified by the rudeness of some of the descriptions and amazed that I would read them such a grown-up story. At times, they were convulsed with laughter and at other times saddened then horrified by the events described. When I finished reading the first chapter, I said: 'I have bought a copy of this book for each of you. If you want to find out what happens next, you'll have to read it for yourself.'

I didn't have to wait long to see whether any of them had

accepted the challenge. Two of them appeared in the classroom the next morning looking very glassy eyed.

'What's wrong?' I asked.

Their explanation for their tiredness was that they had stayed up reading till the early hours of the morning. Over the next couple of days, a couple more of the girls started talking about what they had read. Over the next few weeks, four of the girls finished reading the book. Before the end of the term, several others had finished it. Discussing the book one afternoon, one of the girls asked about the author, Bryce Courtenay.

'Was the story true?' she wanted to know.

'You could write to him and ask him', I suggested. 'He might even write back to you. I'm sure he would be thrilled to hear how much you enjoyed reading his book.'

She became very excited about this idea and volunteered to write a letter. She spent three weeks composing her letter and finding out how to type it on one of the school's computers. Then she had to learn how to print it. 'Please come to school and have lunch with us,' she wrote. I sent off her letter and a separate one explaining what the girls had achieved.

It didn't take long for Bryce Courtenay to reply. He wanted to meet the girls, so he invited them to visit the advertising agency where he worked. We accepted his invitation. The letter writer was thrilled to have confirmation that Courtenay had indeed been thrilled to receive her letter. As we walked into the office reception there it was on the notice board for everyone to see. The girls spent quite a long time chatting to their new hero and then had a tour of inspection to discover what went on in an advertising agency. For two girls in the group this was the first time they had ever visited the city and it was certainly a new experience for all of them being shown around a very modern and successful advertising agency, and being able to talk to someone who was so well known. Bryce was the writer of the *Louis the Fly* jingle, which advertised a well-known flyspray. Everyone knew the words of this jingle and could sing it, so, in the eyes of the girls, Bryce Courtenay had to be famous. *The Power of One* was his first novel so he had not, at that time, achieved fame and recognition as an author. That came later. A few days after our visit, Bryce Courtney wrote a full-page account describing their visit and what they had accomplished in the *Sydney Morning Herald*. A couple of months after the girls' visit to the city, Bryce Courtenay followed up on their invitation to visit the school and have lunch with them. This time he brought with him a film crew from the Australian *60 Minutes* program.

§

At the end of Term 3 it was agreed that those girls from the original group of twelve who could now read would manage in the mainstream classes. This caused a great upheaval. The few who had made little progress were understandably upset by the fact that some of their classmates had done so well. Two of the replacement students were in the group not because of learning difficulties but because of behavioural problems.

The teachers couldn't cope with them, so the program I was working with provided an easy solution to their difficulties.

This new situation brought with it a whole range of new problems and some more breakthroughs in understanding, which enabled me to help more girls.

Chapter 5
Stress: Origins and Responses

The breakthrough in Term 2 when girls suddenly started being able to read fluently and learn with ease provided the results that I hoped for but not in the way I had expected. The principal assured me that I wasn't imagining things. He told me that he was getting reports from the parents of the students with whom I was working. They were very pleased by the changes they were seeing in their daughters and they were talking to their friends in the schools that the girls had attended prior to entering high school. Advanced enrolments for the high school were higher than for previous years and the principal at the high school was not quite sure whether this was a good thing or not. Many parents of students with learning problems wanted to enrol their daughters for the following year.

Staff members were less enthusiastic than the Principal. They didn't want to talk to me about what I was doing. They felt threatened by something that was different from the commonly accepted practices that they knew. I felt very much the outsider. I was well aware that I had been given special treatment and had special privileges. For this reason alone, I was resented. The publicity the girls had received hadn't helped. In spite of the antagonism I felt from fellow staff members, I was determined to find out why the changes I had observed were occurring.

§

Prior to working at the high school, I had studied accelerated learning techniques and I understood the detrimental effect of stress on brain function and I knew that this was a significant factor when it came to skills such as reading. What I didn't understand was the cause for the students' high levels of stress. I formulated a hypothesis in order to help me understand what was happening: if a girl had decided, years earlier, that she was stupid, because of some incident in her life where she couldn't do what she thought she ought to be able to do, that became her reality from then on. She would have strongly disliked the label that she had given herself and she really wanted to prove to herself and to others that she was not stupid. Her conscious desire to be clever meant that she had laid a conscious positive affirmation over a deeply held, subconscious decision. This created two conflicting and irreconcilable programs for her. She strived to achieve something that she had already decided she could not do, and the negative, subconscious program remained stronger than the positive affirmation. Until the dilemma could be resolved, the harder she tried the higher the level of stress she experienced. Stress would affect her ability to learn and this scenario would cause difficulties to become more and more serious.

I felt Miranda's problems could be explained with this sort of scenario.

Miranda was one the students who came into the group in Term 3. Her reading levels had gone backward from the time she entered high school. Miranda was probably the most ambitious of all the Year 7 girls I worked with. She found it difficult to cope with the immaturity of her fellow classmates and her self-righteous attitude landed her in many difficult situations.

At this stage of development of the Stress Defusion process, I hadn't yet worked out the relationship between stress and learning difficulties and it wasn't until later that I realised that stress was Miranda's problem, and it was a problem of her own making. She really wanted to be successful and she was anxious about her inability to perform at the level she expected. The stress that resulted meant that she was able to do less and less as the year progressed.

Miranda was determined to succeed and was open to trying anything I suggested. There were times when Miranda seemed to be doing well with her reading and others when she could not read very well at all. Foolishly, I told her that I would continue to work with her until she could read fluently, and even more foolishly, I guaranteed her that she would be able to read fluently by the end of the year – a guarantee that I failed to honour.

On the first day of school, the following year, Miranda was waiting for me. She announced that she could now read. It appeared that her reading ability had shifted at the end of the year when she suddenly found that she could read fluently and understand what she read. I immediately realised that I had created a situation for her such that she couldn't let go of the program that she had been running any earlier than she did. She believed me implicitly. I had guaranteed to her that she would be able to read at the end of the year. That was exactly what happened: she was able to read at the end of the year but not before.

§

Stress adversely affects an individual's ability to learn. It does this by inhibiting the operation of the cerebral cortex. Under stress an individual's ability to perceive and link incoming information with information already known, is hampered. From what I saw when working with people with a variety of different problems and different life situations, it became evident that stress had a continuing and long-lasting effect on performance. I realised that when I tried to help someone who was dealing with an on-going stressful situation, nothing shifted. Not shifting was the body's protection mechanism.

I decided that the reason that work I was doing had no effect for some of the girls was because it was counter to their overall well-being. My work facilitated the processing of information faster than the brain had been capable of doing previously. The technique I was using also caused an expansion of the visual field so that the eyes were able to take in more information. With faster processing capacity and an expanded visual field, an increased level of incoming information was available to the brain. This was not in someone's best interest if they were in a situation of on-going stress and trauma. For them, incoming information represented a threat and they needed to stay shut down for their own protection.

My research indicated that in order to minimise stress levels, the human brain functions in a way designed to reduce, or cancel out, incoming information that is likely to cause stress. It does this by shutting down information traffic between the various parts of the brain, and filters out information that causes strong feelings of fear or anger.

This is due to the fact that, as individuals, our primary goal is survival. Stress is actually an indication that our survival, in terms either of our physical safety or in terms of our representation of who we are to ourselves, is threatened. Ego survival is very important to us and we all have a variety of strategies to ensure that our concept of who we think we are and what we think we know, remain intact.

To reduce stress, we use a variety of very powerful strategies. One is to shut down our brain processing capacity. The most common form of brain shut down involves separating the functions of the right and the left hemispheres. This strategy effectively reduces the speed at which the brain can process information. Alternatively, we develop a strategy of switching between right and left hemispheres of the brain instead of operating with both sides concurrently.

The effect of left/right brain separation is illustrated by the following facts. When it works independently, the left side of the brain has the ability to work at the rate of 40 bits of information per second. When it works independently, the right side of the brain has the ability to work at the rate of

40^3 bits of information per second. In combination, the two sides of the brain have the ability to operate at a speed of 40^4 or 2,560,000 bits of information per second. At this level of brain function, coping with information that threatens our sense of self because it doesn't fit with what we *know*, can cause major stress. High stress levels are life threatening or can be perceived to be so.

My research revealed the significance of a second strategy that reduces the impact of incoming information on our self-image by shifting responsibility from ourselves to others or to factors over which we have no control. We do this by going into strategies of blame, justification, denial and quitting and/or by deleting and distorting incoming information.

Blame

When we resort to blame, we ensure that something or someone other than ourselves is responsible for the problems we are experiencing. By making what happens someone else's fault, we shift responsibility from ourselves to someone or something over which we have no control. If we can't control the situation, then we can't do anything about it. If there is nothing we can do about it, then we are absolved of responsibility. Blaming doesn't provide solutions, but it does make us feel better about ourselves.

Justification

We move into justification when we identify reasons for not being able to do something that we feel we ought to be able to do. We find a reason that acts as an excuse: 'You know I have no aptitude for technical things.' With this attitude, we have no reason to make the effort to learn or understand what we cannot do or do not know. We absolve ourselves of responsibility when we find excuses or reasons to explain the problem away. Again, we do this to avoid taking responsibility, because we are not willing to be honest with ourselves about our shortcomings.

We accept things and adopt the view: 'That's the way it is and the way it has always been'. We feel sorry for ourselves and sad about the situation we find ourselves in, but lack the understanding that we could actually change the situation by making the effort to do something different.

Denial

The third strategy is denial. We move into a state of denial when we are too fearful to face whatever it is that we are fearful of. Denial takes many forms. For some, it involves a life that is so full of action that there isn't time to just *be*. For others, it involves creating continual crises so that they keep themselves very busy fixing everything for everyone. Denial might involve talking endlessly on the phone, meeting friends for coffee, shopping, or playing computer games for hours at a time. By keeping busy with mind-numbing activities, they can deny that there is something in their life that they don't like.

Denial is the means used to avoid facing the truth. Someone whose life isn't what they would like it to be doesn't have to acknowledge even to themselves that they are in any way short-changing themselves or living in a way that is less than meaningful.

A strange incident helped me to understand the power of denial:

As part of my study to identify strategies that would help overcome learning difficulties, I researched the application of accelerated learning techniques. I was given the opportunity to market a sophisticated language learning system, which was developed by accelerated learning guru Colin Rose. Wanting to demonstrate how well the technique worked, I decided to provide the opportunity for a couple of high schools to use it for a trial period. At one school I spoke at length to the language master. He listened to my explanation and he said that he would like to see how the boys reacted to it so I spent a period with a class demonstrating the program. The language master and the class teacher were both present during the demonstration. Whilst the boys reacted positively, the language master wasn't convinced that accelerated learning could speed up the learning process. To convince him I left a copy of Colin Rose's book 'Accelerated Learning'.

Several months after this demonstration, I was invited to talk to teachers who were involved with the Saturday Language Schools in Sydney. These schools were designed for children whose parents spoke English as a second language and who wanted to improve fluency in their parents' native language. The meeting was held in the school that I had visited earlier and I was met by the teacher who I had spoken to at that time.

'Hello Ken. It is good to see you again.' I was surprised by Ken's response.

'We've not met before.'

'Don't you remember, I visited your school and showed you this language program.' With this I produced the large folder of books and tapes. It was a colourful presentation and not one that could be easily forgotten.

'I have never seen that,' Ken responded.

'Don't you remember, I demonstrated the program to a class of boys in that room,' I said, as I pointed to the room where I had done the demonstration.

'No. That never happened.'

'And I left you a copy of this book for you to read.'

'I don't have that book. What's more, I have a very good memory for people and I have never met you before.' At that moment, another teacher walked by. It was the teacher in whose class I had done the demonstration.

'Are you here to do the demonstration of the accelerated learning language program?' This teacher obviously remembered me. When I demonstrated the program that morning Ken, who was in charge of the meeting, was absent. He had other, more important, matters to attend to.

This story demonstrates the power of the mind to filter every-day experiences so that they agree with what is already known to be true. When new information does not fit in with what we know, or threatens what we know, we change the incoming information so that it agrees with what we *know* by deleting it in the way I have described, or by distorting and/or generalising it.

Quitting

Quitting is the ultimate low point because quitting represents the choice of *non-life*. It means refusing to take responsibility for oneself and handing over that responsibility to someone else. Fortunately, there are many who enjoy taking on the responsibility that others hand them. Doing so makes them feel important.

Quitting takes many forms. The ultimate form is suicide. More often it takes the form of shutting down feelings, perceptions, and/or breathing. Emotionally, physically and mentally we go into a state of numbness, unable to think or feel fully.

Quitting may involve shutting down one aspect of ourselves. We shut off our brains from our hearts or our minds from our spirit. When we deny our feelings, we shut down physically by breathing shallowly which causes us to restrict the intake of oxygen. We may shut down the ability to see, hear and feel. This affects every aspect of life. Some people quit by becoming unthinking robots who perform the same routine tasks every day with no sense of purpose and very little feeling of accomplishment. Some quit through terminal illness or mental or physical ill-health.

Medication

A common strategy designed to reduce the impact of stress is to resort to medication to mask stress symptoms. Beyond Blue, an Australian organisation, states that 45% of Australian people experience mental health conditions during the course of their lifetime. The most common conditions are anxiety, ongoing stress with no particular reason or cause, and depression.

According to the *Beyond Blue* website, the benefits of medication are a decrease in symptoms such as heart palpitation, sweating and shaking, a reduction in negative thoughts and improved mood. Countering the benefits are side effects such as nausea, sexual disfunction, poor memory, impaired co-ordination, sleep disturbance and increased blood pressure. Some medications require a strict diet because foods such as cheese and alcohol can increase blood pressure leading to stroke or death. Medication can lead to drug dependence. According to *Beyond Blue*, rebound anxiety and withdrawal symptoms are common when drugs are withdrawn.

Acceptance

Just allowing what happens just to happen can actually work to reduce stress levels without the need for any form of intervention, and accepting that stress exists for a reason is a first step to identifying the cause. Stress is the consequence of things in our life that need investigation and is an appropriate response to what is happening.

It is also important to understand that emotional energy associated with the underlying cause of the stress attracts life experiences to us that are likely to increase stress levels. Each experience, similar in some way to the one responsible for our stress situation in the first place, adds to the energy associated with this issue. We eventually reach a point where we can no longer deny the emotion. That is what I did to allow the emotions attached to the wool press incident, which I described in chapter 2, to surface.

§

In order to release emotional energy, people have to be open to the idea that feeling really sad, angry or fearful is actually OK. Allowing themselves to feel emotions that have been triggered by the events in their lives, or sometimes for no apparent reason, may actually be all that is needed to resolve issue-related stress. People don't even need to identify the cause for healing to occur. Doctors call this spontaneous recovery and whilst it may seemingly occur spontaneously, it is possible to dig deeply into the subconscious thought processes and realise that a thought has been the cause of the stress condition. Allowing feelings to surface, however bad it feels to do this, actually helps healing to occur and allows restoration of full body and mental function. This is because the body has its own strategies of stress reduction. What looks like magical intervention, may actually be triggered by an individual's preparedness to just allow what happens, to happen.

There might still be times when the situation has become so severe that intervention is required. Additionally, impaired health due to poor diet, inadequate rest and physical activity, and stress conditions themselves, which are tremendously enervating, mean that the body simply does not have sufficient energy to activate the processes designed to restore health.

§

The fight, flight, freeze response.

Term 3 of my first year at the high school presented me with a series of new challenges, the result of which was to greatly increase stress levels in the classroom. The students for whom I had not yet found the key needed for them to make a breakthrough felt that they were failures. Some of the others profoundly resented the fact that they had been put into the *dummies* class. Girls who had replaced those who had returned to mainstream classes were not necessarily poor readers when they first arrived at the school but had gone backwards during the first two terms. A couple of the newcomers had serious behavioural problems. The newcomers knew exactly why they were in my class: they were failures.

In addition, problems such as hyperactivity, which I attributed mostly to poor diet and the school's resistance to remove drink vending machines, didn't help. Sugar and caffeine-filled drinks adversely affected the girls' ability to concentrate. My assertion that diet had a major impact on learning ability had one positive outcome: the school changed its policy in relation to food sold at the tuck shop. Foods that were considered to be healthier were substituted for the sugar buns and lollies that were sold previously.

Mid-way through the final term of that year I discussed the problems I was having with the principal, and we decided that the arrangement of trying to help the girls by putting them in a special class was not working. We decided to disband the special class at the end of the year. Until the new plan was to be put in place, I had to continue with a less than optimal situation. Even so, whilst I was not happy about what was happening in my little class, Term 3 provided some valuable insights as stress levels increased.

§

In stress situations people respond as animals do in the wild. The first response is to fight. The second is to flee or run away from the situation. In today's world, the more common response is to freeze, which is what animals do in the hope that they will not be noticed. One of the consequences of the freeze response is to store tension in the backs of the legs.

The fight, flight, freeze response can be explained in the following way. If a threat is perceived, a person's immediate response is to do whatever is needed to survive. The body responds without conscious thought. A high level of energy is generated and directed to where it will be needed most: the leg muscles. If the situation is a one off and if this energy is not used by running or fighting, it gradually dissipates, and things return to normal. If someone lives in a situation of constantly recurring threat, without being able to run or fight, then they go into freeze mode. Energy builds up over time and becomes blocked to such an extent that the leg muscles become very tight and sore. Many people with severe mental problems walk on their toes because of the tight muscles in the backs of their legs.

I was fascinated to discover that if I massaged the students' legs without using my other hand to bridge the vertical auricular line above their ears, the muscles in their legs were not sore. Some of the girls were intrigued that I could make pain come and go just by taking my hand away from their heads. Occasionally, girls would identify memories that were associated with particular areas of soreness as I worked to release the blocked energy.

I particularly noticed the link between the flight/fight/freeze response when I worked with Salimeh. Few teachers were able to cope with this child in a normal classroom situation. Her behaviour was disruptive and attention seeking. When things became too difficult, she absented herself from lessons and hid in the toilets. If there was a fracas in the classroom, Salimeh was invariably in the middle of it. Academically, she was reasonably proficient, but she lacked interest or motivation. All she wanted was to have friends and to have people like her.

Once I got to know Salimeh, I understood why she behaved as she did. I also knew that there was very little I could do to help her. The situation in which she was placed, the one that was creating her stress, was ongoing. She needed to stay shut down for her own protection.

Salimeh was the eldest of six children. Her family was Lebanese and her mother was living on a deserted wife's pension in a housing commission flat. They were very poor. By the time Salimeh was thirteen, her mother, who was still only twenty-nine years old, was overweight and diabetic. She was often sick and in hospital and when this happened Salimeh was expected to look after her younger brothers and sisters. Regardless of whether her mother was home or not, she took care of the children after school. I heard that there was a court order in place, which prohibited Salimeh's father from seeing his eldest daughter. She never told me the reason for this. She came to school to have a rest and to have a bit of time out from the responsibility of looking after the family.

In my attempts to help her I used the Stress Defusion process regularly with Salimeh and massaged her legs to release blocked energy. The pain that she experienced as I worked with her was excruciating. I repeatedly asked her if she wanted me to stop but she insisted that I continue. I understood the reason one day when, as she came into the classroom, she 'said: 'I just walked up the stairs and it didn't hurt nearly as much as it used to.' Until then, she had not mentioned that she was in constant pain.

The following year, when she returned to regular classes, Salimeh's work and behaviour became progressively more troubling. She started truanting from school and wandering the streets. She was a beautiful child and her naivety, and her need for attention, put her in danger. Teachers were relieved when, after her fourteenth birthday, she was sent back to Lebanon to an arranged marriage.

The stress that Salimeh was experiencing was ongoing during the time I knew her. I was unable to help her.

§

Initially, I was only able to identify the location of blocked energy in the backs of the legs, because that was where the girls felt pain. As I gained more experience, I developed great insight as to where the blockages were located. Muscle tone felt a little different in some areas compared with others. With experience, I picked up more and more subtle clues.

When I was working with Irene, I located a really sore area on the inside of her right leg, and I was really surprised when she said, without being asked: 'When you were working on my leg, three separate incidents came to mind.'

'What did you remember?'

'The first incident was when my mother refused to let me see my grandfather when he was in hospital. I knew he was dying. I was very angry with my mother. The second one was when I was quite small. I was asleep on the back seat of the car and my head must have been resting on the door. A motorcyclist swerved and hit the car. I woke up because of the terrible noise just as he was thrown up into the air by the force of the impact. It is a terrifying memory.'

'What is the third memory?' I asked.

'Well, my Mum has been very sick since she had a hysterectomy and she gets really bad pains in her stomach and she gets ulcers. She's really very sick.'

'Are you frightened for her?'

'Yes.'

'Do you try and hide your fear because you don't want to upset her?'

'Yes.'

'Do you have a Dad?'

'Yes'

'Perhaps you could share your fears with your Dad. Perhaps he is afraid, too.' This idea caused Irene to start crying. As she did, I felt energy release from her leg. Later, when I checked what progress she had made in terms of her reading ability, I was pleased that her fluency had improved remarkably.

§

I needed to delve into much deeper territory when Rachel came to me for help.

In Year 7, Rachel was the school's champion swimmer. She was also an A grade scholar. Her work during Year 8 had deteriorated quite remarkably and teachers put this down to her busy training schedule and to the stress of competitive sport.

I didn't have any contact with Rachel until she was in Year 9. She complained about pain caused by her knee joint slipping out of its socket. As she started investigating the cause for this, Rachel reported that her legs had lost all feeling. I had no idea why this had happened.

Resistance to letting go of blocked energy can lead to headaches, and Rachel's mother was understandably concerned by the headaches that Rachel experienced following the session that I had with her. I spoke to her mother and told her that I was quite concerned for her daughter. For the next few months, Rachel did the rounds of doctors, psychologists and psychiatrists but she was forbidden to work with me. She stopped competitive swimming but her knee joint kept pulling out of its socket and Rachel spent months on crutches with her knee bandaged. During this time, her relationship with her parents deteriorated. They had been her most ardent supporters and now it seemed that their talented daughter would never swim competitively again. Understandably they were disappointed.

At the end of the following year, Rachel came to me in tears asking for help. Her knee condition had continued to deteriorate and doctors were insisting on surgery to permanently stiffen it. Rachel had suffered constant pain for over two years and she was desperate. The resistance she put up previously was no longer a problem. Rachel was now ready to look at whatever had been worrying her earlier. As soon as we started, she saw clear pictures that explained to her what had happened. The pictures weren't real. She saw what was happening as a sort of dream state. The picture she described was of herself in an operating theatre as a skeleton without a face. It was a death scene. 'Death' was at the end of the bed. Lying on the floor beside her was her leg, which had been cut off. Blood was pouring out from the leg. Around her, sitting in tiered seats and looking through a window were her friends, parents and teachers. They were all laughing at her.

'Who cut off your leg?' I asked.

'I did.'

'What was the intention behind cutting your leg off?'

'I wanted to punish my parents. They expected too much

of me and I couldn't do what they wanted. It was too hard and no matter what I did, I couldn't meet their expectations.'

'Who suffered most from your decision to punish your parents?'

'I did.'

'Was that a good decision?'

'No.'

'Is there perhaps some other decision that you could make that would be more useful?'

'Yes.'

'Can you do that?'

'Yes.'

I didn't ask what decision Rachel made but I do know that her knee started to heal shortly after. Three months later she was able to discard her crutches.

§

Towards the end of that year I was summoned to the office of the Student Counsellor. Someone had reported me for massaging the girls.

'Are you touching the girls?' she asked, clearly embarrassed to be put into a situation where she had to ask this question.

'Yes. I massage their legs,' I replied. 'Would you like me to show you what I am doing?' She agreed that I could demonstrate my technique on her, so I sat alongside her, made her put her leg up on a chair so that I could reach it, and held *my hand cupping her ear and started to massage her leg. Almost immediately she demanded that I stop.*

'That hurts. That really hurts. That's enough. Stop.'

She didn't ask me to explain but seemed satisfied that I was not interfering with the girls.

Two years later I heard that the counsellor had left the school shortly after this episode. She had been diagnosed with cancer of the legs and she died soon after. At the time I heard this news I regretted that I hadn't understood the link between sore legs resulting from ongoing stress, and the consequences of holding that stress in the body. That understanding came much later when I realised that when issues were resolved in the mind, the body benefitted.

Chapter 6
Eyes: Filing Clerks of the Mind

Shakespeare wrote that the 'eyes are the windows of the soul' and he was right.

Jacob Liberman[5], an American optometrist who decided that glasses were not the best solution to eye problems, taught me that visual constriction occurred in conditions of stress. It was this idea that caused me to think about the connection between specific areas of avoidance in the visual field and a possible connection to traumatic memories. The intention behind restricting the visual field is to shut down access to memories that cause us to become emotional. The strategy is only marginally effective in reducing stress levels which decrease dramatically only when we understand the cause of the problem we are attempting to hide from.

I think of the eyes as the filing clerks of the mind. Their role is to both store and retrieve information from our memory files. When there are memories that we prefer not to remember, we train the eyes so that they do not access those parts of the visual field that provide an entry point to those memories. Reluctance to focus in particular areas

---

5   Jacob Liberman, OD, PhD *Light: Medicine of the Future*, Published by Simon and Schuster, 1991

of the visual field when thinking something like: 'I'm not safe,' causes a person to avoid the area that provides access to memories associated with that decision. Other avoidance strategies include defocusing and/or restricting the visual field in an attempt to not see, or more accurately, not remember, the events associated with intense trauma and the emotions that were associated with these memories at the time of the experience. Patterns of restriction in our peripheral vision change, depending on our thoughts at a particular time.

Over time, because we choose to not remember traumatic events, the muscles in our eyes constrict so that accessing specific areas of peripheral vision becomes difficult and, eventually, painful. Pain causes us to restrict our visual field and change our ability to see so that the pain that arises from past memory is translated into pain when we try to remember. Jacob Liberman's research provided evidence that eyesight problems are created by our need to not remember.

I realised that refusal to access an area of the visual field, while thinking about something that caused distress at some time in the past indicates that this area holds the key to retrieving significant memories. These memories provide the data needed to reconstruct the events that caused a negative decision to be made: a decision that became a program that the brain obeys. Because the program that arises from this process is generally negative, it follows that the consequence for our life's experiences is also negative. Because we don't understand that we have been responsible for creating the negative programs that control our lives, we tend to blame others, circumstances, or bad luck for what happens in our lives.

Before attempting to locate the areas of resistance, it is necessary to talk about the perceived problems and develop a hypothesis relating to what the original decision *might* have been. The reason for doing this is because the entry point to past memories in the eyes depends on the thought that is being investigated. The entry point for one thought will be different from the entry point for a different thought. The thought doesn't have to be exactly the same as the original one: a close approximation is sufficient. Having identified a negative statement that approximates the original thought, I always ask clients to focus on this statement while I work with the eyes by drawing an infinity sign with my hand and asking them to follow this pattern with their eyes. When I see avoidance, skipping, twitching, jumping or refusal to access a particular point of peripheral vision I can identify the area where work is needed. By *work* I mean strategies to encourage the client to access the area that they are avoiding so that they can retrieve lost memories.

> *Stephanie was an extremely retarded 14-year-old who had created a very effective method of making sure she could not use her eyes to access information. Because of this, she couldn't find her way to the shops, use money, or remember anything she had learned. She was in a special class in high school.*
>
> *It was significant that when Stephanie was asked a question, she moved her eyes randomly. The movements were very*

fast, and sometimes she also became cross-eyed. Stephanie couldn't find the information she needed to answer questions. It looked to me as if she knew it was there somewhere — but she couldn't find it.

Stephanie couldn't function in life because she was unable to locate the appropriate information that she needed. Possibly she had decided, at some point in her life, that she did not want to remember what she had seen, and her eyes had shut off all communication between her eyes and her brain. Fortunately, with the Stress Defusion process it was possible to restore this link so that her eyes could function normally and with this reconnection came immediate improvement in her ability to function in life.

§

My understanding of the role of the eyes in storing and retrieving memories came in a moment of insight, which allowed me to see the connection between various disciplines and to identify a pattern that was common to all of them.

In my kinesiology studies I had been taught to replace negative thoughts with positive ones using a variety of strategies involving the eyes. I had learned how to install positive thoughts in different parts of the brain using different eye positions. Like circus tricks, these methodologies are clever, but I felt they were covering problems with Band-Aids, rather than addressing the issues and finding solutions to them.

When I studied Neuro Linguistic Programming with Stephanie Burns and Marvin Oka I came to understand the importance of the eyes in filing and accessing memories. I went a little beyond the work that was being done in the field of NLP in the 1990s when I realised that the eyes are the key to accessing both subconscious and conscious memories, and the emotion associated with those memories.

Identifying how we access memory is the foundation of Neurolinguistic Programming[6]. Richard Bandler and John Grinder documented the now commonly accepted relationship between the position of eyes and the types of information that is accessed, in particular eye positions. They then developed techniques to find out the sequence of thought that we use to act or to make decisions and how we use different strategies to code information, so that we know how we feel about it. For example, we might file happy pictures in colour and unhappy pictures might be in black and white, perhaps even with a frame around them. Bandler and Grinder discovered that it is possible to change how we feel about our memories, simply by changing how we store memory.

My experience confirmed Bandler and Grinder's findings about specific eye positions that are accessed in order to find visual, auditory and kinaesthetic memories. Additionally, I discovered that when we look down and to the left to access feelings or emotions there is a specific location for each

---

6   Richard Bandler, John Grinder, *Frogs in Princes: Neuro Linguistic Programming*, Real People Press, 1979

emotion. Terror, for example, is accessed when we look down and to the far left, but we access sadness when we look straight down. My experience confirmed the Neuro Linguistic Programming model, which shows that when we look directly left or right, we access auditory memories, and when we look up, we access visual memories. I also realised that predominantly visual people tend to defocus or look inwards when they think deeply. Perhaps this happens as a way to access the memory bank in the posterior part of the brain, which is where we store visual memories. I also found that future fears are accessed by focussing on points straight ahead at various distances from the eyes. This is the area cleared last in a session after all the peripheral vision glitches are identified and defused.

I had worked with accelerated learning techniques developing teaching strategies that access individual's visual, auditory and kinaesthetic learning strategies to enhance information input for those who could learn easily. To my surprise, I discovered that these strategies didn't help people with existing learning problems. They simply helped people who were able to learn become more efficient in the learning process.

For me, everything came together when I realised that eye movement shows exactly where the eyes need to be to recall specific traumatic memories, even those that aren't consciously remembered. I also realised that the eyes could be used to release energy associated with traumatic memories. This understanding was particularly significant because nothing can change until the emotional energy that is associated with the memories is released. Until the link between a strong negative emotion and the memory is broken, it is not possible to access the memories without judgement. When a particular memory is associated with, for example, fear, sadness or anger we judge the memory as being something bad, rather than as just a memory. I suspected that the energy that was released during the process was the energy of blocked emotion that had become associated with the memories, at their time of origin.

Understanding the need to split the memories of past traumatic events from the emotions fused with those memories led me to adopt the name Stress Defusion. Once the association between memory and emotion is broken, it becomes possible to use strategies to release energy associated with trapped emotion and process memories in a way that leads to a non-judgemental recollection of an event. Only then, when judgement is released, is it possible to come to understand what the process involving the creation of negative programs is designed to teach.

When someone holds onto a thought about a problem being experienced and holds their eyes in a position that they normally avoid when thinking about this problem, they can experience discomfort, pain, nausea and strong emotions. Prolonged holding can create major discomfort. For some people, memories that have been buried for years come to the conscious mind and might be emotionally and physically distressing. I have seen people feel sick, and be sick, or become extremely angry or fearful as a consequence of bringing long hidden memories to conscious awareness. When people are unable or unwilling to consciously access these memories, the physical feelings and pain associated with the memories may surface, but not the information.

A session with James illustrated the power of the eyes to access body memory and re-create physical responses that were outside the ability of the conscious mind to control.

James came to me because he was so depressed that he found it very difficult to get out of bed in the morning. Accessing one part of his peripheral vision caused him intense physical discomfort. Almost immediately, he felt nauseous. Seconds later he raced to the bathroom to throw up. When he returned and we resumed work the same thing happened. Again, he rushed to the bathroom. I used a kinesiology technique called muscle testing, to find out how old he had been when the incident that was triggering the nausea had occurred.

'What happened when you were six?'

'I was really happy when I was six. I remember it as being one of the happiest times of my life. I was living in Canada at the time and...' At this point James stopped. Then he continued. 'I was six when I fell through the ice into the river. It was mid-winter and the river had frozen over. I was with my brother. I fell through a hole. I couldn't swim.'

'What do you remember about that?'

'I remember looking up and seeing the light coming through the hole. I couldn't reach it because I couldn't swim.'

This was only one incident but it was a start in James's

Chapter 6   Eyes: Filing Clerks of the Mind

journey to recover lost memories and discover the cause of his depression.

§

By working with James and others I understood that the eye positions which we find difficult to access are issue specific, and the eyes have a different pattern of energy blockage when we think of one area of difficulty in our lives, compared with another problem. Clearing one problem did not necessarily help with others but it soon became apparent that separate fears could become grouped together in bigger and bigger bundles, because they have a similar origin. These memory systems are called engrams, or meta-programs, and some are so powerful they affect every aspect of our lives. It is possible to peel away a significant block, incident by incident, by holding onto the thought of the overall problem and finding the different locations in the visual field that are avoided. This is necessary in order to identify and clear different aspects of the problem.

Anna showed me how a range of apparently separate problems become linked. Resolving her difficulties involved working with many areas of her visual field, tackling one incident at a time.

Anna's problem arose because, while still very small, someone must have told her she was wrong when she showed fear when something frightened her. From that moment on, she felt it wrong to show that she was afraid of anything. Whenever she became frightened, she tried to hide her fear. When I met Anna, it appeared that her life was governed by a large number of what appeared to be totally irrational fears. She was afraid of storms, of big waves, of falling off the trampoline, of falling off a play gym, of being alone on her own.

Having been told she was wrong the first time, she had a double dilemma from then on: not only was she afraid, but also she was wrong for feeling afraid. Finding the memories of many times when she had been afraid, and encouraging her to feel her fear and creating a situation where it was all right for her to feel her fear was all that was needed. She just had to feel it and allow the fear to dissipate.

§

I understood the importance of the eyes when I realised that much of the information that forms the building blocks of our conceptual thinking come through the senses. Our eyes, nose, ears, skin are the organs that translate what is occurring around us into electrically transmitted codes, which end up in our brains for a complicated process of unscrambling, encoding, processing and subsequent decoding. Just how important our eyes are in terms of information input, is demonstrated by the fact that each eye contains more than 1 billion moving parts and 137 million light receptors. For all except those who are blind, our eyes provide us with 90% of the information we receive in a lifetime. Of the three billion messages relayed to the brain every second, two billion are received through the eyes.

Concentrating on a question or problem, while stretching

the optic nerve and holding the eyes at the limit of focus, facilitates energy release. Energy release is followed by restoration of the ability to see more easily, frequently with a wider visual field than was possible before. Sometimes a memory, devoid of any strong emotional attachment, identifies the origin of the problem.

Perhaps one of the keys to explaining why holding the eyes at a point on the periphery of our visual field allows access to hidden memories accompanied by a release of energy is that in this position we defocus our eyes and in a defocused state, thinking stops. Defocusing therefore allows us to be *in the present*. When both the person being cleared and the person facilitating the clearing are in a state of defocus, there is a totally clear space in which to work. Working with blocked areas of peripheral vision pulls childhood memories to conscious awareness. This is the time when many of the problems we experience in life, originate.

§

Bringing hidden memories to conscious awareness is not something that should be done without due regard for the consequences. Many clients were stunned by the memories that they retrieved. They had no idea that the events that they recalled had occurred, and they were often incredulous about what was revealed to them when they were able to access their subconscious memories. My concern was always that I should never hint or suggest a possible explanation for the consequences of events in their lives. That would always be something they needed to work out for themselves.

We hide some memories as a form of self-protection. Some can be hugely distressing when they resurface. Unless the memories can be processed at the conscious level, allowing unconscious memories to resurface means they may cause a resurgence of the emotional distress that was appropriate at the time of the original event. Processing requires letting go of judgement around the event and releasing the emotional energy associated with the event. It takes skilled counselling to facilitate this process.

§

At the physical level, experiencing stress that arises from memories and decisions made at the time of the events related to those memories, causes the pupils of our eyes to contract. In an effort not to see or remember, the iris constricts, as does the visual field. Progressively, we develop tunnel vision. By our refusal to acknowledge anything scary or unpleasant, we control both the physical apparatus that allows us to see and the ability to access our emotions. Over time, refusal to access traumatic memories and the shutdown of emotions that are linked to those memories can affect our whole body. Our eyes change to accommodate our decisions about not seeing, becoming short sighted when we choose not to see the big picture, and long sighted if we choose to not see detail. Our bodies may, over time, become inflexible or misshapen as a side effect of the shutting down.

§

A particularly astute client drew my attention to the fact that the release of blocked energy in the legs can be speeded up by moving the eyes to the position that corresponds to the area of soreness in the legs. This involved a process of working alternatively with the eyes and then with the legs. Clearing an area of blocked energy in the legs facilitated the identification of deeper memories that could then be accessed through the eyes. As each layer is removed, more and more deeply unconscious memories come to the surface.

Once the leg/eye connection became apparent, the correlation between the location of eye dysfunction and the location of leg pain became clear. Having made this connection, it was easy to generalise the idea that physical pain or inflexibility in any part of the body can be associated with memories of traumatic events. This understanding made it easier to clear energy blockages in those people who demonstrated energy blocks in the form of physical pain or physical rigidity.

Working with physical inflexibility or pain meant working backwards by first locating the pain caused by stretching or bending the body, and then finding where this area was located in the visual field. Werner illustrated this connection really well.

As a 10-year-old Werner couldn't bend forward. When sitting on the ground, he sat back on his hips with his back rounded. When asked to lean forward, he just rounded his back more and more and pushed his head forward. His hip joints were totally rigid.

Confirmation that the eye clearing process was connected to physical rigidity occurred as Werner cleared areas of his peripheral vision. As he did this he progressively released the rigidity in his hips so that he was able, when sitting, to move from an angle of 130 degrees with his legs outstretched, and bend forward so that his torso and head touched the floor. It took about half an hour to achieve this result.

Testing the improvement in Werner's reading ability at the end of this session illustrated the link between intellectual capability and physical flexibility. When tested at the beginning of the session, Werner had been a slow, stumbling reader with poor comprehension. At the end he was reading far faster than would have been normal for a boy of his age.

§

During the years following the time I spent at the high school, the Stress Defusion process developed quickly as I incorporated new discoveries and worked with a wide variety of issues. At the high school my primary goal was to release blocked energy so that whole brain operation could be restored. This work provided the basis for what was to follow: a much more complex series of challenges involving adult clients with a variety of life problems.

Initially I didn't understand the process that caused blocked energy. Once I realised the connection between the unwillingness to feel emotion and the way we block energy, I developed visualisation techniques to facilitate people's ability to get in touch with their emotions. Intensive questioning provided a way to identify the origin of the problem and, over time, I defined specific questioning techniques to identify exactly what sort of approach was required for each client. Some clients were unable to access memories, but their bodies contained all the information that was required to identify the cause of problems, so I worked with pain and inflexibility to bring the issues to conscious awareness and to test progress. For some clients, conflict resolution counselling was helpful when there was conflict between what they consciously wanted and couldn't have, because they were reluctant or unable to access emotions. Sometimes, I asked clients to walk the pattern of the infinity sign and as they walked for an hour or more, I could see by their walking pattern the location of the problems. By questioning them about aspects of their experience, I was able to facilitate their understanding of the issue being investigated. Each case was different and different strategies were required for every client.

§

I have mentioned several times the idea that people create

lifetimes of extreme difficulty because of decisions they made as children in response to traumatic events or circumstances. By working with the Stress Defusion process, I soon understood that this was not something that had happened by accident. It was designed as a way to teach each person something that was significant in terms of their soul journey. When I came to this understanding, I realised that part of my role was to facilitate the learning that their experiences had been designed to teach. Two questions became important to the process: 'What have you learned from your experiences that resulted from the decision you made as a child?' and 'Who do you blame for what happened?' Accepting without judgement that their experiences were designed to teach them something significant, without resorting to blame of others, was an important aspect of the Stress Defusion process. Identifying what they had learned was also important.

The Elohim explained these ideas in the following way: *Every experience we have is for a purpose. There is no such thing as chance. We choose to experience life and we choose the experiences that life has to offer. This is part of the contractual agreement we enter into before we are born. Of course, we have free will. We can choose not to follow the blueprint. When we make such a choice, our route through life becomes an even more interesting experience. Fear of facing the experience is the reason we choose not to. Opting out is not an option. Even opting out through death by suicide or illness merely postpones the inevitable. When we look at life as a game to be played, we lose our attachment to having things the way we think they ought to be.*

§

Early on, I understood that once the issue they were investigating had been cleared, clients would be tested in a way that would confirm that the lesson their experiences had been designed to teach them had actually been learned. A change in response indicated that learning had occurred. As they completed their session, I warned each client: 'You will be tested. Something will happen in the near future that will show you whether or not you have truly understood what this life experience was designed to teach you.' Most didn't believe me at the time, but later confirmed that what I had predicted would happen, actually happened. The test involved being put into a situation similar to the one that had started off the whole process. Their response to being in a similar situation allowed them to discover whether they had repeated the decision they had made originally, or whether they had responded more appropriately. For those that failed the test, their lives reverted to patterns similar to the ones they had experienced before. Passing the test meant they could move on to a new set of challenges.

§

Birth is a transition between a warm, safe, comfortable

environment in the womb and an unknown, uncertain world. In chapter 2, I told the story of Andrew, the teenager who had chosen to paralyse one side of his body rather than experience the pain he was suffering during his passage down the birth canal. If, as Andrew indicated, a baby has awareness of what the future holds, birth would be accompanied by a level of trepidation and fear. Perhaps it was this fear that held Andrew in the birth canal.

Following the work he did to understand how he had created the difficulties that he had experienced since birth, Andrew had the opportunity to make the transition from a safe environment at his school, where he knew what was expected of him, into a far more demanding college environment. Whilst this was a very different experience from being born, it had elements of the same situation: transition from the known into the unknown and a need to confront fear and self-doubt that accompanies all such transitions. Graduating from school and going to college was the test that Andrew was given to show him that he had learned what he needed to learn from everything that had happened in his life. He failed to make the transition, choosing to move back into the school situation, which represented safety. He failed again when he was given the opportunity to study music in Australia and he chose to return to Canada and to his mother. Had he chosen to confront his fears he would have moved on to a new set of challenges, designed to prepare him for what he had come to Earth to do.

When I understood what was happening, I chose to cut

all ties with Andrew. I suspected it could take him a long time before the frustrations and disappointment that would accompany his decision to stay stuck in a safe place, would be sufficient to force him out of his comfort zone and accept the challenges that moving forward would provide. Had he chosen to move forward, I suspect my reaction would have been different and I would have chosen to assist him overcome any resistance that prevented him from achieving his goal.

Releasing energy and clearing blocks has always been the easy part of the Stress Defusion process. The more difficult task was to get clients to understand what their experiences were designed to teach them. Even more difficult was facilitating each client in letting go judgement of the manner in which their lessons had been learned. Clients needed to understand that their experiences, regardless of how bad they had been, were for a purpose: to teach them something important or to allow them to understand something they had not previously known or understood. Once this was identified, they realised that when decisions are made from a point of trust in some higher guidance, the consequences arising from making those decisions were for the greater good of all.

Chapter 7
Decisions, memories, values, attitudes and beliefs

I believe that the life we create for ourselves is the outcome of a complex variety of experiences from which we build our decisions, memories, values, attitudes and beliefs. These determine how we operate in the world and also determine the sorts of experiences we have. If we are angry and fearful, for example, we will attract angry, fearful people to us, and our experiences occur as a consequence of those interactions.

In my experience, few people attempt to work out why things happen as they do, preferring simply to accept that things are as they are. Bad things are generally accepted without question except perhaps for a rather plaintive, 'Why me?' Alternatively, people blame something or someone else for their life situation. When we start to examine the origin of the circumstances of our lives, it is necessary to go within because it is here that all the answers can be found.

One significant concept is reincarnation, which is basic to many Eastern philosophies as it was to Christianity until 533CE. In that year, the Ecumenical Council of the Catholic Church in Constantinople voted to strike all references to it from the Bible in order to solidify church control. Some people who do believe in reincarnation suggest that prior to coming to Earth in each lifetime, we decide the purpose for our life and develop a plan so that we can achieve our purpose. Even though we may not be consciously aware that there is a plan, we are drawn towards it by a sense of inner knowing, although we have a choice as to whether or not we will follow the plan.

Some people go even further, suggesting we have a purpose for being alive at this time and believe that we also choose the family into which we will be born. These people also believe that we choose the circumstances of our childhood and the experiences that we have will allow us to learn what it is we have come to Earth to learn.

In the introduction to *Everything in Its Place* I told the story of a meditation session after which I accessed information relating to my life purpose and higher purpose. Because of this experience, and what has happened subsequently, I believe that the idea of having a purpose for being on Earth at this time and choosing the circumstances of life that assist the achievement of that purpose is true. It has certainly been true for me. Initially, I thought that the insights I gained from attending the meditation were fascinating, but unrealistic. I had no concept that what I learned that day was the blueprint for what was to come. I had no understanding that, from then on, my life's path would be determined by my need to do what I had decided I would do prior to coming to Earth. Trust was required, and, as each step was successfully accomplished, trust grew. The manner in which I would achieve my goals was determined by the decisions I made as I progressed along a non-defined path. What I did find was that working to achieve the goals that were outlined for me at that meditation has made me happy.

Looking back, I know that my life since that day has been lived with purpose and that everything foretold on that day has come to pass. The things that I needed to learn as prerequisite to the development of Stress Defusion, and the circumstances that allowed the process to be developed, were provided. The information that I received from the *Elohim*, gave me a framework for my thinking and an understanding of why things happen as they do. I passed some of this information on when I trained others in the Stress Defusion process and when I wrote *Final Days of Judgement*. For me, the Stress Defusion process allowed me to bring my own forgotten memories and decisions to conscious awareness and to let go of the negative programs that I had written for myself. Remembering allowed me to recognise the values, attitudes and beliefs that have determined my life's path since that time.

It has not always been easy. There have been many times when I have questioned why things have happened as they have, rather than in the way I would have preferred. I have berated myself for lacking clarity regarding the choices I made.

The most significant thing that I learned as a result of my own journey was that we create our own reality. I have already explained how we do this, but because our most significant decisions have been made as a consequence of events that we often choose to forget, we have no idea that these decisions even exist. Without this information we have no way of explaining to ourselves why our lives play out in the way they do.

Decisions, and the values, attitudes and beliefs that arise from them, are important because they determine the success of future actions. The outcome of actions we plan for the future is determined by the decisions we made in the past. This is true until such time as we remember that the decisions we made in the past were appropriate at the time they were made, but do not have to provide a blueprint for future actions.

§

In *The Secret of Creating Your Future*,[7] Tad James investigated decisions, memories, values and attitudes and concluded that they are organised in a hierarchy of significance and level of subconsciousness. He also concludes that we make decisions to support our values, attitudes and beliefs.

My findings differ from those of Tad James. My research indicates that decisions are the vital component that explains how we organise our thinking and how we select our experiences. Decisions are where everything starts and are fundamental to the whole process of explaining how we create our reality. Over time we generalise our decisions to create our values, attitudes and beliefs, which are the filters that determine how we perceive our world. They have the power

---

7   Tad James, Richard Ro, Richard Roop, *Time Line Therapy: The Secret of Creating your Future*, Published by NeuroDynamics Incorporated, 1989

to override our perceptions and our conscious decisions so that they fit in with what we already know.

Decisions

I believe that the process starts with a decision or a range of decisions. Once made, reality is interpreted through that decision or decisions and our perception of truth is coloured by decisions that we have made in the past. From then on, experiences, similar in some way to the original one which caused us to make a significant decision, are filed in the appropriate filing cabinet in our brain. These files are ready to be accessed, and referred to, whenever we experience similar challenges.

Decisions can be investigated at increasingly deeper levels of complexity, and at each step we remember more. In doing so we start to see patterns and gain understanding of how we perceive the world and how we operate within it. The only thing stopping us from discovering this is our reluctance to feel strong negative emotions that are associated with our memories of the events that gave rise to the decisions. This is because significant decisions are usually made at times of deeply distressing experiences, which we are reluctant to revisit. Until we learn what those experiences are designed to teach us, we keep repeating the same sort of experiences over and over again so that, with each repetition, we see things from a slightly different perspective. Eventually we learn what the experiences are designed to teach us.

Sara illustrated the power of decisions to control our lives in ways that are sometimes hard to comprehend.

In Sara's case, the mysteries of her life were revealed when she investigated the consequence of always thinking, 'I can't have what I want'. In a discussion of what she saw as her problem, Sara spoke of her tendency to destroy the things that actually were what she wanted.

Speaking about her experiences at school she remembered that her 'friends' were not the friends she wanted. The children she did not like were the ones that wanted to be her friends. She did not have the father she wanted. Her biological father left her mother, so she had lived with a stepfather.

She remembered her stepfather telling her, 'You can't always have what you want,' and how angry she felt about this statement. She also remembered her mother telling her: 'You can't have everything you want,' over and over again.

Sara explained that she found herself playing the words, 'You can't have what you want' in her head. She replayed the words in different tones and at different speeds, sometimes slowing them down as if she were speaking to herself as a child.

One Christmas, Sara was given the bike she had yearned for. She smashed it up the same day. Having the bike that she wanted didn't fit in with her decision, 'I can't have what I want', so she had to do something to make the facts fit the decision. The bike was never repaired.

This pattern of destruction of anything she had that she really wanted continued for many years until she found herself with a major dilemma. She had no future because she couldn't decide what to do. This was understandable, because the subconscious program that she was running guaranteed that she couldn't have the job she wanted, the love she wanted, the happiness she wanted, the family she wanted. She couldn't have the belongings that she wanted, and she had long since given up trying to get them. This made her both sad and angry because she had decided that this was how life was, for her.

Each of us has a range of decisions, which are the outcome of many experiences. Some are positive. Some are negative. The decision from each distinct experience is filed in our subconscious minds. Whenever we encounter an experience that is in some way similar to the original one, we check what is in the filing cabinet and re-enforce the original decision by making another decision which is the same or similar. We add this incident to the file and build the power of its contents with emotional energy. Some of the files become very large indeed and influence very important aspects of our lives.

When we tap into memories of past lives, we find that the issues we are investigating in this lifetime have their origins in decisions made hundreds, possibly thousands of years previously. By investigating at this level, we discover that the patterns have been repeated over and over again for lifetime after lifetime and, each time, the issue is investigated from a different perspective.

Memories

Over time, our experiences transform into memories. The *Elohim* explained the significance of memories to me:

Memories are the most conscious of the brain programs we run. Our memories play a large part in providing us with choices, which we make on the basis of 'how it was before'. If we remember that things normally turn out well for us, we are prepared to take action. When we remember that this sort of action provides us with an unpleasant response, we frequently choose not to continue.

Without the experiences of life, we would have no memories, and we would make no decisions, good or bad. Without experience we would not develop attitudes about others, the world and ourselves. The problem with memories is overwhelmingly that peoples' attention is focused on the past rather than in the now. Memories prevent us from focusing our attention where it needs to be focused.

Memories allow us to identify patterns. That is their only value. Through the process of juxtaposition, we see linkages between events — cause and effect, matches and mismatches, increases and decreases. Memories allow us to realise that things don't just happen in isolation. Each event is part of a much larger whole. Memories allow us perspective. That is their purpose and their only purpose. Perspective allows us to judge the progress we are making. If what is happening now is less powerful than what happened in the past, then we can assume that something has been learned.

More important than the memories we retain, are those events of our lives which we do not remember. 'Not remembering' is significant. Forgotten memories are often painful and avoidance of pain is something mankind has perfected as a fine art. Forgotten memories are significant because they are indications of the things we need to investigate.

If we are smart, we can use memories and the patterns they create to understand the whole. When we block our memories, we are denying ourselves vital clues. In fact, the missing memories are probably more significant than the existing ones, because missing memories contain the really important data we are searching for in order to make meaning of our lives. Without these memories we live in a fog and things happen without reason. When we refuse to see, there is no pattern and no meaning.

Problems in life arise when the memories we have of the world in which we live are distorted to the extent that the filters through which they pass are a reflection of our negative beliefs and attitudes. It is like clean air passing through a pile of cow dung. When it comes out the other side it smells of dung. In the same way, our experiences of today take on the smell of the past. Today's experiences are distorted to the extent that they are a repeat of our decisions about past experiences. Mostly, we are unaware that this is happening.

Another problem with memories is that they cause people to focus their attention too often on the past, rather than on the present. Many spiritual teachers advocate living in the present but it is something that is almost impossible to do until we let go emotions associated with each past memory file.

Values

Values are generalised principles derived to provide us with our own personal rules for who we are and how the world is. The importance of values is that they govern all behaviour by determining how we spend our time. They determine whether we decide what we are doing is good or bad, valuable or useless, right or wrong. The basis of our whole personality derives from our values.

Attitudes

Attitudes arise out of our value systems. Attitudes provide the guidelines for judging how we feel about what happens on the basis of decisions made at an earlier time. We develop attitudes about everything; ourselves, our family, other races, black cats, doing the washing up and street litter.

Beliefs

Studies on the importance of beliefs provided the basis for many books in the 1990s. *You'll see it When You Believe it* by Wayne Dyer[8] is a study of the importance of beliefs and their role in determining how each of us lives. Beliefs are ideas about what is true or real. They are also generalisations. Beliefs are the things that take away or create personal power. They are the on/off switches that regulate our ability to do anything in the world.

§

---

8   Dr. Wayne Dyer, *You'll See It When You Believe It*, Harper Collins Publishers, 2001

As I have already stated at the beginning of this chapter, people rarely take the time to find out why things happen as they do or to investigate the programs they run, which, in turn, determine the quality of their lives. There are several reasons for this.

The first is that people generally believe that if they want to change something, they must change it in the external world. Positive change is thought of as being the consequence of doing things differently, being smarter or being more efficient. What is not understood is the principle that what happens in the external world is a reflection of what is held within: as within, so without. If someone's view of the world is one of poverty and deprivation, they must first investigate their attitudes towards themselves if they want their experience of the world to change. As long as they hold onto an attitude of *poor me*, that is what they will experience. Once a person's negative internal programs are identified and released, their experience of the external world also changes. This is the evidence needed to show that internal change has occurred.

A second reason why people don't make the effort to identify and release the negative programs that determine the quality of their lives is because they do not realise the significance of releasing these programs. When they do, they have the opportunity to experience life from a very different, and much more positive, perspective.

Another reason is that, whilst people might realise from their mind chatter that they constantly demean themselves, they don't know how to identify and release the programs that they are running. Life coaches advocate such things as positive thinking, but positive thoughts that overlie negative ones create stress, so this may not be the best strategy. Positive thinking only works when negative thoughts have been eliminated.

Possibly the most important reason why people don't seek to let go the programs that are holding us in a bad place is that they feel comfortable being who they are, knowing what they know, and having what they have. For things to change they have to change themselves, and that is a scary idea. Many clients have expressed the idea: 'Who will I be if I could do what I wanted?' Change is threatening because it is a deeply held fear that if things were to change, they would likely become worse, rather than better. Change involves risk and in general, risk is something that we avoid at all costs.

Chapter 8
Strategies for handling negative decisions

In the previous chapter I discussed how memories, values, attitudes and beliefs structure our lives and that they arise from decisions we have made. Decisions provide the first step in the process of creating filters through which we view subsequent events in our lives. Once the filters are in place, we develop strategies for handling them.

Decisions that operate in our subconscious determine what we experience thereafter, through the power of attraction. The universal law of attraction explains that the energy frequency of emotions that are fused with decisions attracts experiences of similar frequency to us. Since the emotion associated with significant traumatic decisions is often of low frequency, what we subsequently experience is often different from what we would like to experience.

When a person makes an emotion-charged decision, that decision has creative power and it creates the patterns of our lives. In consequence, we decide that this is who we are, not realising that it is actually not who we are but rather that this is what we have decided to be, do, or to have. Thereafter, people make choices regarding how they will handle the situation that they have created, and these choices can only be from three available options: acceptance, control and investigation.

Acceptance

When someone accepts that the decisions they have made, or the labels they have been given by others, are the truth, they allow their lives to be controlled by those decisions and labels. Once they are in place, people rarely question the validity of the decisions or the labels.

Phillip believed he couldn't get things right. A participant in my yoga group, I had been amazed by his flexibility. I suspected that his mind was similarly flexible. His language, however, supported my suspicion that he was someone who believed he 'couldn't get it right'.

During our first Stress Defusion session, knowing a little of Phillip's background, I commented, 'You don't appear to have a problem with the fact that you can't get things right, Phillip.' I had made this observation after I tested the level of left/right brain separation while Phillip concentrated on the thought, 'I can't get things right'. There was nothing to indicate that this thought caused him any stress.

'No. I'm OK with that idea. I learned that when I was very small, and I've lived with it all my life. I've designed my life to compensate for the fact that I make a lot of mistakes. I've never had very demanding jobs. I was content with being a postman,' he said.

'But what I've picked up, from various conversations we have had, is that you get really angry when other people,

people who call themselves experts, don't get things right.' Testing this thought had shown that Phillip went into a state of split-brain separation indicating a high level of stress when he thought about having to consult 'experts' on occasions when he didn't know how to do something.

'I get really angry with lots of experts. They set themselves up as knowing everything but when I want them to perform, they don't know as much as I do. They call themselves experts and they charge huge amounts of money for advice. And then they get it wrong.' Phillip summed up the situation perfectly. He had a real issue with incompetent experts.

When I questioned Phillip about his childhood, in order to find what might be the source of his stress, I learned that, even as a small child, he had extraordinary insight into big picture concepts, and he was often so engaged in thinking about such things that he didn't handle routine day-to-day tasks well. Reminded regularly by an authoritarian stepfather that he wasn't getting it right, he had taken on this label as a child. As an adult, he had worked in menial jobs, but in his spare time had learned to build and renovate houses and had developed a high level of expertise in this area, a level of expertise far higher than most experts possess. Even so, Phillip had never thought to investigate the idea that he couldn't get it right. He told me that he had resisted getting help because most of the people that offered help in this area called themselves experts, and he didn't think they really knew what they were doing.

At the end of the session, Phillip could think of experts

getting things wrong without this thought causing him to shift into split-brain operation, as he had done at the beginning of the session. This meant a change had taken place in Phillip's evaluation of himself in relation to others who called themselves experts. His stress level dropped quite noticeably over the next few weeks, opening the door to the possibility that he would be able to re-evaluate his own level of expertise at some time in the future and realise that in many things, he had been getting it right all along.

In the year that followed these two sessions, Phillip completed the building and interior of a modern, hemp-walled house that he had designed himself and in doing so, conclusively demonstrated that he no longer had problems 'getting it right.'

Control

The second and most common way of dealing with negative subconscious programs is to take control of negative situations and make them right. This is hard work. Such an approach can be extremely debilitating in terms of physical health over an extended period of time. Changing detrimental life situations by controlling what we do and what everyone else around us does, is extremely demanding in terms of energy expenditure. It requires constantly being on the lookout for possible problems, working hard to prevent them and fixing any that occur.

Alice's life path illustrated what happens when someone resorts to control as a life strategy. From the time she was still a teenager, Alice looked after children: her own, the children from her ex-husband's former relationship, the children from her husband's former relationship and her sister's son who suffered from epilepsy.

When she came to see me, Alice already had a great understanding of why things had happened in the way they had. As a child she had strong psychic capabilities, but these had been dismissed by her parents. Those in charge of the fundamentalist church the family attended has seen these attributes as the work of the devil. Having walked away from this church and the teachings that they espoused, Alice had followed a spiritual path of her own devising. She was at peace with what had happened, but aware that several things were still not working in her life. All but two of the children she had taken care of for most of her life lived interstate and she rarely saw them. She understood that she still tried to control the children's lives but was working hard to allow them to work through their own problems, rather than providing solutions for them.

During an investigation of why Alice's life had followed the path it had, she was able to trace some of the patterns back to a decision she made as a two-year-old, which had its origin in a bizarre set of circumstances. Alice's parents spent time on a boat in the Mediterranean when she was tiny. One day, they left her alone asleep on the boat and it drifted from its mooring. Alice survived at sea for two days until she was rescued. During her Stress Defusion session Alice discovered that during those two days she made a number of decisions, some of which she identified as: 'No one can hear me', 'No one can help me', 'and, 'No one cares for me'. These decisions became the pattern for Alice's life. She had to do everything for herself. Her partners didn't help her and she took on responsibility not only for eleven children in total, but also for financially supporting them. Because she had decided that no one cared for her when she was a child, she compensated for this by caring for her own and other peoples' children.

When I first met Alice, she had been seriously ill with a variety of problems including cancer, a heart attack, diabetes and liver problems. She was working hard to lose weight and improve her level of fitness. It was not surprising that Alice's health was poor. She had spent her whole life taking care of everyone else and had taken little notice of her own needs.

There was a positive aspect to Alice's situation. By doing what she had done she had benefitted as well. Whilst her life demonstrated constant struggle in the face of adversity, Alice had developed many skills, great wisdom, fortitude, strength of character and determination. Once she let go her need to control, she was in a position to use these attributes in a meaningful way that would benefit herself as well as others.

Investigation

The third alternative is to check into our subconscious and investigate whether we are running programs which are stopping us from getting what we want in life. When we choose to look within for the source of our problems, we find ways to release the programs that have created the difficulties we seek to overcome. Thereafter, we can then consciously choose what we want to experience in life, without having to wage constant war with our subconscious mind. Brenda is someone who had, after a series of disappointments, decided to investigate why her love life was as it was. A few hours before she was due for her second appointment, she telephoned to cancel.

'I've a terrible throat,' she explained. 'It feels as if someone is slashing at me with razor blades.'

'How long has your throat been sore?'

'Just since this morning.'

'I think you should keep your appointment. It seems to me that your sore throat is telling you something, and it is an excellent time to find out what that is.'

When Brenda arrived, she was in considerable pain. She was aching all over in addition to having a sore throat. It seemed that she had suffered from sore throats as a child, and these started to recur when she was engaged to Peter. She and Peter had broken off their engagement before she came to see me initially, and she hadn't suffered from sore throats since that happened.

'What changes have you noticed since your last appointment?' I asked.

'Well, I feel much happier with myself. In fact, I've decided that I quite like myself and that I don't need Peter. That's very different from the way I felt before, when I didn't think I amounted to anything without him. I always bent over backwards to do what he wanted, and then I resented him. The other thing that has happened is that I have met another man. He is really nice. But what is so different now is that whether or not I'm in a relationship with someone, I still like myself. He's just an added bonus.'

With this comment, I realised that we had just hit the jackpot with regards to identifying the cause of Brenda's sore throat. It was somehow connected with the new man in her life. Half an hour later, Brenda's sore throat was much improved. In order for this change to occur, she had experienced some painful childhood memories and severe nausea, to the point of feeling physically sick. The decision she had made as a small child was, 'I'm useless'. Identifying this decision allowed Brenda to understand some of the difficulties she had experienced with Peter. As she went out the door she said, 'Peter kept telling me how useless I was. When I was around him, I was useless. He used to say that he didn't know how I survived when he wasn't around.'

Investigation is by far the easiest strategy for resolution of life's challenges, but it is the one that most people fear. Possibly, this is because people are concerned that they are going to have to relive the periods of greatest emotional turmoil in their lives. They will put up with years of untold misery to avoid doing this. Even knowing that re-experiencing memories of past traumatic events can be accomplished very fast, literally within minutes, many still balk at the idea, fearing that they will be left forever in a devastating emotional nightmare. I suspect that others fear that they will be *found out* and this is something that must be avoided at all costs. Perhaps some don't want to look stupid or unworthy, having spent most of their lives working hard to not be thought of as stupid or unworthy.

When they release the negative programs they have chosen for themselves, they can start to live in the *now* rather than from habitual responses that are anchored in past decisions and blocked emotions. Once they do this, it is possible to build the future from the basis of their present actions, rather than from past negative programs.

It is only when people decide that they are truly responsible for their lives, and what happens in their lives, that they have the opportunity to find true happiness and true fulfilment, which they yearn for so deeply. It is only when they stop looking outside themselves for the source of that fulfilment and understand that the answers are within them, that they have any chance of finding what they are seeking. Unfortunately, few have the courage or the understanding that is necessary, to look within to find the source of their pain. The good news is that regardless of the choice they make, from the three choices that are available to them, they learn. Eventually, they come to realise that they have created their problems in order to learn something of great value. The end result is, in my opinion, inevitable. The only variable is the time it will take to get there.

§

Whichever strategy people use to resolve the difficulties in their lives, self-esteem and self-confidence play a major part in determining how easy the task is. Self-confidence is certainly the key to the achievement of any goal and this is necessary before anything worthwhile can be accomplished. Self-confidence comes from having the ability to control ourselves, and our environment.

Nothing works when someone believes that he or she has no control over the outcome, regardless of what they do or how well they do it. This behavioural response was examined in Martin Seligman's book *Learned Helplessness*,[9].

Seligman defined learned helplessness as the giving up reaction, the quitting response that follows on from the belief that nothing you do will make a difference. He then demonstrated that this response is a learned one, which is dependent on the language used by someone to habitually explain to themselves why things happen as they do.

Seligman's study of learned helplessness started in 1964 as the result of an experiment on dogs, which went awry. The experiment was designed to test whether the dogs would learn to link noise with electric shocks, and act to avoid the shock by jumping over a wall.

During the first stage of the experiment, the dogs were put into a pen where they learned to expect a high-pitched tone to be followed by an electric shock, which they were unable to avoid. In the second learning stage of the experiment, the dogs were taught to jump a low wall. The third phase of the

---

[9] Christopher Peterson, Steen F Maier, Martin E.P. Seligman *Learned Helplessness A theory for the Age of Personal Control*. Project Gutenberg Self Publishing, Published 1995

experiment was designed to see whether the dogs would hear the high-pitched tone, link it to the memory of the electric shock, and jump the wall to avoid feeling the pain.

The dogs were put into a double pen with a low wall separating the two compartments. To the amazement of the experimenters, when the noise of the high-pitched tone was heard, the dogs didn't even try to jump the wall. They just lay whimpering. The experiment was designed to discover whether the dogs would learn to link the shock with pain. What the dogs actually learned was helplessness, a level of helplessness so high that they made no attempt to avoid the pain.

Learned helplessness was what I was seeing with people of all ages who had come to me with a variety of problems. When Phillip came to see me, it was obviously that he had accepted the label of helplessness from an early age. Because I understood the implications of Seligman's work, I recognised the power of both thought and the spoken word to create the situations of our lives that we are helpless to change, because we do not question why things are as they are.

I regularly heard my clients describe themselves negatively. The words they used about themselves were also the words that I would have used to describe their experiences in life. In addition to the words they spoke out loud, they told me that in their minds they repeated negative words and instructions over and over. It was as if their brains contained a file of recorded instructions, which they repeated over and over. I called this *mind chatter*, and I realised that mind chatter files contained all the decisions that these people had made about themselves, and the world. Mind chatter reinforces negative decisions that keep people stuck. Over time I realised that once judgement of events of the past no longer existed, mind chatter diminished to a point where it ceased. Once mind chatter is extinguished, people operate in the *now* rather than finding themselves being constantly pulled back into the past.

§

I came to the conclusion that the decisions people made at the time of particularly traumatic events were a logical interpretation of the situation because, like the dogs in Seligman's experiments, they hadn't identified the solution. When they decided they couldn't do something, or when they thought they couldn't do something, that became their reality. At the time of the event some of them didn't have the skills or knowledge to do what they wanted to do, or what was asked of them by others, and they didn't ever make the effort to acquire the appropriate skills or knowledge. Perhaps in the original situation they weren't strong enough to tackle a really difficult physical challenge and from that time on, they accepted their weakness. Perhaps the odds against them were overwhelming, and from that point on, everyone and everything seemed to conspire against them. The problem was that they had made the decision that they were helpless and they didn't make the effort to change either themselves or the situation from then on. Even though they managed to survive a difficult situation, because of their own actions or by being helped by others, they never re-evaluated the decision that they had made. This is what happened for Nicolas when he was convinced that he was going to die.

Nicolas was 16 when his father brought him to see me. He didn't want to come and wasn't very co-operative. He was finishing Year 11 at a prestigious private college and was doing very badly both with his studies and in relation to his attitude. Nicolas denied that anything was wrong.

'How are you going at school, Nicolas?'

'School sucks.'

'Are you happy with the progress you are making?'

'No.'

'Your Dad tells me that you were doing really well at school until a few years ago. Is that right?'

'Yes. I was top of the class all the way through primary school'.

'When did things start to go wrong?'

'Dunno.'

'Was it at the beginning of high school?'

'Don't remember.'

'Did you do well at the end of Year 7?'

'Yes.'

'What about Year 8.'

'Nup. My marks slipped badly when I was in Year 8.'

'Do you remember anything that happened between the end of Year 7 and the end of Year 8 that was out of the ordinary?'

'Can't remember.'

'Did you do anything special that year?'

> 'Went skiing in Austria during the Christmas holidays.'
> 'Did anything happen when you went skiing in Austria?'
> 'I got lost. It got dark and I couldn't find my way back to the village where we were staying. Ended up the next morning in the next valley, miles away.'

It was not what Nicolas told me that alerted me to the seriousness of the situation he had found himself in. He was not at all willing to share the details of what had happened but it wasn't hard to imagine the trauma associated with a twelve year old boy, cold, lost and frightened, on his own, in the dark, in the middle of winter, walking and skiing across mountains and down into a strange valley, miles from where he set out. Nicolas didn't tell me what decisions he made that night. He possibly didn't remember. The thought was sufficiently powerful to control his life from that point on and must have been something like: 'No matter how hard I try, or what I do, I'm going to die.' In spite of these fears he persevered until he worked his way down off the mountain to safety.

I was fascinated that neither he nor his parents saw the connection between that incident and his change in attitude and academic performance immediately afterwards and I wondered how many people fail to see the connection between traumatic life events and the way their lives crumble in consequence.

Nicolas left school shortly after he came to see me. He enrolled at TAFE and spent the next two years studying for his Higher School Certificate, which he completed with high marks.

§

A second problem is that having made very powerful negative decision on several occasions, people then generalise, or expand their *I can't* thinking patterns to include a wider and wider range of experiences that are similar but not quite the same as the original one. They reinforce their decisions with spoken excuses for themselves. They replay their mind chatter tapes over and over so that these decisions determine who they are and the sum of what they are capable of achieving. They limit their lives according to their beliefs and then they judge themselves as being *less than* others, who seem to be more adept at life than they are. This becomes a self-fulfilling prophecy. After many experiences when they *can't* they stop trying, which guarantees that what they decided becomes their reality. Over time, their bodies adapt to the decisions they made, to ensure that what they chose to experience becomes their reality. Their beliefs are translated into the reality of who they are and how they operate in the world. What is most interesting is that people's attitudes and beliefs about themselves often have little basis in reality.

> Sybil came into the room, looked around and said, 'Thank heavens you are here on your own. You mentioned that you might have a student observing the session and I didn't want anyone else to know my problem. It's bad enough having to share it just with you'.
>
> 'So, what's worrying you so much?' I asked.
>
> 'I'm fat.'

'I'm sorry, I must have misunderstood. Did I hear you say that you are fat and that is what is worrying you?'

'Yes,' she replied. 'I'm fat and I don't know what to do about it. I'm a tennis coach so I am physically active for many hours every day, and I can't do more than I am already doing. I watch my diet. I just don't know what else to do? I diet constantly, and if I allow myself to eat anything the slightest bit fattening, I just balloon out. It's awful. How can I continue working as a tennis coach while I am so fat? My students look to me as an example.'

Whilst I didn't think that being fat was a life-shattering problem, the situation would not have been so peculiar if she had actually been fat. She was very slightly overweight.

Working through the problem, Sybil remembered that as a small child, her father's favourite term of endearment was 'My little fat piglet' and she had, as a consequence, made the decision that 'I am daddy's little fat piglet'. In her mind, she was still her father's 'little fat piglet' regardless of how false the description was of her as a 40-year-old, or that her father had died several years earlier.

I had no idea how Sybil had processed the 'little fat piglet' label she had given herself as a small child, but her body created the fat pig image most effectively. I didn't know how it had become the obsession that it had clearly become, but once she understood the association between her father's term of endearment and her inability to be slim, her obsession about being fat vanished. As she walked out the door Sybil looked as if she had let go a great weight. She actually laughed about how sensitive she had been about her weight problem and said, 'How could I have got myself into such a state about something so unimportant.'

§

Mark's story illustrates what happens when a decision about one aspect of his life came to be extended to cover a whole range of situations where it didn't apply. Mark described himself as a slow learner. He was a long term, loyal employee of his company who thought highly of Mark and wanted to help him. He was getting older and just wasn't coping with the physical demands of the job that he had done for many years. The company wanted him to retrain as a forklift driver so that they could keep employing him. The problem was that Mark couldn't read. Mark was brought to his appointment by the company's Personnel Officer. The company's office was about an hour's drive from where I saw clients and they knew that Mark couldn't read a map.

At the end of the first session, I asked 'How will you get here next time, Mark?'

'I'll drive,' replied Mark.

'How will you find this place?' I queried.

'I'll take the same route we took today,' said Mark. I knew that doing this involved a really difficult route involving lots of changes of direction.

'But you've only been once. Are you able to read the road signs?'

'No.'

'How will you remember?' His answer astounded me.

'I only need to go over a route once. I never get lost because I remember exactly where I have been before.' Mark might not have been able to read the road signs or follow written directions, but there was nothing wrong with his spatial memory.

For most people, learning difficulties occur in specific areas. Because of the emphasis that is placed on academic achievement, children with reading or mathematics difficulties then judge themselves as dumb and generalise one area of learning difficulty across the whole spectrum of learning, discounting and ignoring those areas of their lives in which there is no problem. For such people, it is as if they have excelled in their ability to not learn and then they have applied this ability in lots of different areas. Additionally, educational institutions provide many opportunities for children to practise being unable to do what they can't do. Children who can't read are provided with remedial reading programs. The effect of encouraging children to concentrate much of their time and effort into doing things that they actually can't do, reinforces their inability and make them feel ashamed as well as useless. Intervention programs are intended to help the children, and some children do benefit, but in many cases the remediation approach destroys self-esteem and with it any belief that the situation can ever be different. This is what happened in Karen's case.

Karen left school at the end of Grade 10 unable to admit she could not read. As a child she felt that there was a key missing for some part of her brain that had become locked. It caused her immense embarrassment and suffering. Shame was a familiar feeling for her. One of her parents was a school teacher and the other a journalist, and she didn't understand why she had problems. Genetics certainly weren't to blame.

At her parents' urging, Karen went to Secretarial School but didn't finish the training. From then on, the jobs that she got were the result of personal interviews and the work usually involved manual labour because, once she left school, tasks such as filling in forms, writing letters, or completing job applications were a nightmare. It was not possible for her to apply for jobs in writing. What had been ignored both by her parents, and her school counsellors, was that Karen was really good at art. She eventually got work as a self-taught graphic designer and later designed and manufactured clothing, which she sold at markets. She cleverly worked around her problems by concentrating on the areas where she excelled. This was a great strategy because it allowed her to build confidence in her abilities.

By the time she was in her 30s, Karen was determined to overcome her reading problems and let go the of label that she had carried around with her for too long. She attended an adult literacy program and went on to do a tertiary preparation course at TAFE. These helped boost her confidence even further, so she continued her studies and completed a Diploma in Counselling several years later. Doing this had been difficult for her but she had persevered and been successful.

I met Karen while she was studying at TAFE and spoke with her about the relationship between stress and learning problems. I mentioned to her that I thought that there was a link between childhood trauma and reading difficulties. Part of her course at the Adult Literacy Centre involved a research project and she chose to do a survey of the students attending the classes. The results of her survey confirmed my hypothesis and convinced Karen that trauma in childhood was a major factor contributing to literacy problems. All the students she had surveyed indicated that they had experienced one or more traumatic events as children.

Stress Defusion allowed Karen to identify the decisions that were basic to her belief that she was stupid. She remembered becoming what she thought of as 'stupid', overnight. Something happened one night when she was seven years old and the next day, she was unable to read or learn. She was not prepared to share what actually happened. Until then, she had been doing really well in school. Following her work with Stress Defusion, Karen was aware of a steady improvement in her ability to read and spell, but the most important change was in her level of self-esteem. She came to realise that the label 'illiterate' was not who she was. She also realised that illiteracy had been a tool that had forced her to gain a huge variety of experiences as a result of which she learned things that she would not have learned had her life followed a more orthodox path. Illiteracy opened the door to situations *and experiences that she was able to embrace as having been beneficial even though, at the time they happened, they were intensely distressing. In Karen's words: 'Stress Defusion allowed me to separate my reading difficulties from who I am. I am no longer just the label and the label no longer hurts'.*

Karen's case, and several similar ones, provided me with confirmation that the hypotheses that I had developed over several years were correct. I had suspected for a long time that learning difficulties were associated with one, or perhaps several traumatic incidents, which caused left/right brain separation. I believed that inability to perform certain tasks, such as reading, was not the problem that needed to be addressed. Inability to read was a symptom of a much deeper problem. Another important hypothesis I had developed was that belief about one's ability was a major factor in a person's ability or inability to perform in particular situations and that belief in oneself is a core aspect of behaviour.

§

From the beginning of the development of the Stress Defusion process, I suspected that changing negative beliefs was not a matter of making a conscious decision. It was my belief that positive affirmations were ineffective. It was not the conscious beliefs and decisions that were causing the problems. It was the decisions that were hidden in the subconscious that were basic to the problems people experienced. Furthermore, I came to the realisation that bringing about change involved more than replacing negative decisions with positive ones, which at first seemed the obvious solution. This approach would have caused a variety of different stress-inducing problems. It took me a long time to understand this and to realise that an issue didn't shift completely until energy around both the negative and the positive aspects of a decision were released. Acceptance, instead of judgement, was what was required. In response to witnessing something that is deeply distressing, someone might make a decision *I don't want to see* and *I don't want to be seen*. The judgement arising from such a decision is that *seeing* causes distress, and *being seen* can be dangerous. The effect of these decisions could be loss of visual acuity, which will not be reversed until both decisions are identified and defused.

I had learned how to install supportive, positive beliefs into the subconscious as part of my kinesiology studies, but I didn't feel that it was right to do this. Kinesiology, when I studied it, didn't explain how to eliminate already existing negative beliefs. It simply provided techniques to override them. Such an approach, I thought, must create stress because this involved two conflicting beliefs, each struggling for supremacy in any given moment.

My breakthrough came when I developed a strategy not to override or to eliminate negative beliefs but to identify them, accept them without judgement and provide understanding of where they originated and what they were designed to teach. When this was done, they lost their power to control.

Discovering the benefits to be gained from operating with beliefs that originated in negative decisions provided an added bonus: acknowledgement of learning that is the consequence of having lived our lives from the base of a negative decision. Working through this process involved counselling, the purpose of which was to explore the idea that negative beliefs and decisions are valid at the time they are installed but need not form the basis for a variety of mindsets that persist for the whole of life. Negative decisions propel people into experiences and environments that I believe are part of the training they undergo to achieve their life's purpose. Karen summed it up beautifully when she explained that her illiteracy provided her with an entrée to a variety of different experiences; experiences she would not have had, if she had not been illiterate.

Holding onto blame and judgement around the painful aspects of our lives keeps us from moving forward. What is needed is to let go of all judgement. It is a matter of accepting that negative experience is a learning tool, which provides an opportunity to learn something important. It is neither good nor bad even though it might make you feel bad. It feels bad because it is linked to emotions: hate, fear, terror, sadness, shame, guilt and/or jealousy. Reluctance to allow ourselves to feel these emotions at the time when they were appropriate, causes them to be associated with the original decisions and are locked away so that they persist over long periods of time. Until people are able to release the emotional energy that keeps them stuck, the patterns they have created for themselves keep repeating.

§

I recognised the importance of self-confidence when I tackled the problems arising from my son's brain damage and I helped him to work through a difficult period with his self-confidence intact. What I didn't realise until much later was that the idea of self-esteem goes much deeper than I originally thought.

Low self-esteem and self-defeating labels lead to unhappy lives for those who carry these labels. Unreasonably and unquestioned high self-esteem, based on an unrealistic evaluation of skills and abilities, and an unrealistic expectation of the benefits that such skills and talents bestow, has an even more devastating consequence than having low self-esteem. The sufferer is not the individual who is supremely confident in his or her own abilities. Rather, it is the person who becomes the victim of someone who has grandiose ideas of their own invincibility and self-importance.

We are told that it is a good thing to think positively about ourselves, to believe that we are capable and intelligent. Such beliefs are certainly beneficial as long as they are related to specific areas of achievement. They make life easy because confident people accept challenges and have the motivation to work hard to meet the challenges that they set for themselves and/or the ability to motivate others to make the effort on their behalf.

However, those who have superior abilities and have a history of high achievement may discover that an excessive sense of entitlement results from decisions such as *I can do this better than they can* and *I'm smarter than everyone else*. Sometimes these decisions are made consciously and deliberately as a strategy to override fear and lead to belligerent, aggressive, dominating behaviour that is designed to intimidate others. As with negative decisions, positive decisions made on the basis of one or two instances or as a deliberate strategy of control, can be generalised to include all aspects of life. Grandiose self-delusion is the result.

Having fallen into the trap of judging themselves to be invincible, some people become so convinced of their own superiority that they become supremely arrogant. Some go even further and slip into narcissism, becoming convinced that their self-importance and invincibility are incontrovertibly true.

Unfortunately for the rest of humanity, such people often work their way into positions of power with control over the lives and destinies of others. Problems are inevitable because narcissists are exploitative of others, easily corrupted and preoccupied with fantasies of unlimited success and power.

Those who are at the other end of the spectrum sit back feeling helpless, whilst complaining that power rests in the hands of those who are unscrupulous and exploitive. Those in power pass laws to guarantee that they gain privilege and financial wealth, which is commensurate with their status, thus cementing the positions of power that they occupy.

Interestingly, the behaviours of these two personality types, one that is submissive and ineffective, and the other that is belligerent and self-serving often have, as their basis, a deep fear of insecurity, which arises from the decision that they are not good enough. What we see in both are two sides of the same coin.

§

Change on a world scale will only occur when the weak and powerless people of this world, those who have learned to be helpless, accept that they have chosen to live a lie. Powerful people who believe themselves to be invincible generalise one area of expertise to describe everything they do. Powerless people do the same thing. They generalise one area of deficiency to include everything they do. Feeling powerless, they then give away what remains of their power as a strategy of gain. In the hope that they will receive privileges, they subordinate themselves to those who have fame and power. Their objective is to tap into the bucket of *goodies* that is available from others rather than become the provider of their own *goodies*. In the longer term those who abdicate responsibility for using their skills, resources and energy for their own benefit, become the energy source by which narcissists gain even greater power and control. Those in control make many promises designed to convince that their approach provides solutions such as support, safety, and security, but what these promises actually do is drain energy in the form of money and resources and funnel it into the hands of those who are already powerful.

It is unlikely that those with narcissistic tendencies will change until they are forced to do so. Change, on a world scale, is in the hands of the majority, those who have decided they are not good enough but who will be good enough when they look within and find the truth about themselves.

Chapter 9
Identifying the Patterns of our Lives

Following my years at the high school, I had a constant stream of people wanting help to resolve problems in their lives. Those who had experienced the Stress Defusion process wanted to know more so that they could use it for themselves. I facilitated the investigation of a range of life problems for clients of all ages.

Children were easy to work with. For some of them, showing them how to find where blocks were located so that they recognised how they felt, was all that was needed for them to identify and clear additional blocks. I would say to them: 'Find the blocks in your eyes.' They could do this easily. Ken was ten years old when I saw him. After explaining that my job was to help him find energy blockages using his eyes, and showing him how to do that, he decided that he didn't need my help. He could do it on his own.

'There's a block when I look up there?'

'What's it about?'

'I don't know. I just know that it's a big rectangle. It's gone now.'

'Can you find another one?'

'Yes. There's one when I look down there. It's a round

block. I've got it. When I move my eyes a little, there's a small block. That one was easy to get rid of. Now I've found a really big one. It's a large square. It's grey. It's taking a lot to get rid of that one. OK. It's gone now.'

Alternatively, it was possible to say to some children, 'Tell me where your arm doesn't feel right,' and they would identify positions where it didn't feel right. Even more, they would suggest which emotions were being accessed when their arms were held in a particular position, and then, without being asked, locate other areas of the body where the same emotion was being held.

Working with children was magical but I worried whether I was playing God by helping to dis-create problems that would, over their lifetimes, lead to situations from which they would learn. For this reason, I decided I shouldn't work with children any longer. Years later, I don't know if my decision was the right one.

Once I started working solely with adults, the problems needing attention became more complex and more difficult to unravel. With some of the girls that I had worked with at the school, I had encountered similarly complex problems. Because the girls were reluctant to talk with me about what they were remembering, I wasn't able to see the patterns. Additionally, it was rare for me to need to work with a student more than twice. My Than was one of the exceptions.

My Than had been in Australia for three years when she came to the high school. She was born in Vietnam. Her father had fled from Vietnam when she was only a year old. He had decided that it was too dangerous for My Than and her mother to leave with him at that time. They were reunited as a family nine years later.

In May of her first year in high school, My Than's reading was slow and disjointed. She read one word at a time and her comprehension was that of a seven or eight-year-old. When I tested her ability to cross the midline with her arms, she was unable to do it, which indicated that there was a separation between her left and right brain functioning. She could not cross-crawl, another test that determines the extent of the degree of right or left sided brain dominance, a condition referred to as ipsilaterality.

Working with her for the first time in May, My Than investigated the idea, 'I feel confused'. Tested at the end of the session, My Than was able to cross the midline with her arms while doing the infinity exercise that I used to determine the level of ipsilaterality. This indicated that some connection between the right and left hemispheres of her brain had been restored

In June, she worked with the issue 'I can't read English'. During this session she was not prepared to share any of the memories she had accessed, but it was obvious from the expression on her face that her memories were particularly nasty.

During the next session My Than worked with the issue 'I feel frightened'. She had problems looking up and to her left when she concentrated on the thought, 'I feel frightened' and this was a difficult area to clear. It appeared that many things in her life had frightened her.

By July, My Than reported that her schoolbooks were neater. She understood more in class, talked less and she was working harder, so that she was able to complete the work that was set for the class. In this session her problem area was in looking upwards to the right, and she investigated the idea, 'I feel sad'. Doing this caused her considerable eye pain but, at the end of the session, testing indicated a marked lessening of left/right brain separation.

My Than's last session was in August. Her good news was that her results in mathematics had improved from 17% to 77%. Her reading was fluent, and she didn't feel sad anymore. She investigated ideas relating to 'I can't breathe' and 'I feel disconnected'. That was the last time I worked with her.

I have no idea what sort of a life My Than had before she came to Australia after the Vietnam war. I can only suppose that it must have been an awful situation for her and her mother. Whatever happened, it certainly left a very traumatised child, who, without the intervention provided, would not have been able to perform academically to the level that she was capable of achieving when she eventually felt safe.

§

With children it didn't appear necessary to do more than bring the hidden memories to conscious awareness or perhaps, because I worked with children first, I didn't realise the necessity to do anything more than that. With adults, it was different. They were as fascinated as I was by the circumstances that explained why things had happened in their lives. Many were willing to share their stories with me. Frequently, they wanted to understand the significance of their memories, identify the benefits they had gained from their experiences and, on occasion, discuss in detail the process that they had put in place to create the events of their lives. Sometimes, to fully understand a life pattern, it was necessary to see the connection between a number of different incidents in this lifetime, or even to include a number of past life situations.

Tad James, whose work I referred to in chapter 8, gave the name meta program to the complex and many-faceted programs that run over long periods in one lifetime, or even over many lifetimes. Whilst one specific decision may control an aspect of life, meta programs are basic to our personality and the influence they exert over our lives is extraordinarily powerful. Where inconsistencies exist, stress occurs as the brain attempts to find ways to reconcile conflicting programs. Over time, the power of the persistent mass of experiences and decisions increases to the point where it controls a person's life and attracts to them experiences similar to the one that established the process. Progressively, their whole energy field is distorted by this energy draining area of tension. The more they consciously attempt to change the situation by willpower, the more stress results.

I can illustrate what happens within a person's life by

relating a story that explained to me how meta programs develop. The story does not concern a person, but rather a small area of land on my farm.

Down by the creek, there was a small unkempt area. There the grass grew tall and tree saplings and large bushes were sprouting. I watched as the area grew larger and larger over time. This area annoyed me every time I mowed. I didn't dare put the tractor into the area, scared of what might be hidden by the long grass. I was certain that huge boulders lay in the midst of this unsightly mess. After years of mowing around the area, and watching as it grew thicker and larger, I decided to ask a friend to clear it by hand. He worked for a couple of hours before appearing with a small rock in his hand. This was at the heart of the problem. And so it is that the weed-infested areas of our lives can originate in a seemingly insignificant event in the same way that my weed-filled area originated with a small rock.

Defusing a persistent mass involves following each strand as far as possible and working with each decision point as it rises to conscious awareness. Only when the various strands of linked blocks are removed is it possible to locate, identify and release the original decision that triggered off the whole sequence. Since we are very clever at hiding the truth about ourselves from ourselves, the decision we are seeking is generally a denial of who we really are. We shield ourselves from this knowledge by denial. Sometimes, it is simply the number and complexity of the circumstances of our lives that stops us from identifying the pattern.

The *Elohim* explained the significance of a persistent mass with the observation that:

Defusing the prime core of a persistent mass frees us to be who we really are in relation to that issue. Its ramifications go far beyond an easily identified problem that gives us trouble. The problem is the end result of a much deeper and more fundamental issue. As each negative core belief mass is identified and defused, the vibrational energy of the person changes, becoming lighter and smoother with all the distortions ironed out. It gets nearer the energy vibration pattern of what has been called unconditional or universal love.

§

Katrina experienced the changes that occur as she progressively cleared a range of issues associated with a persistent mass, so that she was eventually able to reach the core and to clear that. This wasn't something that happened overnight. Unravelling meta programs can take months or even years.

Katrina's memories of her school years were of trying hard, having no success and feeling hopeless as a result. Awarded the Achiever's Certificate (the award for those that try hard but don't succeed) for six years in a row didn't help. Stringing cotton on nails to make mathematically even designs was no substitute for learning actual maths. With the help of tutors and teachers, Katrina completed high school and gained a traineeship with a large and prestigious retailer. She rapidly rose to the position of section manager overseeing twenty-five staff. In spite of her academic difficulties Katrina started a B.A. degree course in Secretarial Studies. Excelling in assessment tasks and struggling through examinations that terrified her, she completed her course and vowed never to study again.

Returning to the workforce she moved from one job to the next for five years. Then she moved to a managerial position in a sales promotion agency where she was totally out of her depth and was asked to resign. Three more jobs followed with the same result. She was asked to resign from all of them. Intellectually, Katrina knew that she was sabotaging herself by convincing the people around her that she was hopeless. She was also aware that she was unable to stop the pattern of self-sabotage.

Clearly, secretarial and office work were not appropriate, so Katrina returned to study. This time she chose naturopathy and she struggled to understand chemistry and other science-based disciplines. Eventually, she graduated but not before someone recommended she investigate the Stress Defusion process.

Katrina's first session allowed her to release much of the pent-up anger she had felt since childhood. In her words, 'I uttered profanities that shocked even me.' A month later, during her second session, she had a similar experience of anger. Over the following year she worked to unravel issues such as 'I'm hopeless', 'I can't trust myself' and 'I'm not good enough'. The list seemed endless, until one day it occurred to her that she was no longer suffering from feelings of utter hopelessness. To her surprise she started to feel comfortable with herself and with what she knew by then to be her life's purpose.

A series of events indicated that things had changed. Now fully trained as a naturopath, Katrina realised that she was under-charging for her consultancy work. She phoned the company she consulted for and told them she was planning to charge more. They agreed to double her hourly rate. A second company also agreed to pay far more than she would have charged only a few months earlier. Clients came because their doctors had referred them. These changes indicated that a shift had taken place. From these incidences, Katrina came to understand the idea that life is an external mirror of what she held within and this understanding provided her with a totally different perspective on life's challenges and opportunities.

§

Decisions that have the power to create a persistent mass are core to every part of our life and are the filters through which everything we experience is viewed. Identification and unblocking of one such core issue has the potential to restore whole brain operation and the ability to see patterns and what has caused them. Defusing a persistent mass makes life meaningful. A sense of balance and harmony in relation to that issue is restored and defusion of one such mass of blocks may be sufficient to change lives as dramatically as it did for Katrina.

When working with the Stress Defusion process I assist

clients to investigate each issue from the evidence that presents itself. This may come in the form of repeating patterns of relationships, physical injuries, compulsive behaviours, co-dependency situations or people and situations that bring up extreme negative feelings or tension. Each of these must be cleared. Initially this may lead to a feeling of euphoria because the clients believe that the problem has been overcome, but this feeling is likely to be temporary. For as long as hidden decisions can be triggered by everyday events, the problem will return whenever a similar associated experience occurs. Perhaps the problem doesn't return with the same level of intensity as previously, but sufficient to indicate that more work is needed. Rather than judging this as a negative, people are far better served to see it as the tool they need that causes them to investigate at an even deeper level.

I suspect that it is too simplistic to suggest that meta program systems are linked in a random pattern. Possibly each of us has a job to clear some part of the meta program that connects all mankind and has at its core, a denial of connection to All That Is. Defusing each part facilitates others in doing the same. If there is a meta program that holds all of mankind stuck in third dimensional reality, at some point it will be defused and we will have the ability to create the next episode in man's evolution based on the learning from this one. I believe that as this happens it is being marked by a huge shift in energy frequency felt throughout Earth in much the same way people shift in energy frequency when they resolve their own meta programs.

Chapter 9 Identifying the Patterns of our Lives

The shift will be from 3rd to 5th dimensional reality.

Within the 3rd dimension the major theme is competition: being smarter, richer, prettier, better than others. People are identified in terms of labels: good/bad, smart/stupid. People see themselves as separate from others and their major goal is to become the best they can be in terms of education, status, financial standing, material possessions, appearance and achievement. Such things are seen as the key to happiness. Others are judged on the basis of social standing, colour, age, gender and financial status.

Change in attitudes and perceptions away from pursuits in the material world towards knowledge and understanding indicate a shift to 4th dimension. Knowledge and understanding are perceived to be the key to fulfilment. Operating within 4th dimensional frequency, people are aware of having been conditioned to think as they do.

Within the 5th dimension, the emphasis is on co-operation rather than competition and there is a new level of reality in which the consciousness of love, joy, peace, freedom, compassion and spiritual wisdom prevail. Labels become unimportant; nothing is inherently good or bad. Those who operate in the 5th dimension understand that their major task is to heal themselves because they know that everything they experience is a reflection of what they hold within. Emphasis changes from changing the world to letting go judgement of themselves and others. People who operate in 5th dimensional frequency understand that they have the power to create their own reality and that no one has power over them unless they agree to it. Within this frequency it is understood that true power comes from unconditional love.

Suggesting that each of us is responsible for unravelling a bit of the puzzle that holds humanity in its current reality involves the idea of Earth being a hologram and each of us being part of that hologram. My understanding is that each person has a job to learn something or understand something that they didn't know prior to this lifetime. As each person learns, this knowledge is added to the universal knowledge bank. As each person understands what they have chosen to understand in this lifetime, they complete one of the many steps needed for Earth to evolve to a higher stage of consciousness. Earth's history has provided its people with the experience needed to understand whatever it is that Earth's purpose is to understand, but Earth's history has been shrouded in lies and obfuscation. That is now ending, and the true history of Earth is being revealed as a strange and wondrous tale. All that remains is for us to see the patterns.

§

The development of holograms revolutionised my thinking about the way the world works. Holographic images rely on laser light, which is an orderly form of light in which the energy waves are uniform. A hologram is a special three-dimensional picture created by energy interference patterns. It is created by sending a single laser beam through a device called a beam splitter. The beam of light separates into two, both originating from the same source. One of the beams then passes through a diffusing lens, which spreads it from a very narrow ray into a wide-spreading one. This beam is then directed by mirrors to shine on an unexposed photographic plate.

While this is happening a second beam passes through a second lens, bounces off the object being photographed, and then onto the same photographic plate. When both light beams meet, an interference pattern is created with the light waves from both lasers interacting.

The remarkable thing about the hologram is that it is three-dimensional. It is possible to walk around it. It appears real. Even more interesting is that one can cut away a small piece of the holographic film, hold it up to laser light, and see the entire image.

What happens with the photographic plate allows us to understand the universe in a new way. Like the hologram, the universe is an energy interference pattern. Each part, no matter how small, is part of, and at the same time separate from, the whole. Change one piece and change occurs for the whole.

The holographic nature of the human physical body and Earth itself is illustrated graphically by two facts. The first is that both are 70% water. Another interesting fact is that the human body and Earth are made up of the same elements, each in the same proportion. These facts were identified by philosopher Buckminster Fuller, who argued that the same patterns are true for Earth itself as it is for those who live on Earth.

Working with Debbie illustrated the interconnectedness

of people, and in particular, the interconnectedness of family members.

Debbie came to do an extended training program because she wanted to help her son who had learning problems and was unable to read. She was very surprised when I suggested that investigating and healing her own issues would probably also help her son. She couldn't understand this concept. A couple of days into the program, Debbie received a phone call from her son. He was excited and he wanted to share his news. His teacher had just given him an award for improvement in reading.

When Debbie arrived home a few days later her son was waiting for her. He gave her a list of things he thought she needed to research for her 'special project'. The list was a summary of his research on the internet. Research requires the ability to read. This was something he could not do a week earlier. The change had happened when Debbie had been away.

Debbie didn't need to help him. She'd already done that by working on her own issues. When she phoned to give me the good news, she still couldn't believe what had happened.

For the same reason that Debbie's son was able to read, each person doesn't have to start from scratch to clear issues that are keeping the whole world stuck in negativity and fear. Each has to do only what is relevant for them and, over time, everyone and everything is changing. Whilst many are sceptical that this is happening, because our mainstream news is full of stories of terror and brutality, it is actually true.

People are becoming much more aware and compassionate and in time a *100th monkey* situation will prevail. This 100th monkey phenomenon[10] is described in this way: Monkeys on the island of Koshima liked to eat sweet potato but they didn't like it when the sweet potato became covered in sand. One day, in 1952, scientists observed one monkey take his potato down to the sea and wash off the sand. A second monkey saw what the first monkey did and followed his example. Within a few weeks several more monkeys learned that they could make their sweet potato more palatable by washing them. Eventually, all the monkeys on the island washed their sweet potatoes in the sea before they ate them. They saw what the first monkey did, they followed his example and behaviour gradually changed.

This example is easy to understand within the context of a logical sequence of events. The strange thing is that the anthropologists who observed the change in monkey behaviour then discovered that it wasn't a change of behaviour for just the monkeys on the one island. Monkeys on all the islands nearby also started washing their sweet potatoes. Monkeys on the other islands hadn't learned from observation. There had been no communication between the monkeys on the different islands or any way of them learning this new behaviour. But that is what happened.

§

---

10 www.worldtrans.org/pos/monkeys.html

Cells in the human body illustrate the principle of the hologram. Every cell contains the DNA of the whole. If the DNA in one cell changes or the chemical composition in one cell changes, then all cells change. In the same way, clearing an issue for one person allows that issue to be cleared for all. This doesn't mean that everyone changes at that point because patterns of behaviour and thinking are habitual and difficult to shift. Over time, however, change has been happening, and it is happening exponentially.

The fact that what is true for the individual is also true for the world demonstrates that an intimate relationship exists between individuals, Earth, the universe and everything in it. To illustrate this idea, let's look at the problem of garbage and effluent. Seas and rivers are polluted with plastic. Seas and rivers are used as man's waste repository. Rivers are polluted with chemical and industrial waste. Soils are polluted by insecticides and pesticides, chemical and industrial waste. Air, the waste disposal system for gases and particulate matter, is polluted with industrial chemicals and, more recently, with toxic substances such as barium and aluminium, as a consequence of chemtrails. Chemtrails are explained as a strategy to control weather but they may also have a different, a possibly more sinister purpose involving barium and aluminium contamination of forests, food and water.

In the same way that the Earth is polluted, we, as individuals, suffer from pollution of the body. Through a build-up of poisons and waste, our elimination systems are overloaded and inefficient. Overloading the body with toxins interferes with the body's waste disposal in just the same way that too much garbage overloads our cities.

Decline in individual health, which is illustrated for the first time in decades by a decrease in longevity in some countries, is mirrored in the decay in the health of our cities. In spite of advances in health treatment, technology and an ever-increasing amount of money being spent on health infrastructure, health for the general population is maintained only through elaborate and expensive intervention procedures, such as joint replacement, organ transplants and dialysis, because kidneys don't work properly. Individual health will improve when we improve the health of our planet.

Planet health will improve when, as individuals, we start to eliminate poisons from our minds so that we can see clearly what is happening. It is crucial for us to maintain our bodies by keeping hydrated with clean drinking water, by eating chemical-free foods and breathing air that is pure and clean. When we clear the poisons from our minds and our bodies, we will understand the connection that exists between our wellbeing and the wellbeing of Earth. Both are inextricably linked.

When we have the eyes to see, we will understand that all around us are clues as to the true nature of man. What we are creating is a reflection of ourselves and it is ugly. When we don't like our creations, the place to start correcting it is within ourselves. Once this happens, solutions will be found to restore the Earth systems that are struggling to operate in the face of overpopulation, pollution and exploitation. This is starting to happen. The building of a tree belt across Africa to stop the expansion of sand dunes is a sign of large-scale community action taking place. Increase in organic farming production is another sign that change is occurring. Organic farming is growing fast but from a small base. In 2017, it represented only 1.4% of total farming but showed a 20% increase in land under organic production compared with the previous year.[11] This trend will be boosted by Russia in 2020,[12] when all agrochemicals, pesticides, antibiotic growth stimulants and hormones will be banned in that country and regulations and controls over producing, storing, labelling, selling and transporting organically grown food will be enforced. Another sign of change is the setting aside of areas of ocean where commercial fishing is banned so that fish populations can be replenished.

Understanding that the world is a mirror of what is happening within us, explains what is happening in the external, physical world. This realisation allows us to understand that if we want to create positive outcomes for our world, we need to fix ourselves as the first priority.

---

11 Organicwithoutboundaries.bio/2019/02/28/organic-agricu-lural-statistics-book.2019

12 https://www.rt.com/business/435219-putin-organic-pro-duce-regulatiom

Chapter 10
Energy

Everything in Its Place starts with the story of Helen, the high school girl who would not, or could not, participate in school activities. In the eighteen months between starting work at the high school and the time I worked with Helen, I was flying blind. When working with the Stress Defusion process I became aware that I was working with energy. When the girls brought hidden memories to conscious awareness, or understood something that they hadn't understood earlier, a strong outpouring of energy from the eyes often occurred. What followed was an immediate and dramatic improvement in academic performance, as the brain returned to full operation with both left and right hemispheres connected. Gradually, I became more and more attuned to the energy release and there was no mistaking that it was happening.

I had confirmation that I was working with blocked energy on the day I found myself spread-eagled against a wall following a strong energy release from someone I was working with. The force of the energy was so strong that I was literally blown a metre or more backwards. Somehow, I was causing the release of huge energy stores from within the brain and/or body, and perhaps it was this that had somehow blocked my client's ability to live their life in the way they wanted.

I was able to confirm that I was releasing blocked energy when I discovered Somato Emotional Release, developed by the Upledger Institute[13] in the United States. The institute was training people to identify and release what they referred to as energy cysts, which were trapped in the body as a consequence of traumatic physical injury.

Upledger realised that energy, which had entered the body as a result of a blow or from impact, and travelled into the body following the line of impact. If this energy became trapped in the body it could be released by allowing the body to return to the position it was in when the injury occurred and holding it in that position. Doing this allowed the trapped energy to release back along the line of entry.

It was an understanding of Dr Upledger's work that led me to postulate whether, when trauma occurs as a result of something seen or heard, there is a similar injection of energy through the eyes and possibly the ears, as it did when the energy was injected into the body by a blow or some form of impact. And just as it had been found possible to release the energy through the body by placing the body in the same position as it was when the physical impact occurred, I wondered whether release of energy occurred through the eyes when they were placed in the same position as they were in when the emotional trauma associated with strong emotion was experienced. I have no idea whether this idea

---

13   The Upledger Institute International
     https:// www. upledger.com.au

is true or if it explains the sudden release of energy through the eyes.

For a deeper understanding of the process I have just described, I needed to accept that we are beings of energy and that the world we live in consists of energy in different forms. This notion has been confirmed by particle physicists such as Allan Hegland, who maintain that Universe is a unified field of intelligence. His theory extends the Willard Gibbs' phase rule[14], which states that the physical universe breaks down into three categories: gas, liquid and crystal and that these distinct states of matter arise as a result in changes of temperature or pressure.

Without being a physicist, I could accept the idea of the same substance taking on different forms because as a teenager at school I had learned that water was state specific. I was taught that water changed from ice to liquid then to gas when temperature was increased. From my research into energy I learned that energy forms are also state specific. In conditions of low frequency, energy takes on solid crystalline form. At a higher frequency, energy takes on atomic structure and at an even higher frequency, energy assumes wave form.

Understanding this caused me to consider the following questions:

- Are energy blocks actually low vibrational frequency

---

14 https://www.historyofinformation.com/
detailptp?entry=3341

emotional energy that has changed state to become minute crystals within the brain or the body?
- Does the Stress Defusion process cause an increase in energy frequency such that the crystalline energy blocks are transformed into wave form, which allows the energy to be released through the eyes?

Whilst I still don't know whether or not the release of energy occurred because it had changed from crystal to wave form as a consequence of an input of energy from an external source, I do know that energy was being released. I felt it. It was a conclusion that made sense in terms of the research that had been done at the Upledger Institute even though the cause of the energy being trapped was different.

The idea that I was actually inputting energy through the eyes explained why I had changed how I worked with the eyes a few years after developing the Stress Defusion process. Without having any specific reason for doing so, I started using a crystal to give people something to look at when working with their eyes. Perhaps by using the crystal I was somehow increasing the energy frequency by focusing my own energy through the crystal? Perhaps I was directing energy to the location of the block through the crystal? By asking my clients to concentrate on thoughts that seemed to be connected to the problems they were experiencing, the process was causing an increase in energy frequency so that the energy changed from solid to wave form. This idea would explain why I was experiencing an outpouring of energy.

Scientific research confirms the idea that energy changes

in form. Quantum physics demonstrates that electrons display interchangeable characteristics depending on their vibrational frequency. Electrons have the ability to appear as particles or waves of light — mutually exclusive characteristics. Observation of this phenomenon has led scientists to the extraordinary conclusion that matter and energy are interchangeable.

§

We see the effect that different frequencies of energy have on matter when we see the effect music has on something like iron filings. Under certain conditions, iron filings move and form patterns in response to the vibrational frequency of sound. The complexity and the beauty of the pattern that is created is a reflection of the type of music that is played. Even more fascinating is the demonstration that the Sanskrit alphabet's letters are formed in sand in response to sounds of a particular frequency.[15]

I considered the possibility that we might have created the patterns of our lives to conform to certain patterns depending on the energy frequency of our thoughts and emotions. If the majority of these thoughts and emotions are generated from memories and decisions held deep in our subconscious, then it follows that we have neither knowledge of their existence nor control over their effect. This means that we are the creators of our own reality without even realising it. I wondered if such a

---

15 Vimeo.com/207708176

simple process could be the explanation for the circumstances of our lives and whether or not this could be so powerful that it overrides conscious control, and remains hidden, so that people have no clue that it even exists.

Research by Japanese scientist Dr Masaru Emoto, shows that this thought might have some substance. Dr. Emoto's experiments demonstrate how the energy frequency of emotions associated with thoughts or words create patterns in water crystals. Water subjected to strong, negative, low frequency emotions creates crystals that are deformed when water is frozen. The crystals formed from water that is spoken to in terms of love and acceptance, are coherent and intricately shaped.

Similarly, an experiment by Dr Emoto[16] that has been replicated many times involved putting rice in three beakers of water. Every day for a month, Dr Emoto said 'Thank you' to the rice in the first beaker and 'You're an idiot' to the rice in the second beaker. The rice in the third beaker was ignored. After a month the rice in the first beaker fermented, giving off a strong and pleasant odour. The rice is the second beaker turned black and the rice in the third beaker started to rot. From these examples one can see that the energy of thought plus emotion affects matter.

Knowing that the human body is about 70% water, it made sense that strong, negative thought held as crystal

---

16 Emoto Rice experiment https://www.youtube.com/watch?v=Enlw-9PJklE

energy cysts could have the power to affect our bodies. It did not seem unreasonable to believe that thought, both conscious and unconscious, associated with strong, low vibrational negative emotion might be capable of changing the state of energy within the body and forming tiny crystals. I concluded that *blocks* in alternative healing parlance are literally energy, which has become crystal in form because it is of low vibrational frequency.

This idea was confirmed when an eye doctor explained to me that progressive deterioration of sight is a function of crystal-like deposits, which enlarge the lens in the eye. Thickening of the lens reduces its flexibility and ability to change shape quickly in response to change in light and distance. Similarly, arthritis is caused by crystalline deposits in the joints, which cause swelling and distortion. Kidney stones are formed by crystal-like substances, which can be shattered by laser technology.

Understanding how negative thought patterns end up as energy blockages provided the key to accepting that they could be removed by directing energy of a higher frequency into the area of the energy blockage. I concluded that this was what I was doing. I was creating an interference pattern by directing my own energy through massage and through the eyes to where energy blocks existed. This was what was making it possible for the blocked energy to change to a wave form state, flow out through the eyes and be released from the body.

Other modalities work from a similar basis. Higher energy

frequencies occur in sound, music, colour, or the emotions of happiness and unconditional love. People also vary in their frequency levels, depending on the frequency of emotional energy that they store in their physical bodies. Those who hold a lot of fear or anger operate at a lower frequency than those who operate in a frequency of love. Being around people of high vibrational frequency can cause blocks to release spontaneously. This is why people flock to spend time with spiritual gurus.

By moving from the specific example of the importance of energy frequency within the body to a much wider sphere relating to the energy frequency on Earth, I learned that there is a standard energy frequency on Earth. It is called the Schumann Resonance[17] and it measures the quasi-steady electromagnetic waves that exist between the surface of Earth and the inner edge of the ionosphere. These waves have been thought to occur over a range between 7.83 Hz, which is the frequency of Earth's heartbeat, and 59 Hz.[18]

There was very little information relating to the Schumann Resonance available prior to 1987 and the information that was available indicated that the Schumann Resonance was stable at 7.83Hz prior to that time. Since 1987 it has been notable for increasingly higher variations in amplitude, often

---

17   Schumann Resonance https://drjoedispenze.net/blog/../what-does-the-spike-in-the-schumann-resonance-mean?
18   Dr Annette Deyhle, Research Co-ordinator, Heartmath Institute http://www.stillnessinthestorm/2017/05/heartmath-institute-the-schumann-resonances-are-not-increasing

reaching what was thought to be the highest level of 59Hz and staying there for increasingly longer periods of time before returning to the base level of 7.83 Hz. Early in 2019 the Schumann Resonance shot up to 150 Hz, far higher than was thought possible previously.

When the Schumann resonance increases, over a period of a few hours or days, it has been noted that those who are holding onto emotions like fear and anger or negative thoughts that are of low frequency, feel quite fragile. Subjective observation undertaken in 1978 by Robert C Beck[19] demonstrated that when we are exposed to Extremely Low Frequency (ELF) fields of around 6.6Hz we experience confusion, fear and nausea. When the frequency range is increased to 7.8 Hz, we move into a more meditative state and when it goes into high ranges some people become deeply stressed and paranoid.

Studies undertaken by Dr Beck confirm other research that shows that Earth's resonance affects our emotional states and ties in with the idea that emotional states are affected by the Earth's frequency. It also connects with research done since 1992 on magnetite crystals, millions of which are found in the brain[20]. Magnetite, it seems, is synthesised by the brain and scientists believe magnetite crystals provide a link between Earth's electro-magnetic field and cognitive/emotional function.

---

19 *Robert C `Beck — 1978 ELF frequencies /emotional state
20 https://www.realclearscience.com/blog/2019/06/11/why-is-there-magnetite-in-the-brain

Research by Dr Michael Persinger[21] of Laurieton University in Canada indicates that brain responses confirm a definite connection between our brain and the planet's geomagnetic field. Dr Persinger's experiments also indicate that matter is created by universal consciousness in which sub-atomic particles, which are vibrating packets of energy, are trading information within a background energy field. Their conclusions confirmed one I had already reached, based on information from the *Elohim*. The information was as follows:

Universe is cellular memory magnified to the limits of our imagination. It exists as a result of universal belief that it exists. In reality there is no such thing. Everything we experience, we create. It is no different for the universe.

Matter manifests when the mind chooses that it manifest. Universe is everything — and nothing. It contains all the thoughts that have ever existed and since there is nothing other than thought that is all there is. At the same time, it is nothing because thought is nothing but vibration.

Matter manifests because we choose it to be this way. We design our experience and our perceptions. We experience what we choose to experience and when we do not learn the essential meaning from that experience, we give the responsibility of the experience to someone or something else.

Hallucination is what we do when we trick ourselves into believing that what we see is real. For each of us, reality is

---

21   https:/<u>www.youtube.cpm/?v=Enlw</u> — JklE (Magnetite) Proc.Natl.Sa.USA pp7687, August 1992 Biophysics

different because we create our own reality on the basis of our past experiences. Everything that we create is a hallucination because, in truth, the only thing that is, is energy. Thought is energy. We have the power to manipulate this energy from flowing waves, to static particles or to solid crystal by thought. Energy in motion is created by thought and contains all the information of universe.

Through my research into energy, I realised that what started as an exploration of learning problems in children, did not end there. Instead, it opened up a kaleidoscope of ideas and possibilities that had not occurred to me previously.

Chapter 11
Energy of the Body

When I worked with clients, I was working to release energy that was locked into the physical body. It was for this reason that I needed to learn about the energy of the human body in order to understand what I was witnessing.

Much has been written about the idea that the human body is more than the physical body that we see. It can be described as a complex energetic interference pattern or hologram, superimposed upon and interpenetrated by non-physical patterns of energy called the etheric, emotional, mental and astral, each of which operates at a frequency higher than the physical body. Each is a highly complex and infinitely orchestrated field.

Whilst physics studies have shown that things cannot occupy the same space at the same time according to the Pauli exclusion principle, multiple electromagnetic waves do not obey this rule because they mediate the interactions between matter rather than being matter themselves. Thus, multiple energy bodies occupy the same space in and around the body. It is now scientifically accepted, but not widely understood, that the body is an electric machine and there are a variety of instruments that measure energy fields of the body and movement of energy within the body[22]. Cells conduct electricity, create electrical fields and function as electrical generators and batteries. Cells are designed to run at 25mV (millivolts) but drop below 15mV when they are dying. When cells are injured or need repair, the energy level is boosted to 50 mV to increase blood circulation, which brings an extra load of protein to the cell and removes waste. This causes inflammation and pain, which are indicators of both damage and healing.

When we are young, our energy field is pure and corresponds most closely with the universal energy field. The field is pure because it has not yet been contaminated by the programs that we create in response to life. As time passes and life becomes more difficult, our energy field becomes progressively more contaminated by negative programs and this causes our energy frequency to decrease. By consciously accessing the deeply held negative programs that we hold in our subconscious and then releasing them, we have the ability to increase the energy frequency in our body. This allows people to change the reality of their lives because under conditions of energy purity, there is unobstructed communication between human consciousness and universal consciousness making possible such things as intuition, clairvoyance and the ability to tap into energy dimensions that are outside the normal range.

---

22 Global Advances in Health and Medicine 2015 ncbi.nm.nih.gov/pms/articles/PMC4654784

§

Research into energy flows between cells, [23]within and around the human body is relatively recent. I remember having a kirlian [24]photograph in the 1980s to find out what my aura looked like. Kirlian photography photographed energy emissions. In 2003, photon emissions from the human body were measured [25]and more recently research in a study involving the channelling of information and energy relayed by electromagnetic waves of light[26]has proved that energy meridians exist. The basic energy structure within the human body has been understood for centuries in Indian esoteric teaching and boosting energy flow in eastern medicine is the basis for such things as acupuncture and cupping.

At the start of this chapter, I referred to the etheric body, the energy field that surrounds the physical body, which is often referred to as the aura. This energy field contains the blueprint for future physical growth and development. Psychics and clairvoyants describe this energy pattern in terms of colours. An aura can be seen as a variety of colours.[27] Each colour corresponds to a specific frequency range. Measurements

---

23 graduate.maryland.edu/gsa/gazette/February-2016/How-the-human-body-uses-electricity
24 https://www.livinglifeinfullspectrum.com.what-is-kirlian-photography
25 ncbi.nih.gov/pubmed/15244265 May 2003
26 upliftconnect.com/science/science-proves-meridians-exist
27 p 133 *Vibrational Medicine*, Gerber, Richard, M.D. Published by Bear Company, 1988

using EMG electrodes have shown that the frequency of the energy in the etheric field is far higher than the brain's normal range of 0-100 Hz.

Energy Transfer System

Within the body, *meridians* comprise the major energy network transfer system. There are twelve pairs of meridians, each of which supports a specific organ. Associated with the meridians is an internal duct system linked to the endocrine, lymph, blood and organ surfaces. *Nadis* are the minor energy distribution channels which distribute energy from the meridians to the cells.

Energy transfer also involves cells which contain microcrystalline sub-elements, which act as electron transport chains. Cell membranes are the capacitors and the mitochondria are batteries. Thus cells, in addition to all their other tasks, are electronic switching and transmission centres.

Acupuncture is used to stimulate energy flow by stimulating different points along the medians. Korean research[28] in the 1960s demonstrated that beneath the acupuncture points, special corpuscles are located and the tests carried out by this research showed that these points are unusually high in DNA, RNA, amino acids, nucleotides, adrenalines and 16 free hormones.

---

28 https://www.buddhistdoor.net/.../korean-researchers-claim-scientific-evidence-of-meridians..

Energy Frequency Moderators

Located along the backbone are centres called *chakras*. The job of the chakras is to change the energy vibration levels of the energy fields extending out from the body to a level that is usable by the organs. There are seven major chakras along the spine. In the same way that each energy body operates at a particular frequency, each chakra has a specific energy field ranging from 100 to 1600 Hz. Again, chakra energy is perceived as colour by those who have the ability to see energy fields. The base chakra at the bottom of the spine is seen as red. The solar plexus chakra is yellow and the throat chakra is blue. Each of the seven major chakras is associated with specific endocrine glands and organs and is the centre for a particular emotion. For example, the throat chakra is associated with the cervical ganglia medulla, the respiratory system and the thyroid. Because of the connections between the chakras and the glands, blocked chakras affect emotions because emotions are subject to influence by the hormonal/chemical compositions that affect the whole nervous system. Clairvoyants, who are able to see energy fields, have observed that during Stress Defusion sessions chakras open and close, and the whole of the body's energy system is affected by the decisions that are being addressed at a particular time. During a Stress Defusion session, energy is inserted into the system through the eyes and flows via the pineal gland to the areas of greatest tension. The organ and chakra affected by blocked energy determine whether physical sensation is felt as a result of the blockage, as well as the location of that sensation: nausea in the stomach, pain in the heart, choking in the throat and/ or headaches in the third eye location.

Energy systems which are blocked or distorted may well be at the core of physical problems. Michelle provided me with the opportunity to see the connection between physical problems and energy system distortion:

Michelle was nine years old when her mother brought her to me. Like her mother, she was psychic and had the ability to see energy flows and auras.

Testing during her first session showed that Michelle was operating ipsilaterally. Her mother was in the room as we worked and after the session was complete, she shared what she had seen.

The blocks that I was working with were visible in Michelle's brain. They appeared as different coloured lights. Some areas showed up as grey and Michelle's mother presumed that these indicated parts of the brain that had shut down. She voiced her concern that the grey colour was an indication of initial stages of disease. When I worked with Michelle's legs, the blocked areas in the legs also showed up as coloured light linked to the corresponding area in the brain by narrow ribbons of coloured energy.

In Michelle's case, the flow of energy linking legs and head went from the left brain down to the left leg. As the blocks were progressively released, the brilliance of the light gradually diminished. As this happened, Michelle's mother noticed that the aura surrounding Michelle, which had contained areas of distorted energy, became smoother.

When she understood the meaning of the term ipsilaterality, Michelle volunteered the information that she had seen her own aura and it appeared as if it were split. The aura on the right-hand side was a different colour from the aura on the left and there was a break at the crown chakra.

I tested Michelle a month after this session and the test showed that all evidence of ipsilaterally had disappeared. Again, the lines connecting her head and legs, which had been blocked, were visible. This time, however, the lines went from the right brain to the left leg indicating that Michelle's energy system was now in balance. Additionally, she was much more centred and had literally regained her balance. Much of the muscle tension in her legs was gone and she was much improved in flexibility. Her understanding of maths, which had earlier been a cause of concern, had improved dramatically.

§

A complication regarding blockages in energy systems arises because decisions made as a result of traumatic events attract similar, perhaps less traumatic, emotionally charged events and this causes the energy block to become bigger and bigger. Blocked energy has the same sort of effect as a stalled car at a busy intersection. Other cars are blocked by the stalled car, and these, in turn, block other vehicles. After a while, no cars can move. The only way to untangle the snarl is to remove the outside cars, the ones that are easy to see, until it is finally possible to get to the stalled car in the middle of the traffic jam.

Working with the eyes around the visual periphery works in a similar way to removing blocked cars caught up in a traffic jam. The most visible ones are dealt with first. People are very conscious of the superficial issues that are impacting on their lives thinking they are *the problem*. These are actually not the problem. They are the unintended side effects of something that is buried much deeper. As the blocks are identified and removed, more and more of the issues that someone is consciously aware of are identified and eliminated making it possible to go deeper into the subconscious, which is where the original stalled car is located, deeply buried and hidden.

Traffic jam removal initially requires an input of external energy because the stalled cars don't start easily. Sometimes energy from another car is needed via jump leads. So too, the Stress Defusion process needs to be jump started using the energy of a second person. This happens because individuals experiencing significant blocks generally have low energy levels which deny energy to essential organs of the body. Frequently, through bad diet, inadequate exercise, poor breathing techniques, medication, alcohol, nicotine, drugs, polluted air and water, energy systems have become clogged.

Once the process of unblocking is started, provided the individual is prepared to take responsibility for unclogging their own systems by making positive adjustments to their diet and exercise routines, it is fuelled by the individual's own energy.

When someone is investigating an event, which has resulted in a particular negative decision being made, the energy field closes down. When the decision is brought to conscious awareness and processed so that all judgement around the decision is removed, the chakras unblock, and the energy field expands. From observations by clairvoyants who have witnessed the Stress Defusion process, it seems that the decisions from which we operate, affect our energy system.

§

Understanding the energy flows within and around the physical body enabled me to take the Stress Defusion process beyond a purely mental exercise, which is where I started. In its development phase, Stress Defusion work was done with the mind, identifying and releasing blocked energy which interfered with the brain's ability to work according to its design. The Stress Defusion process created changes to mental function and effectiveness. Techniques to locate and clear blocked emotional energy were required to start the energy flow, and then it was necessary to identify the origin of the blocks in order to reduce stress levels. When clients identified the origin of each problem, they felt less confused. Understanding what had happened, and knowing why they had experienced immense challenges, made a huge difference to each client's peace of mind. Release of blocked emotional energy was all that was required to allow the body and brain to relax and heal sufficiently and to allow physical and mental systems to operate at improved levels of efficiency. But before this could happen, a detoxification process was needed to remove the toxins that had accumulated because of the blocked energy flow. Whilst the detoxification process was uncomfortable and occasionally painful, it was short-lived and the benefits from releasing toxins from the body were immediately identified.

Whilst releasing blockages through the eyes was easiest, sometimes there were blockages in the physical body that were easily identified, and I developed techniques to clear blockages from the body. These techniques involved stretching, massage and/or pressure whilst simultaneously working with the eyes.

Within the body, blockages were identified by such things as extreme inflexibility, muscle soreness and sometimes pain associated with energy that was so blocked that it had become crystalline in form and had caused problems such as arthritis. Having understood this, the issue being investigated was stated in terms of a physical disability or problem such as *I can't straighten my arm* or *I have pain in my back*. Once the problem that had caused the energy blockage to occur was identified and released, the physical condition often improved.

Catherine complained to her mother about her eyesight and an appointment had been made for her to visit the optometrist. Catherine explained that when she watched television, she saw two images superimposed, one on top of the other.

Working with the issue 'I can't see' restored Catherine's eyesight. When she told her mother that there was no longer any reason to have her eyesight checked, her mother said that eyesight didn't improve just like that and took her anyway. Catherine's vision was tested and shown to be excellent.

§

Over time, I realised that all three aspects — mind, body and emotions — needed to be cleared for the issue being investigated to be resolved fully, and then, by understanding the energetic connection between blocked chakras and the health of specific organs I was able to explain why physical complaints could suddenly vanish. Once energy flow has been restored, the body has the ability to heal.

During her session, Phyllis mentioned that she was booked to go into hospital a week or so later to have surgery. The plan was to remove an internal organ that was causing problems.

When I checked on her a week or so after the session, Phyllis told me that our session hadn't been successful. Nothing had changed.

'So, you're booked into hospital for your operation?'

'No. I went to see the doctor a couple of days ago and he did some tests and he told me that the problem I was having seems to have gone away. I don't need surgery.'

'Well I'm delighted you don't have to have surgery but very sorry that nothing has shifted for you.' What else could I say?

This conversation clarified for me something I had noticed previously but hadn't fully realised its significance. It seemed that once a problem was 100% cleared, it was as if it had never existed. Physical symptoms as well as memories simply vanished.

§

My next epiphany came when I realised that clearing energy blocks within the body facilitated energy flow to specific organs, so that they could heal, because the chakra associated with that organ had become unblocked. For energy to be available from the universe, people needed their chakras to be open, because the chakra's job is to lower the frequency level of universal energy to a level that is appropriate for the physical needs of specific organs, and to open meridians to transport that energy where it is needed. Blocked chakras represent a totally closed energy system and unfortunately this is the reality for many people.

The society in which we live restricts our uptake of universal energy. The great majority of Earth's people live in artificial environments, devoid of natural vegetation and running water. People rarely walk on the earth with bare feet so they are unable to tap into the energy that is naturally available to them. City dwellers spend most of their time in air-conditioned environments, with artificial lighting, breathing polluted air.

Energy deficiency shows itself in people living in a state of numbness, unable to feel, communicate or respond to those around them. Others practise a form of *energy vampirism:* taking energy from people rather than using the unlimited supply that is available from the universe.

Energy vampires don't even know that they are taking energy from others, they just know that they feel energised when they belittle or criticise others. When people are angry, energy flows from those who are the object of the anger to the one who is violent and abusive. When people cause others to feel afraid, they sap energy from those around them.

There are many instances where people are valued only in terms of energy and what can be produced from that energy. Inequality results from the stealing of energy, or life force, from vast numbers of people who spend their lives working long hours for a pittance. These practices are not new. They have been a feature in many societies over much of Earth's history. Sacrifice to the gods was a fundamental aspect of spiritual practice in Mayan culture and I believe in Atlantean culture. If greater equality is to be gained, those who are subservient must step into their own power and those who use the energy of others must understand that energy is readily available from the universe and does not need to be taken from others.

Chapter 12
Emotions

The Stress Defusion process was so named because it splits apart, or defuses, memories of a traumatic event, the unexpressed emotions associated with that event and the decisions or judgements made at the time of the event. When these three components of memory are locked together, they cannot be shifted. But once the elements are split apart it is possible to deal with each separately: to *identify and feel the emotion* that was felt but not expressed at the time, *recall* the events that evoked these emotions and *identify the decisions* that were made at the time. Once that is done, it is possible to investigate the memories and to realise that the decisions made were probably appropriate in view of what was happening at the time. The emotions that were aroused as a consequence of the event, were also appropriate. What was not appropriate, was emotion that was unexpressed, so that emotional energy was stored somewhere in the body. Stored low vibrational energy provided the energy to attract similar events and experiences.

Emotional pain is appropriate in specific circumstances. It is appropriate to feel sad when someone loses the person they love, or to feel inadequate in the face of a challenge and uncertainty. Fear is a totally rational response to a dangerous situation. If someone has ventured beyond the bounds of safety, fear alerts them to possible danger. It is absolutely right to feel angry when you see those who are weak being physically abused or when you are being abused.

But society tells us to hide our feelings: *big boys don't cry.* The reason for people not wanting others to express their emotions is that when they do, it triggers an emotional response in those who are present and people do not enjoy feeling sad, fearful, ashamed or weak. In fact, people will often avoid feeling anything at all. Some people have perfected non-feeling to such an extent that they are unable to feel emotion of any kind. Others just feel bad all the time and become depressed. Depression is treated as an illness rather than as an appropriate response to a disastrous life situation in which a person always seems to sabotage themselves regardless of the situation in which they find themselves.

What is not generally appreciated is that emotional pain is carried forever when people shut their emotions down. The energy of emotional pain becomes trapped in their physical and auric bodies. That is why it is crucial to understand that identifying and feeling emotional baggage is all that is required for it to be released.

There is a difference between feeling and expressing. For example, people can feel anger without expressing anger. Expressing anger may actually be a way of avoiding feeling. Someone may act angrily but not necessarily feel angry. Acting angrily is a way of giving the energy of our anger to others so that they do not have to feel it themselves. The difference is subtle, but significant.

Where someone does not wish to consciously remember specific events, they file them away. But blocking memories by *forgetting* creates strain, and the memories become unwanted baggage that the person carries around with them. Thereafter, everything that happens in their life is filtered through their memories, so that subconscious memories have the potential to become unintentionally associated with a range of subsequent events and experiences, which attract the same degree of emotional intensity to them as was attached to the initial events. This happens even though subsequent events may not, in themselves, be emotionally significant.

§

The problem with holding onto unexpressed emotion is that it distorts the auric energy field, disrupts energy flow through the physical and subtle bodies and may, over time, cause physical problems due to the negative effect on the body's biochemistry. Anger, when not expressed, is held in the body. This causes a variety of biochemical reactions that translate thought into chemical codes in the brain and the body[29] and upset the hormonal balance. People respond to trauma by activating the limbic system, triggering the release of ligands such as peptides, hormones, cortisol and a variety of other agents. The intensity of the emotional experience dictates how much, and which specific ligand, is activated.

---

29 https://experiencelife.com/article/emotional — biochemistry.

What happens to peptides following their release has been observed by using an electron microscope.[30] They flow towards thousands of receptor cells, which, depending on the vibrational frequency of the cells, may allow them entry. Once incorporated, peptides have the potential to change the cell's composition dramatically. A chain reaction of biochemical events is initiated, causing cell functions to alter. In turn, the input of a peptide may alter the cell's way of adding or subtracting energetic chemical groups such as phosphates into its composition or it may change the cell's dividing processes.

These minute physiological changes at the cellular level can translate into large-scale changes in behaviour, physical activity and mood. When unresolved anger or fear and anxiety persist, people experience stress. Under stressful conditions, specific areas of the brain are activated. One brain area that gets involved is the amygdala, which is associated with fear and aggression. Activation of the amygdala causes the release of a hormone which prompts the adrenal glands to release chemicals that cause non-essential functions such as digestion and growth to slow down. When the stress issue is not resolved in the short term, another part of the brain gets involved. Its function is to release norepinephrine which signals the amygdala to produce more hormones to reactivate the stress pathways. In this way, the problems caused by repressed emotion are re-activated over and over again. It is easy to see that holding onto emotion creates a whole series of potential health problems.

---

30   candacepert.com.

The nature of emotion

Dr Manfred Clynes, chief research scientist and director of the biocybernetics laboratories at Rockland State Hospital in the USA, studied the nature of emotions. He explained his findings in his 1989 book *Sentics*.[31]

Dr Clynes, states that emotions can be experienced independently, as pure qualities independent of a context. Associated with each emotion, or sentic state to use Dr Clyne's terminology, hormonal and body changes exist together with a variety of physical sensations. Joy, for example, is accompanied by a feeling of lightness, and grief by a feeling of heaviness.

Dr Clynes observed that each emotion has a particular vibrational pattern, which is generated by the brain. I understand emotion as being the brain's response to something that is perceived. If there is nothing to impede response from all areas of the brain, the response will be simultaneous. If this response is monitored and graphed, the graph is of a gently undulating electrical pattern, which has been identified as the pattern of *universal love*. If, on the other hand, the stimulus triggers *time-delayed* responses from different parts of the brain so that the response is sequential rather than simultaneous, the pattern generated will be uneven. According to Dr Clynes, each emotion has different characteristics related to the synchronicity of the electrical activity. Where there is little synchronicity, the emotion experienced is a very intense, negative one. Anger,

---

31 Dr Manfred Klyne *Sentics* Prism Press 1989

when graphed, is shown to have a sharp angular pattern. Dr. Clynes concluded that the degree of synchronicity is the key to explaining sentic patterns.

My hypothesis is that lack of synchronicity depends on the existence of blocks, which prevent the various parts of the brain from working in unison. When all blocks are removed, every part of the brain operates synchronistically. When this happens, the emotional state felt will be one of universal love regardless of the stimulus. Possibly, this is the ultimate outcome for Stress Defusion: removal of all blocks created by holding onto emotions, which then affect both brain and body operation. When no tension exists, all parts of the brain and body operate synchronistically.

According to Dr Clynes, the feeling of universal love creates a smoothly undulating pattern of energy. Love encompasses minor vibrational energies such as reverence, joy, interest, enthusiasm and excitement. All other emotional patterns represent a distortion of this ideal.

§

Each person has a unique energy profile; a unique way of *being*. Their *being-ness* determines how they interpret the world, and how the world interprets them and acts as filter for their life's experiences.

Since the frequency of the emotions being held coalesces into a unique vibrational pattern for each person, it is easy to understand why people respond to others in a particular way.

They *read* their energy frequency at the subconscious level. The good news is that this frequency changes positively as energy garbage is released.

At any point of time in someone's life, they are the sum total of the emotional energy frequency left from the events of their lives, and possibly their past lives, overlaying the energy frequency of love, which cannot contain negative emotional frequencies without itself changing. For example, love plus sadness creates melancholy. It seems evident that a person's experience and interpretation of the world depends on the vibrational level at which they operate, because this acts as a filter for all their experiences.

Whilst a person may suppress recollection or be in denial of some aspects of who they are, they move into negative emotional states every time an opportunity arises that connects with emotions they hold onto. To ensure this happens, the vibrational energy that they hold onto is magnetic in its effect, so that they attract people to them who have the same vibrational energy as themselves. Each time they experience envy and jealousy in others, if they also hold onto feelings of envy and jealousy, their own energy pattern becomes more intense. The purpose for this is to eventually force them to acknowledge their envy and jealousy, feel these emotional responses and release them.

Healing also requires people to release judgement of negative emotional responses, which are valid in view of the situation that they are faced with. When they judge jealousy, and judge themselves for feeling jealous, they shut down their own ability to feel it. This response causes them to hold the jealousy within. Feeling the emotion and letting go of judgment that this is what they are feeling means that they cease to attract things to themselves that cause them to feel jealous.

I believe that judgement of emotional pain started the whole process of separation from universal love. When we let go of judgement, we realise that it is appropriate to feel an emotion such as fear, when a situation is likely to cause us harm. All that we need to do is to feel the emotion appropriate to the situation, and let go of it rather than delete, distort, justify or deny it, which is what we have all tended to do. Denial was certainly Mark's response to a childhood experience:

Mark had lost touch with reality by the time he came to see me. He had lost his ability to communicate or to work. A brilliant scholar at the college he had attended, he had dropped out of university after failing Medicine for two consecutive years. His life had gone downhill progressively since then. At the age of 30 he was diagnosed as schizophrenic. He had disturbing nightmares and he heard voices in his head.

When he walked in, I found it difficult to hide my dismay. He sat rigidly, his hands held stiffly in front of him. He was stooped like an old man. He shuffled as he walked, could no longer use his hands and he had difficulty concentrating.

I already had some insights into the possible cause of Mark's problems. I had worked with his sister previously and had a suspicion that she had been subjected to some form of sexual abuse, which was the basis for her back problems. My ideas were vague and unsubstantiated by any concrete facts, but I did know that something had happened when she was ten years old.

As we worked, Mark started talking about how angry he was with his mother for not being around when he needed her as a young child. His next memory was of Jason, his father's stepbrother.

'Was it Jason who raped your sister?' I asked, not sure whether this had, in fact, actually happened. At this, Mark gasped in horror and covered his face. He didn't deny it. He just said, through his tears:

'I couldn't do anything to stop him.'

Mark had been three years old at the time. He had subconsciously carried the guilt of being witness to a particularly nasty event ever since. Until I asked the question, he had forgotten the episode. It had taken the Stress Defusion process to bring it back to conscious memory. His parents had absolutely no idea that anything had ever happened. The children had made a pact not to tell.

Once the truth was out, Mark was able to release the tension that he was holding in his hands. Two months later he was back studying, although he was still a long way from cured.

§

Doctors don't like to have patients who are depressed or in pain. If someone feels depressed or in pain the doctor's response is to prescribe medication to dull the feeling of depression or to dull the pain. The Stress Defusion process acknowledges emotional and physical pain as totally valid responses to events in a person's life, and it works to elicit painful emotions that have been buried or to find the underlying cause of the pain. It does this by encouraging people to re-experience the painful events in their lives.

Like Mark, Garry's schizophrenia was also associated with rape. In his case, he was the victim. Garry was raped by someone, who he referred to as the black tiger, when he was eight years old. Long buried, the emotional impact of this event resurfaced years later, following a homosexual incident or relationship. I never discovered whether this later incident was consensual or if it was another rape, but it certainly involved someone he trusted, as he had trusted the perpetrator of the rape that took place many years previously.

Regardless of what happened, the effect of the second episode was to trigger Garry's feeling of guilt. He was inconsolable for several weeks. Distressed, his mother sought help from the local priest who recommended that Garry seek psychiatric help because he was so seriously disturbed. Garry was admitted to hospital and given drug therapy. The drugs were ineffective. Different drugs were tried. None had the desired effect. This drug cocktail had such an effect on his body that he ended up in a comatose state, needing to be intravenously fed.

I saw Garry at his mother's request. By the time I met him he had been a resident in a mental institution for about ten years. I was surprised that I was allowed access to Garry.

Perhaps that was because his mother had requested it, and she was present during the initial sessions. The first time I saw Garry, much of what he said was unintelligible. One phrase kept coming up. He kept talking about the black tiger. When I asked Garry about the black tiger he jumped out of his chair, crouched against the wall and rocked back and forth. He became very angry and violent, so I achieved very little that session or for the next few weeks. Anger expressed by one inmate had the potential to trigger anger in all the other patients in the ward. Garry's drug dosage was increased as a consequence of my visit and I was unable to see him until he was calm again.

Gradually, Garry came to accept me. I carefully avoided all mention of the black tiger. Sessions took very little time. Garry was able to identify and clear blocks instantaneously. All that was needed was his willingness to participate. That wasn't always forthcoming. Some days Garry surprised me. On one occasion I took Barbara Hand Brennan's book 'Hands of Light' for him to look at. He grabbed it and started studying the pictures showing reflexology points in the feet. He wasn't interested in the pictures of auras, which were the reason I thought the book might interest him. When I asked him about them, he said, 'That picture reminds me of Michelangelo's aura.'

'What do you know of Michelangelo's aura?' I was surprised by the turn that the conversation had taken.

'I was one of his apprentices,' Garry replied.

'Can all the patients in the hospital see auras?' I asked.

'Yes,' said Garry, in an offhand manner, as if I was stupid. 'They're all psychic. The trouble with some of them is that they can't tell the difference between their past lives and the ones they are living now. Gets them all confused. I know which is which, so I'm OK.'

After several months of visiting the asylum, I thought it was time to bring up the subject of the black tiger again. I asked him whether the man who raped him when he was eight years old was dressed in black.

'Yes' replied Garry, 'and he never did give me the chocolate he promised me. He was a bad man.' I wasn't sure whether he was bad because he was a rapist or because he didn't hand over the chocolate.

'Was he the black tiger?' I asked.

'Yes. I hate him.'

'Does the black tiger have a name?'

Garry told me his name.

'Can you get in touch with the hate you feel for the black tiger and let it go.'

'Yes. I can do that now.'

The black tiger was never mentioned after that. More importantly, Garry's anger became less of a problem. The changes following that session were so dramatic that the hospital staff noticed and commented on them. He stopped wetting his bed. His clarity of speech improved as did his concentration. We started having some really interesting conversations. He told me that he was training for the Olympic Games which were to be held in Sydney the following year.

'Well, I'm not really training for the Olympic Games,' he confided. 'That's just the story I'm telling the nurses. They think I'm mad so I can get away with it. I build myself a training circuit in the courtyard and I'm training every day. I pile the chairs and tables up and I jump onto them and over them. I'm piling them high so that eventually I can climb over the wall, but I can't leave till I get fit.'

In fact, Garry had already found a way to get out of the locked ward and he had absented himself in the middle of the night through a window, returning a couple of hours later through the front door so that the staff knew what he had done. While he was gone, he checked out a friend who lived near the hospital and sought his co-operation. He returned because he knew he didn't have the stamina to get away even if he could escape.

A few weeks after this conversation Garry put his plan into action. He went over the wall, ran to his friend's house. The next day he caught a taxi to another friend's house and the following day he contacted his mother who called the police. Garry went straight back to the hospital.

I saw him the day after he returned. He was so drugged he could barely walk and was unable to talk. He was really angry that his mother had sent him back. He was angry that the police had been called. Most of all he was angry with himself.

Although Garry had quite ably demonstrated his ability to leave the hospital if he chose, on another level he wasn't ready. Mental hospitals and gaols are simply a reflection of the walls people build around themselves with their minds. Mental barriers are far more powerful than any walls. Garry freely admitted that he was fearful of the world. The fact that some of these fears had been overcome was demonstrated by his willingness to return to the world, even on a short-term basis and it wasn't long before he was allowed weekend leave. He was no longer judged to be a danger to himself or to society.

§

Garry's escape episode reminded me of time I had spent with Ken Windes, an American who ran a personal development program that he called *The Game*. This was in the late 1980s. Ken's story is about gaols of the mind and how the barriers we build up are of our own making rather than the bars others put up around us.

Ken was on the wrong side of the law from a very early age. He was a car thief and a thug. He spent much of his teenage years in boys' homes and then graduated to gaol. On one of his escape attempts he shot a prison guard. That, plus the number of offences he had already committed including armed robbery, landed him in gaol for a cumulative period of sixty-six years. He was twenty years old at the time.

In gaol Ken had a lot of spare time. He read. His reading led him to meditation and yoga. He read about yogis who could walk through walls. Ken decided that if he could learn to walk through walls he could walk out of gaol. During his time in solitary confinement he perfected his meditation techniques.

Ken needed to find a mentor. This was in the 1960s. The gaol was looking for ways to help prisoners so a counsellor was appointed to run rehabilitation groups at the high security gaol in which Ken was incarcerated, a gaol designated to house the most dangerous criminals.

Ken and the counsellor worked together to develop a program for the prisoners that identified the attitudes and beliefs that were keeping the prisoners where they were. Through their collaboration, Ken realised that the bars that kept him in gaol were of his own making. The technique he and his counsellor developed was so successful that they were asked to work with groups in other gaols. Ultimately Ken was offered release, in recognition of the contribution he had made, but he wasn't ready to leave. He knew that there was still more work to be done. When he finally left gaol, he left through the front door at the time he felt ready to do so. The technique Ken worked with was designed to clear emotional blocks. I was a participant in *The Game* when Ken brought it to Australia, years before I developed the Stress Defusion process.

§

The experience of people who have worked with the Stress Defusion process has demonstrated over and over again what Manfred Clynes' articulated in *Sentics* that

...discharge of accumulated emotional baggage is sufficient to evoke a spontaneous regeneration of well-being and enjoyment of experience, even a specific ecstasy which we call

'peace'. This is accompanied by a surge of energy, no longer directed at the removal of anxiety or at some goal set for satisfaction of a drive. It is energy which joyfully embraces what the world has to offer.' [32]

Discharging emotional baggage is also important in healing physical problems.

Robert held the emotion of terror in his hips but had no memories of the origin of the terror. He could not sit on the floor with a straight back. He sat back on his backbone with a curved spine and concave chest. When he reached his arms out in front of him, he could barely reach his knees. His hips were totally inflexible.

Robert was experienced with the Stress Defusion technique and he chose to find out why he was so inflexible. He recalled the relevant memories, vividly remembering that when he was nine years old, he was playing with his older brother. He crawled into a suitcase to hide but was only able to fit into it by doubling his body into a very tight space. The suitcase fell over, onto the lock, and Robert's brother was unable to unlock it to release him.

Robert was terrified. What had started out as a game became a nightmare. He was in pain because he was in an extremely uncomfortable position for a long time. He was in a dark, confined space. Robert's decision was: 'I'm going to die in here.' He obviously did get out, and the episode was dismissed without further thought. He didn't even tell

---

32   *Sentics* p 181

his parents what had happened. The terror remained fused with the decision, and these were locked in Robert's hip joints causing them to become totally locked up — just as he had been locked in the suitcase. When Robert remembered the incident, and his decision, he was able to re-experience his fear, his hips immediately unlocked and he was able to stretch forward and touch his toes.

Holding onto emotion rather than allowing ourselves to feel it and let it go causes a variety of biochemical reactions which are associated with our chemically-based nervous system, which is in turn, linked to the electrically based central nervous system. Stories such as the ones I have just told convinced me that biochemical reactions affect our mental functioning in a way that can lead to conditions such as schizophrenia and depression. Unexpressed emotion also causes physical inflexibility and a variety of physical problems.

Chapter 13
The Brain

My need to know how stress affected brain operation and why skills such as reading are so dependent on whole brain operation required me to investigate brain research that had been undertaken a few years prior to the development of the Stress Defusion process. There are three widely recognised models of the brain and these allowed me to appreciate the importance of stress and its relationship to whole brain operation. I considered the left/right brain model, the triune brain model and the fore brain/back brain model to be particularly significant. This chapter provides a summary of information that provided me with the opportunity to compare what I was seeing with a scientific explanation of how the brain functions. This information gave me an insight into what I was seeing and allowed me to understand why the things I had thought impossible, before I understood something about brain function, could happen.

Left/right brain model

My understanding of how the brain works was greatly enhanced by the work of neurosurgeons Roger Sperry and Robert Ornstein. Together with Joseph Bogan they won half the Nobel Prize in 1981 for their research into functional specialisation of the cerebral hemispheres. Their research showed that each side of the brain has a different way of processing information and that the two sides are capable of parallel processing. This research was the basis for the accelerated learning techniques that I had studied and applied.

Perry and Ornstein explained that the left brain processes information linearly. It takes each piece of information and adds it logically and sequentially to what is already known, thereby building deeper and deeper understanding. The left brain works with numbers and language, and it operates at a beta level of 14 — 28 Hz, enabling perception of a wide variety of different and separate pieces of information. It is capable of working with split focus, sees time linearly, and operates in present time.

This information was of interest to me because it explained why some children had the ability to read words, and could read a sentence, but didn't seem to understand the meaning of what they were reading. It made sense that these children were relying primarily on their left brain function and, if this was the case, their abilities were slower than optimum because, as I have mentioned previously, the left brain is capable of functioning at the relatively slow rate of 40 pieces of information per second. Perry and Ornstein's findings explained why children were able to read faster and with meaning and learn so much more easily once whole brain function was restored.

The right brain's major goal is to identify patterns. Information is processed holistically, and the right brain can make sense of information that is presented randomly. Right brain processing involves accessing alpha brain wave state which operates at 7 — 14 Hz. It has the ability to recognise patterns including rhythms, concepts, maps and pictures and respond to these with feelings. It processes information globally and understands such complex ideas as love and beauty through imaginative processes. It understands metaphor and how parts go together to make up the whole.

The difference between the left and right brain is similar to the difference between a microscope and a kaleidoscope. Through a microscope we see little bits of detail, but we don't see how they fit into the whole. With a kaleidoscope, we see bits of colour constantly being re-arranged into ever-changing patterns.

The corpus callosum, a broad band of nerve fibres, links the two different sides allowing both perspectives to be reconciled within a framework that is much more meaningful than the information either side provides. Being able to access and synthesise information from both sides of the brain simultaneously provides a much greater understanding than we are capable of when information is available from only one side.

The corpus callous controls information traffic, and its job is to decide when to pass information from the right to the left hemisphere. This is important because the left hemisphere is capable of cutting off from the rest of the brain and working in isolation when a situation has created a stress response. The left hemisphere can also draw information from the limbic and reptilian brain areas, the functions of which I explain later, and work with that information according to abstract ideas of what is possible. With this skill it can actually change or delete incoming information to make it fit in with what is already known. What is *known* is what we have decided is true.

This information explained what had happened at the high school. The teachers weren't deliberately ignoring the information I was showing them. The incoming information I was providing just didn't fit in with what they knew, so they deleted it.

§

Between the ages of 7 and eleven, the left hemisphere develops its language capability and builds a unifying connection with the limbic and reptilian systems, from which it draws information. This communication network allows the left hemisphere to communicate abstract ideas to the rest of the brain.

As I have mentioned earlier, the right brain has the ability to process information at the speed of 40^3 bits of information per second, and its ability to process information fast gives it the power to quickly gain an overview of incoming information. This provides the brain with a framework in which to operate, making subsequent processing far more effective than it is with only left brain operation.

Neither right nor left brain operation is effective on its own. Skill is achieved when both sides work together, simultaneously. This does not happen when someone is stressed. Stress occurs whenever the brain is working with incongruent instructions between the subconscious and the conscious mind reinforced by negative mind chatter which undermines everything we attempt to do. Left/right brain disconnection impacts on high level skills such as reading and comprehension, both of which require the synthesis of different functions.

In reading, word pattern recognition comes through practice, which uses left brain logic. On the basis of past learned experience, the brain works logically and sequentially to sort out the correct arrangements of letters and words. Because verbal and symbol skills are the province of the left brain, anyone who is left brain dominant is able to read slowly and carefully with total attention to detail and sequence. They know what the words are but have little sense of meaning. Neither do they have a sense of context so that they can't identify where this information fits. They sound as if they know what they are doing but, in truth, they don't, and the process they use is slow and laborious.

The right brain, by comparison, is concerned with the big picture. It seeks meaning through generalisation and how things feel. People who are predominantly right brained have strong feelings about things and care little about detail. They have a clearly developed sense of meaning about something that has been read but lack the verbal competence to be able to relay that information to someone else. For all intents and purposes, they look as if they don't know what is going on, but that may not actually be the correct interpretation. They know, but they cannot explain what they know.

Once the blocks that cause the brain to function

ipsilaterally are removed, the brain recovers its ability to combine the functions of both hemispheres and in doing so recovers its ability to work at the level for which it was designed: 40^4 or 2,560,000 bits of information per second. Even more importantly, the brain does not have to work as hard as it did when it was operating with separation between the two hemispheres. So, stress causes the brain to downshift from its amazing ability to work at a speed of 2,560,000 bits of information per second to 40 bits per second. It follows that people have the capacity to achieve at very high levels of brilliance, but only if stress levels are low.

Knowing how much faster we process information when the two sides of the brain start to work together provided me with the means of understanding why the children that I was working with were suddenly able to learn so much faster and more effectively. While they were running competing subconscious and conscious programs, they were operating under huge levels of stress. Once the negative subconscious programs were eliminated, the stress levels decreased, and both sides of the brain were able to work together.

High levels of stress can arise from one terrifying situation. The decisions made as a consequence of one incident may be generalised to include many aspects of life. Identifying the incident that created the stress in the first place and identifying the decisions that were made as a result of that incident, allows dramatic change to occur in someone's life.

James was about four years old when he was left with his nanny while his parents were away. Living next door to

James were two slightly older children. The three of them played together regularly.

James was horrified when his two friends rushed into the kitchen one day with the shocking revelation that they had been digging in James' back garden and had dug up the devil. James was terrified. He had no one to share this terrible secret with. He didn't think Nanny would want to know that the devil had been living in her back garden.

When this incident was remembered and revealed as the source of James' many learning problems, he found it difficult to believe, but subsequent changes in his ability to learn showed that this was the origin of his problems. Fear of the devil had caused the two hemispheres of his brain to separate and shut down his ability to learn effectively.

§

Ipsilaterality can be central to an individual's mode of operation or it may be issue specific. This depends on how fundamental the decision that is controlling the individual's world is to their sense of personal value and to what extent the decision has been generalised across a whole range of activities.

When I was working with a group of ten to eleven-year-old's who were students at a primary school in Sydney, I was able to identify issues that seemed central to whole brain function. Children who identified their belief patterns as *I feel disconnected, I'm not good enough* and *I can't get it right* operated with split brain function. Other belief systems caused them to switch between whole-brain and split-brain operation. Because of their age, I chose to identify the location of blocks through pain and pressure rather than attempting to identify possible problem areas by questioning. Pain that occurred on either side of the backbone, was shown to correlate with an area of peripheral vision. Pain that was central to the body was identified by asking the children to focus both of their eyes towards their noses and move their eyes from the starting point of looking down at the floor and then moving their eyes slowly upwards towards the ceiling. By using their eyes in this way, they were focusing inward and accessing areas of the brain that contained information that was fundamental to their whole way of being. This method provided a way of locating blocks that were preventing the children from reinstating whole brain operation that was very important to their academic achievement. It was a far less intrusive method than asking the children a lot of questions.

Working with a large number of clients over several years showed me how people operate in a balanced, whole-brained way except in relation to specific conditions or in relation to specific issues. Alternatively, some people operate with a time delay in message switching, so that the information available from the two sides of their brain is not available instantaneously and this slows down thought processes. When this happens, they tend to rely on their dominant brain hemisphere to do most of the work. Another strategy is to switch from left brain operation to right brain operation and back again depending on the situation, which is what Alan did.

Alan couldn't do maths. Just thinking about maths caused him to go into split brain operation.

Alan's level of achievement in mathematics was abysmal. Remedial teaching had not helped. Discussion with Alan revealed that his teacher in Year 2 and again in Year 4 got very cranky when children made mistakes. Alan made lots of mistakes. She frightened him so much that he became sick with fear. Alan made the decision: 'I will never be able to do maths. It makes me feel sick.' From then on Alan felt sick whenever it became time to do maths.

After the block caused by the thought that 'mathematics makes me feel sick' was cleared, Alan said he felt much better about mathematics. He agreed that it might be possible to learn his tables and a few weeks later his results started to improve.

§

With re-connection, brain-wave coherence increases so that the brain can downshift its thought-wave activity from the high beta range to alpha brainwave levels. Increased brain coherence enables us to decode holograms. Things start to make sense because they fit into a much bigger picture rather than existing as separate ideas. Focus increases and with it comes an increased ability to concentrate. At the high school, the girls' ability to concentrate was something I had really noticed, right from the beginning when I was developing the Stress Defusion process.

Sandra demonstrated the effect that a sudden switch from whole brain function to ipsilateral brain function can have on a person's ability to learn or perform academically. Sarah's difficulties provided me with considerable insight into what happened when left/right brain function was suddenly reduced to split brain function. Because Sandra had worked with me over a number of years, she understood how her brain functioned and she was able to explain exactly what was going on.

> I had known Sandra for several years prior to the bike accident she had when she was in the final year of study for a bachelor's degree in psychology. Her parents had brought her to see me when she was a teenager because she was experiencing learning difficulties. Later, she was one of the students who had participated in the teenage learning programs that I had run. Over a period of several years, I watched her transform from a mediocre student to an excellent one.
>
> Her bike accident involved an element of extreme fear when she believed she was going to be run over by passing traffic. This caused her to go into split brain operation. Until that time, Sandra had no problems with her university studies, and she was anticipating going on to complete a master's degree. After the accident, she could not concentrate. It took her a long time to read a book and she couldn't remember what she had read. She found it impossible to write essays. She was unmotivated and found it difficult to study. Her marks became progressively worse and her dream of doing a master's degree started to fade.

Sandra came to see me when her back pain and severe headaches, caused by the accident, were under control. It took little more than one hour to identify the decision she had made at the time of her accident and to help her release the fear that had not been expressed at the time and was still linked with her decision. Even so, she had lost a great deal of time and she was worried that she would not be able to catch up. A short time later, she was delighted to tell me that her examination results were far better than she had anticipated, and her enrolment was accepted for the master's degree.

Understanding the difference in operating from a position of left brain dominance, which is common and operating with a brain which communicates spontaneously and efficiently between areas explains, to a large extent, why some people have the ability to learn fast and effectively whilst others do not. It does not appear to be a matter of genetics. Rather, it is a consequence of our experiences, the judgements we have made about these and the level of stress that these judgements engender.

§

The triune brain model

The triune brain model, which describes the brain as having three layers based on an evolutionary view of brain development, was conceived by American physician and neuroscientist Paul D. Maclean in the 1960s and is explained in depth in his book *The Triune Brain in Evolution*. According to Dr MacLean, the brain has three layers: reptilian, limbic and neocortex.

Reptilian Brain

The reptilian brain is the oldest part of the brain and the first to develop in utero. It takes care of survival: food, shelter, procreation and defence. Effective functioning of the reptilian brain is made possible by a brain growth spurt at birth. The birth process triggers off a series of patterned responses which confirm the learning that has occurred when the baby is within the womb and during the birth process. The patterned responses are installed when the newborn baby is lying close to the mother's heart, the position most conducive to development of the sensory systems of sound, taste, sight, smell and touch. Bonding between mother and baby begins here and this is essential to the welfare of the baby and to the development of speech.

The reptilian brain operates at a vibrational frequency that enables it to translate the frequencies of the physical world into meaningful signals so that from the moment of birth we can understand the world we are in. The reptilian brain is the storage place for learnings from the limbic system and neocortex, which have been turned over to our subconscious.

Limbic System

The limbic system is the go-between linking the neocortex and the reptilian brain systems. It enables knowledge of self, relationships and language. Behaviour that incorporates wilfulness, the ability to strive towards a desired goal, is typical of limbic brain function and it is not surprising that development of limbic system occurs in association with a brain growth spurt that occurs when a child is two years old.

The importance of the limbic system is in adding emotional content to everything we experience — cold days, smoky factories, old age. It is in charge of dreaming and intuition, which tend to fade by about the age of seven years, unless these things are deliberately fostered.

Acting as a traffic cop, the limbic system directs the attention of one area to the needs of another. It has the ability to incorporate the functions of the reptilian system into the service of the neocortex, or to shut it off completely. It is the limbic system that shuttles the creations of the neocortex to the reptilian system to give meaning to highly abstract ideas, and then translate the meaning into images for conscious comprehension.

The limbic system organises sounds into meaningful groupings without which the reptilian brain could not prepare a person to speak, read or write. Sensory reports are channelled from the reptilian system through the limbic system for sorting, filing and these sensory reports are then directed into appropriate neuronal filing cabinets.

Neocortex

The neocortex is five times bigger than the other two areas of the brain which is an indication of its importance. A growth spurt at the age of four years builds the neocortex's neural fields. The right hemisphere is the first area to be developed and this allows for systems involving self, the world and language to be put in place. Later, with a further growth spurt at seven years, intellect, reasoning, logic and concrete operational thinking become possible.

The job of the neocortex is to take in incoming information, which it then computes, creates and reflects on depending on what is already stored in the limbic and reptilian systems. This enables the brain to synthesise, predict, plan and control.

By taking information from the limbic system and reptilian systems and by building parallel neural structures, the brain constructs and changes data that would otherwise have been input automatically. This data is collected from the senses of seeing, hearing, taste, feeling, and smell. The neocortex has the power to alter incoming information by referencing what is already available from the limbic and reptilian systems and changing incoming information to fit in with what is already known.

Integration of brain functions

The various areas of the brain have been described as separate entities, but in operation they are not separate. Various functions require links between different areas. Stress is an area of major concern to the brain, and depending on the level of stress, different parts of the brain are either brought into play or are shut off.

For example, the reptilian brain instigates the fight/

flight/freeze response at times perceived to be life or ego threatening. In such situations, the muscles of the legs are notified, adrenalin and other hormones are produced to increase response rate and give the body additional strength and speed. Additionally, the limbic and neocortex systems are blocked off to prevent emotion or thought from interfering with possible life-sustaining activity and this causes the perception that time has slowed down because the reptilian brain has the most rapid response rate of any part of the brain.

Under conditions of moderate stress, the neocortex, including the centres for speech that are located in the left cerebral cortex, shut down. We literally become speechless. When this happens, we switch control of our thinking to the limbic system, which is the storehouse for all behaviours learned as a consequence of past experience. This switch gives us the ability to draw on a learned behaviour pattern that we have stored away. A *something like* approach works well if the new situation resembles something appropriate from the past, but not so well if the brain brings forth a totally inappropriate response to a new situation.

Additionally, because the limbic system is also the storage department for all the emotional baggage, at the point where we adopt the response we used for similar previous events, we also revert to the same emotional response, which may or may not be appropriate. This happens because, under stress, the conscious mind that would normally control our reaction, shuts down.

Under extreme levels of stress, both the neocortex and the

limbic system shut down leaving the reptilian brain in charge. Situations of extreme stress allow no place for emotions or thinking. When a situation is life threatening, the choice is between fighting, fleeing or freezing.

Stress occurs not because of what happens, but because of the judgements and emotional labels that have already been linked to previous similar situations. Where children learn to attach high levels of guilt, sadness, anger and/or frustration to things that happened in the past and play mind chatter tapes that constantly remind them of how they think and feel about what has happened, then the shutdown of the neocortex persists. In time, the neocortex actually atrophies because it is not needed. Unless something changes, they grow into stressed paranoid adults whose lives are dominated by the need to fight and run away from life.

Forebrain/ back brain

The forebrain/back brain model fascinated me because I had seen what happened when I bridged the vertical auricular area between the forebrain and back brain as I was working to ease tension in people's calf muscles. When I did this, memories were accessed, and pain held in the legs was intensified.

The forebrain is where we process information in present time. The forebrain of the dominant hemisphere also contains the common integration area (CIA). For the majority of people, the dominant hemisphere is the left brain which is indicated by the fact that most people are right handed. The dominant hemisphere is the centre of the meta program systems that control our very existence. Meta programs are the control systems we write for ourselves on the basis of experience. They control all future action that is determined by our values, attitudes, beliefs and memories, all of which are derived from our decisions in the past. Knowing this, I came to realise that we program our future on the basis of past decisions, and if we want to change the pattern of our lives, we must first erase the power that these past decisions have to affect the present and the future.

The CIA receives input from what is seen, heard and felt. Input is filtered through the reptilian brain initially. Its job is to sort the information in terms of potential threat. It then connects it with information that is already stored to make it meaningful. Once meaning has been discovered, the CIA selects, according to existing decisions, the best way to react to incoming information. Once this selection has been made, signals are sent to other parts of the brain so that appropriate responses can be made.

There is no choice in this process. There is no rational analysis at the conscious level whether the ensuing behaviour is rational, valid or even destructive. The behaviour is determined on the basis of the judgements that we have made about experiences in the past. These judgements determine the picture we have of *self*. The brain actually selects information on the basis of self-image, distorting or deleting reality so that it fits into the picture of self that already exists. Everything is selected on the basis of an already existing design, which is the design that we have created for ourselves from what we have been told, and from the decisions we have made as a consequence of our experiences.

CIA's priority is survival of the concept of *self*. Its main objective is to keep us from suffering fear, pain or fear of pain. It operates on the basis of what is known and deletes information that causes change, even when change is beneficial.

Under stress, the dominant forebrain's integrative area takes over control of all brain functioning, withdrawing circulation from all brain areas not directly related to physical/emotional survival. It seeks out appropriate response behaviours from the storehouse of memories in our back brain.

The frontal lobes of both hemispheres are also the location of the conscious associational thinking area which has the power to inhibit neurological activity including back brain accessing, heart rate and breathing. There is no function of the body that can be consciously controlled when this area of the brain is in control. Since survival is the single most important function of brain activity, the conscious associational thinking area takes a back seat to the common integrative area's major function, which is preservation: finding the most appropriate behaviour on the basis of past experience.

The back brain is where we store long term memories that we draw on to select appropriate behaviours in response to current happenings. The area of the brain behind the vertical auricular line involves memory. Memories include actual events or perceptions and the sensations attached to those events and perceptions. Sensations include both muscle memories and emotions.

§

The operation of the brain is made even more fascinating when we understand how the brain groups experiences and files them away ready to be re-accessed whenever a *something similar* experience occurs. With new experience, the brain brings in all the information available to it from the subconscious to provide a pattern of response. *Something similar* experiences will re-activate the same sort of emotional response that has been fused with all previous experiences of the same kind together with all the decisions related to similar previous decisions. This occurs whether we consciously want to experience that kind of reaction/response or not.

Understanding how the brain works allowed me to accept that the decisions that we make, the self-talk we use to confirm those decisions, and how we feel about ourselves and the world are powerful enough to create a life path that may not be the one we would prefer to live. It indicated the level of change that could occur if past patterns were resolved. It also allowed me to understand the extremely adverse effect that stress causes on our ability to function physically and intellectually.

Chapter 14
Identifying Issues

It is not difficult to identify and clear blocks using the Stress Defusion process. The difficulty is in identifying that blocks exist and in realising how our lives are affected by them. People who are unaware that their beliefs, attitudes, values have arisen from decisions they have made, think of their experiences as a reflection of who they *are* rather than as something they *do*. I still have a vivid memory of a teenager who, having listened to my explanation of why he hadn't been able to read, wanted to clarify what I was saying.

'Are you telling me that the reason that I couldn't read was not because I'm stupid, but because I've actually made a decision that has created stress and this is what caused my brain to shut down?'

'That's right.'

'Are you telling me I'm not stupid?'

'That right. You've actually been very clever. In spite of all the help from your parents, your friends, and your teachers you've managed to not learn to read. You've done that against a whole lot of opposition. Think of all the time they've spent trying to teach you.'

'But I've always thought I couldn't read because I was stupid.'

'Of course. That's a logical thing to think, but it is actually not true. Of course, when you made the decision that caused your brain to shut down and affected your ability to read, you didn't plan to do that. It was an unintended consequence of a decision you made when you were quite small.'

'Boy! Then if I'm not stupid, I can become an engineer, or a builder. Or anything I want.'

'That's right. You can become whatever you want but it will take time and concentrated effort. You've got a lot of catching up to do.' That young man left feeling much happier about himself and his prospects. Now that he could read and understand what he was reading, a new world had opened up for him.

§

When people understand that the world is like a mirror that gives them information about themselves, they can use that information to identify the issues they need to work with. Once they realise this, they have a choice to change how they experience the world. If they don't like who they are in that world, they can also change that. Stress Defusion is just one of many processes available that allows someone to do this. Understanding that the world is a mirror provides people with major insights, which can permanently change how they view life and the world in which they live.

When they realise that the people who come into their lives and cause them unhappiness, act violently towards them, are thoughtless, rude or abusive are simply mirrors of what is inside themselves, they can stop blaming others and start looking within to find answers. It is they who have attracted these people into their lives to show them who they really are deep inside.

People who create problems in someone's life, do this for a purpose. The purpose is to help others identify the work they need to do to find the programs they have written that control their lives. Those who cause problems will possibly not realise why they do as they do. Possibly they believe that they have no choice. From their perspective, they do what they do because they think of themselves as someone who behaves in the way they do. Understanding this, it is possible to release the villains of this world from judgement and accept, but not necessarily like, the role that they play.

This line of thinking brings up a significant question that relates to children who are brutalised, raped and murdered. They are totally innocent of anything bad. How can what happens to them, be a mirror? The problem of understanding why horrible things happen only exists if people consider that this lifetime is the only one. When someone accepts that past lives *might* exist, it opens up a vast number of possibilities about what has happened in the past, how events from past lives might be playing out in this lifetime, and what lessons need to be learned. This is not Karma in the sense that people are being punished for past sins so much as the possibility that they are carrying guilt and self-blame for what happened in the past. This could mean that they are holding onto the need to be punished for what they perceive as their sins, and that this is what this life is giving them. It could also mean they are still holding onto the fear of being brutalised, tortured or sacrificed, and it is this fear that attracts fearful things to them. Perhaps they are holding onto anger from a previous life. Anger that caused them to inflict harm on others has attracted those who are angry towards them in this lifetime, which results in an experience of being the victim rather than the perpetrator, which was their previous experience.

Understanding that the world is their mirror means that people must forego blame, because blame shifts responsibility to others rather than accepting it for themselves. This means acknowledging that when people that they meet don't acknowledge them, it is because they don't acknowledge themselves. It entails accepting that when people believe they are incapable it is because they have made the decision, at some point in their soul's journey, that they are incapable. It also means that when they are locked up by others, it is because they have decided to lock themselves off from the truth, from their emotions or from the memories that make them feel uncomfortable.

People can blame others for what happens to them or others and nothing changes. They can deny what happens or they can find excuses to justify their experiences, and nothing changes. The only thing that creates change is when someone takes total responsibility for everything in their life and acknowledges that if they don't like what their life is providing, they need to change. Change occurs when they identify and release the programs that they have written for themselves, which determine their experience. Once they do this, everything changes.

§

When someone wishes to improve their life's journey there are six areas to investigate. These are:
1. The people with whom they are closely associated, particularly those with whom they have a long-term relationship.
2. Events and circumstances of their lives.
3. Repeating patterns of events and behaviours.
4. Compulsive behaviours.
5. Physical disabilities, complaints and/or illness.
6. The circumstances of their childhood.

Within these categories there are questions we can ask of ourselves, or others can ask us, that help identify the issues that need attention. Examples of questions that can be asked include:
- What is it about him or her that most annoys me?
- What is it that makes me most angry?
- What is it that I most resent about?
- Of whom am I jealous?
- What is it that I most regret not having?
- What is it that I most regret not doing?
- What scares me?
- What is it that I most want and can't have?

- Who do I most admire?
- What is it that I most desire?
- What would I like to change?
- What would I like to do that I can't do yet?
- Who do I want to be like?
- What do I want to do?
- What have I done, or not done, that I am most ashamed of?
- Who makes me envious?

1. People in our lives

The things about others that annoy, anger, irritate or sadden us reflect what is inside us that causes us to feel annoyed, angry, irritated or sad about ourselves. Our most intense reactions occur in response to things that happen within our immediate family, as Warwick explained, when I asked him who made him angry.

'OK Warwick, if Ben is the person who frustrates you most, what is it about his behaviour that gets you really angry?'

'It's the way he's not using his potential. He's just drifting through school. Everything he does, he does with minimal effort. He's so good at everything yet he accomplishes nothing outstanding. When he gets to the point where he has to put in some really hard effort, he shies away from it. It's such a waste. And he's a slob. His whole personal environment is a mess. His room is untidy. He uses things belonging to other people and never puts them back. He's just crashed both of our cars and only barely managed an apology. He blamed the other drivers for what happened. He refuses to take responsibility for himself.'

'How do you react to the idea that you've just described yourself?'

'What do you mean?'

'From what you have told me it appears that you are not using your potential. You're just skating through life. You're blaming other people, the situation, the circumstances. You're looking everywhere for the answers but you're not looking where the real answer lies.'

'Yes, that is probably true.'

'The things that Ben does that annoy you he is doing for a reason. He's responding to you even though he may not know that this is what he is doing. He's not doing those things deliberately to annoy you, but what he does is bringing to your attention the things about yourself that annoy you. That's why you get so angry. You believe that if you fix Ben, you'll solve your problems. You won't. When you resolve your own issues what Ben does will not affect you in the way it does now. You'll be able to give him the freedom to learn his lessons in his way. What's more, if you take responsibility for yourself, the likelihood is that he'll become more responsible. You, being his father, are his principal teacher. He's only doing what you have taught him to do even though you didn't intend to teach him those things.'

The people in our families and at work, with whom we have long-term relationships, provide us with the most valuable assistance in helping us to identify, in ourselves, those things that we need to work with. However, even people with whom we interact on a casual basis can provide great insight if we take the trouble to find out why we react to them in the manner we do. It is our own reaction that provides the clues. When we react angrily to people who are thoughtless or inconsiderate, it is highly likely that we are not being thoughtful or considerate to some aspect of our own needs. Perhaps we are not giving ourselves time to enjoy what life has to offer. Perhaps we are not paying sufficient attention to our need to have a supportive environment.

Our response to what is going on around us provides the key we need to discover what we need to investigate within ourselves. When we clear our own issues, we discover that the people around us that gave us so much trouble have also changed, or rather, our perception of them has changed so we respond to them differently.

2. Events and circumstances of life.

The most significant circumstances of our lives are those relating to our immediate family because it is within the family that we are provided with the best clues as to what we need to learn to fulfil our life's purpose. Perhaps the family is wealthy and money is spent in order to impress friends and neighbours. In such a situation our job might be to understand that money does not buy happiness. Perhaps the money is used to control others by 'purchasing' their respect or their loyalty and our learning might be that loyalty and respect that is paid for, has little value.

Perhaps we are born into a family that has been abandoned by the mother or the father. The lessons within this family might be to identify some aspect of ourselves that we have 'abandoned'.

If we are born into a family where one parent is harshly controlling and the other is weak, we might need to learn that neither harshness or weakness are the best kind of life strategies, although harshness and weakness might be appropriate in certain circumstances.

In addition to family members, the people with whom we associate provide insight into issues that need to be investigated. Similarly, the events in our lives and the environment in which we live and work provide information about some aspect of ourselves.

If we choose to live in a dark house, it reflects the idea that we are allowing little light or happiness into our lives. Living in a dirty, untidy, uncared for house might reflect how we feel about ourselves; worthless, valueless and ugly. By investigating the circumstances of our lives, we learn much about ourselves.

In my work with clients, identifying issues was frequently the most difficult part of a session, requiring many questions and much probing.

'You tell me you're stressed Kevin, and when you get this way you feel as if your head is going to explode. Can you tell me what sort of situations cause you to feel like this?'

'Standing in queues or having someone stuff around when I'm in a hurry. That makes me really angry. I have to leave.'

'How fast do you drive?'

'Well I used to drive very fast, but I'm learning to go slower. I can't afford the speeding fines.'

'What happens when there's a traffic jam or some driver in front of you is going really slow?' Kevin laughed. I'd touched a nerve. 'What is it about your son that makes you upset?'

'Well, I'm really angry with him because he doesn't listen to me. I tell him that if he's going to move up in life he's got to study. He's got to be more ambitious and he's wasting his time.'

'Is wasting time a problem for you?'

'Yes. I get annoyed when things don't get done on time. I work to very strict deadlines. Things have to be done on time. I'm getting older too. I'm running out of time to get everything completed. I'm developing all this new technology and people are waiting on it.'

'Give me some examples of what happens when things don't get finished on time.'

'Well, there was one occasion when we had this work to complete. It was nearly done, and I had to go overseas so I left it for my partner to complete it and deliver the job. When I got back, five weeks later, it was still sitting there. He'd just wasted the time. That broke up our partnership. I couldn't rely to him to do things on time. My partner wasn't in control of the situation.'

'Do you have a problem with control?' I asked this question because Kevin had told me how annoyed he got with his two young daughters when they got out of control around the house.

'Well, in my work I have to have control. When something goes wrong, I work furiously to get it fixed, no matter how long it takes. I just keep working. I am totally focused on solving the problem. When that happens, I have to be in control. Everyone knows to stand back and not interfere when there's a problem.'

I summed up the conversation with the following observation. 'It seems to me that you have a major conflict. You're in a hurry because you're running out of time, you don't have control over the speed of your life, and you have all these people around you who are slowing you down. How do you feel about that?'

'It sort of sums up my life.'

Having reached this understanding, it became possible to find out why being short of time was such an issue in Kevin's life.

3. Repeating patterns of events and behaviours

Patterns in our lives repeat in various ways. Many people equate who they are and how they behave as the same thing. They do not realise that their behaviours are something they have chosen to do or be, and the events in their lives are the consequence of how they think about themselves. To understand the truth of this, all that is needed to identify the cause of a problem is to listen to people's explanations as to why things happen as they do. 'I'm always late' is their *reason* for being late. 'I'm a spendthrift' is their *explanation* for being regularly overdrawn at the bank.

With Stress Defusion sessions, one never really knows where the session will go. Sue wanted to investigate the idea that she wasn't seeing clearly. She felt that her eyesight was not as clear as it had been a few months earlier and this was of concern. Sue is an artist. As soon as the session to investigate *I can't see clearly* started she started talking about the long-term relationships that she had been in over many years and this investigation allowed her to understand something she hadn't been able to see. Several weeks later, Sue recognised that she could see things much more clearly because she understood the reason for the pattern that was common to all of her relationships.

Throughout her life, Sue's partners were men much older than herself. They were ambitious and high flyers in their various careers. Sue became involved with them because they represented success and security. Although she appeared successful in everything she did, Sue did not feel that way about herself. For her, achievement represented a struggle against her own feelings of insecurity and inadequacy, which is why she worked as hard as she did.

By her late 20s, Sue already had a history of success as a chef. She was married to Richard, whose job involved helping successful people in business become even more successful. Richard was a great deal older than Sue, who he considered had enormous potential if only she could overcome her insecurities. He wanted to help her become successful. The problem was that Sue didn't want to run a successful restaurant. She wanted to be an artist.

Richard and Sue divorced and a few years later she met Luke. Like Richard, Luke was a corporate consultant and he helped companies become more profitable. Wanting to be financially independent, Sue gave up her dream of being an artist and started work in a low-level position with a large, international finance corporation. She thought of this as a short-term solution to her financial situation. She chose not to divulge the extent of her background because she just wanted a mundane job so that she could spend all her spare time developing her artistic skills.

This was not how things worked out. With absolutely no intention of climbing the corporate ladder, Sue soon found herself promoted, several times. Within a few years she was travelling the world as the company's representative and being groomed to become a senior executive. She earned a large salary.

Disappointed by his own career, Luke decided to change course. He still wanted to help people so he chose to study Naturopathy. Sue supported him and helped him achieve his goals but in order to do so, she had to postpone her own desire to work as an artist once again. She continued to work in her corporate job. Shortly after he qualified as a Naturopath, she and Luke separated. She had met Malcolm, an artist. Malcolm was the partner of her dreams. He lived a very simple life in the Barossa Valley in South Australia, worked as an artist and was happy to help Sue develop her talents.

The problem with this plan was that Malcolm earned very little as an artist, his full-time occupation, so Sue had to work to support both of them. She found a job as a lowly paid dishwasher in a local cafe. Little did the cafe owners know that Sue had been a chef in large hotels and high-end restaurants. Explaining her motivation for doing this, Sue said, 'I wanted to think of myself as an artist who supported herself by washing dishes, rather than a chef who dabbled with art on the side.' She bought a run-down country cottage with her savings. Working hard, alongside Malcolm, they turned it into a beautiful home which included a studio designed specially to her needs. Unfortunately, Sue still did not have the time to devote to her art. She was too busy supporting Malcolm.

Angry at the situation she found herself in, she asked Malcolm to leave. She reimbursed him for the time he had spent helping her renovate her cottage and he left, but not until after he had destroyed the studio that he had built for her.

Now on her own, and with a small income from the flat that had been built as part of the renovation, Sue was free at last to develop her artistic career. It took years, but gradually she won recognition for her work and was earning a small income from it.

Thinking that everything was finally heading in the direction she wanted, she built a satisfying life for herself. Then Luke re-appeared. He came for a week and stayed for several with the idea of making the arrangement permanent. Now sick and unable to work, he again wanted Sue to support him. Like Malcolm, he was very angry when she refused to fit in with his plans but this time, she was determined to put herself first and not sacrifice her own goals because of the needs of her ex-partner. It was this decision that helped turn everything around. Almost immediately people wanted to have her do their portraits and gave her commissions for work.

Sue needed to investigate the relationships in her life in order to see that she had chosen men much older than herself with the intention of being emotionally and financially supported by them. She was attracted to them because they were successful and provided her with a sense of security that she lacked as a child. What she didn't see initially, was that their successes were built on shaky foundations and they needed her to validate them as successful people rather than have them validate and support her as she had wanted them to do.

Another thing that she didn't realise was that the emotional security she craved was not something that could be given to her by others. She needed to build that for herself. By working to support her partners in their quest for recognition, she gained resilience, persistence, and belief in herself. It took years, but Sue finally understood why she had chosen her partners. They were the means by which she could grow into the person she needed to be to become a really great artist. That is what she has achieved. Alone for several years now, Sue knows that any future relationship will be between two spiritually evolved people who won't look to another to make up for their deficiencies.

4. Compulsive behaviours

Compulsive behaviours are transparent to us because they are so much a part of us that we never question them. However, they provide the key to unlocking deep core issues which we need to clear in order to know ourselves. Compulsive or obsessive behaviours appear, often without conscious recognition, in many aspects of our lives. They could involve, for example, high levels of competitiveness, or obsessive attention to appearance.

Negative compulsive behaviours are easy to identify. Lying, cheating, gambling, always being late for appointments, drug addiction, smoking and alcoholism are some of the negative compulsive behaviours that people adopt. Some try to overcome these behaviours and are successful in doing so. Many try but cannot. The explanation for their behaviour lies in deeply hidden decisions, long since forgotten. Sophie's compulsive behaviour was that she lied. She didn't like the fact that she was a liar, but she continued to lie. When she discovered why she lied, she was able to change her behaviour.

Sophie received a pink ruffled dress from her Nanna on her fifth birthday.

'Thank Nanna for the lovely dress,' prompted her mother.

'I hate it. I'll never wear it,' responded Sophie, as she burst into tears.

'What a horrible, ungrateful girl you are.' Gasping in shame, guilt and anger, Sophie's mother slapped her hard and in doing so pushed her against the living room wall, causing her to hit her shoulder on the bookcase.

Sophie's decision at the emotionally charged moment was: 'I'll never tell the truth again.' This decision governed Sophie's life from that point on. Every time Sophie lied, she wondered why her shoulder ached badly. Expecting to be found out, she felt shame, guilt and anger and this caused her to lie over and over again.

As an adult she did not want to lie. She made many resolutions to be totally and scrupulously honest. No matter how much she wanted to be truthful at all times, she wasn't, and she never understood why.

Even apparently desirable behaviours, which are beneficial and supportive of the individual can indicate compulsive behaviour that has its origin in some past event. Beneath the obsession may lurk a decision linked to some traumatic event in the past. For example, the need for control can stem from an event where someone experiences disastrous consequences from being out of control. Undue attention to being competent may reflect a time when incompetence caused problems.

The universe works in strange ways and we discover that when obsessive behaviours exist, it is likely that a different aspect of the obsession will be obvious in the family environment or in a long-term relationship. Obsessively tidy people often marry untidy people. Fanatically competent people raise incompetent children. Time conscious people are driven to distraction by colleagues who have little sense of time.

When they are attached to any obsession, people uncover deeply felt emotions that are triggered every time they are frustrated in their obsession. For some people, the sight of a speck of dust can spark a frenzy of housework. Failure to engage in the behaviour associated with obsessions creates tension and/or emotional outburst.

Compulsive behaviours that are seen as worthwhile attributes in society can be just as addictive and destructive as negative ones. The problem with positive addictions is that they are generally rewarded by society and may be difficult to identify. A lifetime characterised by an immense need to be successful may, for example, mask a strongly held belief relating to unworthiness or not being good enough. The reason that a desirable behaviour can be compulsive is that it is frequently used as an attempt to mask or override deeply held negative feelings. Those who are excessive in their need to be successful, caring and loving, security conscious, wealthy, respectful, responsible, busy and knowledgeable may well be exhibiting compulsive behaviours. Massive willpower directed to achieve success may well have its origin in the need to prove that someone is *good enough*, because deep down they know that it is not true. Visible proof is never good enough, no matter how it appears externally.

5. Physical deformities, disabilities or chronic illnesses

Whilst it seems almost impossible to believe, many clients have traced their deformities, disabilities and chronic illnesses back to decisions made in this lifetime or in past lives. The story of Adam, which I told in chapter 2, who was partially paralysed at birth, is one such example. There are many others including Katy who was sceptical about the idea of past lives. She didn't believe that there was such a thing. The fact that she expressed this attitude before starting her session alerted me to the possibility the she might access past life memories during the session.

For Katy, her past life memories were particularly nasty. She recalled an event during an incarnation as an American Indian. She was the spiritual leader of the tribe. The women of the tribe all looked to her for guidance. At a time when all the men were away, the village was attacked. Her children were taken from her and killed as she watched. She was tied up and forced to watch the horrendous slaughter of the other villagers. The decision made as a consequence of these events was: I'll never have children again because it is too heart wrenching to see them killed.

At the time Katy was experiencing these visual memories, she refused to see what was going on, and this decision resulted in immediate blindness in her right eye which stayed closed and unseeing during the time she was accessing these past life memories. She regained her ability to see when she identified the decision that she had made in her past life, and the memories faded.

Katy's feelings of guilt and responsibility for what had happened was awful to watch as she recalled the scenes which came to her as vivid pictures. Her body also remembered. Because she had refused to look at what was happening at the time, her eye was put out and this appeared, in this lifetime, as a distortion of her whole face. In her past life, her throat was eventually cut and Katy now felt this as physical pain.

Her reaction to accessing these memories was one of confusion and disbelief. It had seemed so real. But how could this happen? Discussing the memories, Katy realised the connection between the events she had recalled and her current life decisions: not to have children and not to have a permanent relationship.

The most dramatic outcome from the session was the change in Katy's physical appearance. Her right eye, which at the start of the session had been different from the left one, balanced itself and the dropped lid lifted. As the right side of her face lifted, it caused her to look very different from how she looked when she arrived.

6. Family and childhood situations

Cultures from all over the world suggest that we choose the family and circumstances into which we are born.[33] This idea seems ridiculous to someone born into a dysfunctional family until we realise that the purpose of families is to reveal the pain that the family carries, within ourselves.

The pain might be the pain of separation, in which case the possibility exists that we might lose a dearly loved parent or sibling when we are very young. It could be the pain of physical or sexual abuse, in which case we could be abused as children. Perhaps our purpose in this lifetime is to let go of the judgement of poverty, in which case this issue is likely to feature as part of our family environment as we grow.

John was an asthmatic. He suffered numerous severe asthma attacks and it was normal for him to experience shortness

---

33 cosmiccradle.com/research/birthagreements.

of breath when winter temperatures fell. John's most severe asthma attack occurred when he was travelling through Byron Bay. Fortunately, he was able to get to the hospital where he was told that, if his asthma had not been stabilised quickly, he would have died.

John's asthma originated in his childhood. He and his brother were frequently abandoned by their mother, who thoughtlessly left two tiny children on their own with no food and no heating for days on end whilst she went out partying. The terror of being abandoned and alone was triggered by being alone in Byron Bay, in circumstances where he felt he was abandoning his own children following his marriage breakdown. This event allowed him to make the connection between his childhood experiences and his bouts of asthma. Letting go of the fear of abandonment was necessary before John could let go of this debilitating condition, and also let go of the need to allow for possible negative consequences that he felt might be the consequence of any action he took. Because of this fear, he was always waiting for bad things to happen, which was a really difficult life strategy.

§

Life experiences are designed so that we can resolve issues that we have been investigating over many lifetimes. Resolution comes when we let go of judgement around the issue. We are presented with the issue that we have chosen to investigate in this lifetime, in its various guises, when we are children. The purpose of the behaviours of others and the circumstances of our childhood is to activate the past life programs that we carry, to facilitate resolution which comes, in many cases, as a result of understanding that different attributes and behaviours have both negative and positive aspects to them.

In order to understand this idea, let us look at the issue of sacrifice, which is central to several of the sessions described in this chapter and is a major issue in the world today, as it has been for many lifetimes. It was a key component in Anna's session. Anna had no expectation of delving into past lives when she came to see me. She was hopeful that I might be able to help her with memory problems. The links between traumatic events of Anna's past lives and the circumstances of her current life were dramatic.

Anna, a well-known Australian actress, had been diagnosed with leukaemia two years prior to coming to see me. As a consequence of her disease and the treatment she had received she had the problem that she could not remember the lines she had learned for the television dramas that she was starring in. She had also started to forget things in her everyday life. She knew that this was a consequence of extensive radiation therapy. When she came to see me, she was in remission.

During the first two sessions Anna re-experienced the worst moments of her disease and treatment, in particular the radiation therapy on her brain. It was this that frightened her the most. She feared permanent brain damage. During the third session, Anna's eye glazed over.

'Where are you?' I asked.

'In a camp.'

'Who else is in the camp with you?'

'Just dead bodies.'

'Who are you?'

'I'm a boy. I tell the guards on the other prisoners. That's how I stay alive.'

'How is this memory related to your leukaemia?'

'I have the leukaemia to punish me for what I did in the camp. I caused hundreds of people to die. I sacrificed them in order to stay alive.' After saying this, she opened her eyes and started talking about what she had experienced and the things about the camp that she remembered. It was a vivid recollection.

Intrigued by what had happened, she wanted to continue with the session. Almost immediately Anna slipped into another past life memory. This time, as I walked Anna through what she was experiencing, she described a Roman stadium. She was re-living some event. She talked about what she could see and hear. The crowds in the stands were jeering and booing. When I asked where she was, she said, 'I'm buried up to my neck. My head is above the ground. I'm not the only one. There are chariots. They're being driven wildly around the stadium. I'm feeling absolutely terrified.' *Then she stopped talking, opened her eyes and said, in a normal and matter-of-fact voice,* 'I didn't know they did that sort of thing in Roman times.'

Whatever the significance of these memories, the energy that was released as a result of Anna revisiting these events was very strong. Anna seemed to think that it was this that had caused her leukaemia. Six months later she returned to work. She told me how happy she was being back in front of the cameras and confirmed that she had no problems at all with learning and remembering the scripts.

The key learning from this session was not punishment of those who were responsible. The message of those two lifetimes was that it is not a good idea to sacrifice others for one's own benefit because both the perpetrator and the victim suffer. In not understanding this, as human beings we have glorified sacrifice and accepted it as being a necessary evil or a noble virtue.

Within families, many children are sacrificed. Some are aborted before birth. Some are abused or neglected to such an extent that they are forcibly removed from the family. Some children grow up within a family where neglect, abuse and/or brutality are experienced on a daily basis. This is what happened to John. John understood the long-term effects of neglect.

Within the animal world, the old, young and infirm are preyed upon by predators and in effect are sacrificed for the benefit of the predators. In the same way, human sacrifice has been a feature of many cultures over a long period of time. Young people have been sacrificed for the benefit of rulers for the good of the community, to bring rain, or to appease the gods.[34] The Incas performed child sacrifices during or after important events, such as the death of the leader or during a

---

34 Live science.com/59514-cultures-that-practiced-human-sacrifice.html

famine. Children were selected as sacrificial victims as they were considered to be the purest of beings. Archaeological records also indicate that human sacrifice occurred regularly within the Aztec culture. Remains of skull racks have been found at a temple at Tenochtitlan. Textual references and archaeological remains indicate that the ancient Greeks practised human sacrifice. In 2016, a 3,000-year-old skeleton of a male teenager was found at an altar dedicated to Zeus at Mount Lykaion in Greece. Archaeologists believe that the teen may have been sacrificed to Zeus, an idea supported by ancient texts that tell of child sacrifices that were made on the mountain. Evidence has been found of sacrifice during the Sheng dynasty in China from 1600 — 1040 B.C.E and in Korea, at Mohenjo Daro in the Indus Valley and in Peru.

I have introduced the issue of sacrifice as an example of something that needs to be investigated to determine whether it is ever appropriate. In the past, it was considered an honour to be sacrificed to the gods to ensure they looked on the people of Earth with favour. I have past life memories of what it was like to be thrown into a volcano to appease the gods who, in the opinion of the people and their rulers, were angry and were causing the volcano to erupt. I have had my heart cut out in a Mayan or Inca ceremony. My daughter tells me that in one lifetime I offered her to the temple for the purpose of sacrifice and that I considered it a great honour to do this. I cannot reconnect with this memory.

The idea of sacrifice suggests that some people are expendable if it is for the benefit of others, which in turn suggests that some people are more important than others. This is an idea that the *Elohim* argues against strongly. The message from the Elohim has always been that everyone and everything is of equal value.

So, what is it we need to understand about sacrifice? Is it ever appropriate? Under what circumstances might it be appropriate? Perhaps with regard to an issue such as sacrifice of others, we need to look at the Spiritual Laws of Universe and apply the Law of Obedience,[35] which teaches that if something is wrong in one situation then we must apply the 100% rule and know that it is wrong for every situation. It means understanding the lesson that Sue needed to learn. Whilst she remained angry that she had sacrificed her goals in favour of the goals of her partners, she ignored the fact that in sacrificing herself for others, she actually gained personal strengths that would, at a time in the future, allow her to become a great artist. Perhaps Sue's story suggests that when we choose to make a sacrifice for the benefit of another, the greatest benefactor will be ourselves and not those who appear to be the beneficiaries of our sacrifice. That no one should be sacrificed as entertainment for others and no one should sacrifice others for their own safety or benefit was what Anna learned when she investigated sacrifice in her past lives.

I have discussed the theme of sacrifice because it was central to several of the sessions that I have referred to in this chapter.

---

35 Beverley Buckley, *Final Days of Judgement*, published by Xlibris 2015

Chapter 14 Identifying Issues

§

By looking at the roles played by our parents and siblings in relation to the issues that are uppermost in our lives, we discover that their actions and beliefs represent different aspects of whatever it is we have chosen to investigate. Our job is to understand the consequences of behaving in a particular way and first we need to experience both sides or different aspects of one side. This is what we are given by our parents: the opportunity to establish a base point from which we can start investigating.

The *Elohim* provided insight into the idea that in each lifetime we investigate different issues. They explained it in the following way:

Lives illustrate themes and the choice one makes of one's family provides the data needed for investigation.

Each act in our play investigates a theme. If greed is the aspect of our investigation, we ultimately learn that we have no need for greed which brings with it the need for accumulation of possessions. Possessions become our measurement of success, our safety net against want. Possession accumulation provides the meaning for our lives. Ultimately, we understand that possessions do not make us happy. They are not the answer. The purpose of life is not to accumulate goods or people.

The term possession can be applied to people, goods or ideas. We possess people when we control their lives and benefit materially from their services. Acquisition of possessions arises because we lack appreciation of abundance. We can have anything we desire once we let go the fear of scarcity. Possessions are the way we hide from the real world. They form a barrier between us and others. People who have many possessions spend all their energies protecting and conserving what they have accumulated throughout their lives. They judge themselves to be of value depending on the value of their possessions: the size of their house, the make and model of their car, the brand of their washing machine.

People who have few possessions judge themselves as unworthy, yet possessions are not a true judge of worth. In fact, they are a hindrance, taking as they do, people's attention from what is of real value.

Some lifetimes we investigate greed from the perspective of the victim. Victims see the greed of others and the chaos that comes from accumulation of land or resources into the hands of one individual whose need is rapacious. Caring not for the consequences of their greed, they go to extreme lengths to acquire: theft, misappropriation, force, cheating are some of the means by which possessions are acquired. Look around you and you will identify many individuals who are playing out this scenario. Like any of the world issues, greed does not lead to happiness.

It is OK to play the game of greed. Investigate it fully if you wish. But investigate it with the knowing that you are playing a role and you are not the role. Once the lessons are learned you can move to another role.

Domination is played out in various guises. Within a

family it can be identified in the heavy-handed father, submissive mother and children. At the political level we see domination in the form of dictatorships, military control, legal and economic control.

As we move on from the 90s, mayhem is increasingly being investigated. For no apparent reasons whole communities are involved in mayhem caused by war, or even physical events over which no one has any control.

In the world today, nations are rallying to support those groups of people who are investigating mayhem as an issue, and more and more frequently we find that there is very little that can be done except to stand and watch aghast as groups of mankind self-destruct in the most horrifying of circumstances. There appears to be no logical explanation. In a situation of mayhem there is no rational explanation. Mayhem is frightening enough in the lives of individuals. On a group scale the fear it generates is massive.

All this is a sign of imbalance. The people experiencing mayhem are out of balance. So too, the earth and the people who live on it are out of balance. The earth reflects this imbalance and as it moves further and further into the unbalanced position, it too will struggle to realign. In realigning, there will be physical chaos such as Earth is experiencing: droughts, earthquakes, tidal waves, hurricanes and floods.

Over many lifetimes we have experienced all aspects of the issues that we are investigating in order to understand what the consequences are for the one who indulges in a particular behaviour, or from the perspective of being the victim. Taking, as an example, the issue of adequacy we eventually get to the situation where we realise that no one type of behaviour is acceptable and the other unacceptable. Both are acceptable depending on the circumstances. Sometimes it is appropriate to feel that we are adequately equipped to cope with a situation and can step forward and do what is required, confident that what we do, will be acceptable. In the same circumstance, but with a different type of experience or training, we might feel totally inadequate because we actually do not have what is required by that situation. In this case it is totally appropriate to feel and be inadequate. In this situation we need help. Feeling and being adequate or feeling and being inadequate are both OK but judging another for being inadequate is not an appropriate response. Unfortunately, we tend to judge others far too often.

Because one of the laws of the Universe is balance, families will always be in balance in relation to a specific issue, but individual members of the family are likely to be extremely out of balance. If, for example, we are investigating the issue of inadequacy in taking care of daily chores, we will find one member of the family who is capable, confident, knowledgeable and skilled within the family environment in order to compensate for all the other members of the family who lack these attributes. This is the person who attends to all the chores, maintains the house, cleans, washes, cooks and looks after the finances. They may not be happy within this role, but they fulfil it because there seems no other solution. If that person were to leave because they finally realise that they are not prepared to carry the load for everyone else, the whole situation changes. People take the line of least resistance and will allow others to do what they are not prepared to do, if that is the easy option. Take away the option and they are forced to do things differently.

§

Identifying the issues that need to be cleared isn't always easy. What is significant is that once the process starts, people realise that whatever is happening in their lives isn't a consequence of who they are, rather it is a consequence of what they have chosen to experience. When this is understood, the fact that people are not their labels becomes clear. People give themselves labels then act as if those labels are real. Once they understand that acting the role that the label suggests doesn't give them what they seek, they have the choice of dispensing with it, adopting a different one, or just be. They can go from 'I'm John, the black sheep of the family' to 'I'm John.'

Chapter 15
Mind/Body Connection

Most practitioners of alternative therapies believe that the mind and body are not separate and independent but are intricately connected. Bodywork practitioners accept that emotions are stored in the body and physical and emotional trauma cause blockages in the body, which are also present in the mind. They are familiar with the concept that blocked memories and emotions are the cause of physical tension which leads, over time, to pain.

Blocks that we create by our thoughts, manifest in our body either as disease, pain or some form of physical disability, persistent patterns of walking, standing, slouching and/or stiffness. Work on the mind frees up the energy flow around the body and assists the body to make its own repairs. Bodywork assists in emotional and physical release.

My introduction to the world of personal and spiritual development was through bodywork. In the hope that I would find a magic cure for a variety of physical problems, I investigated many different techniques: rolfing, hellerwork, feldenkrais, rebirthing, kinesiology, shiatsu, acupuncture, sacro-cranial massage, acupressure, float tanks, massage and yoga. Some, like rolfing and hellerwork, involved deep massage to free the fascia, which surrounds the muscles, allowing the body to re-align. These modalities can be painful but are effective. Feldenkrais works by subtle body movements, again to release blocks.

Rebirthing, another popular alternate therapy, uses deep breathing to re-oxygenate the body and assist the clearing process. As a result of oxygenation, parts of the body that have been shut down through oxygen deprivation, re-activate and bring to the surface memories that have been buried.

Shiatsu, acupuncture and acupressure work by assisting energy flow through the body, working through the energy meridian system of the body.

All bodywork makes a difference, but my experience is that improvement is maintained for only a short period of time unless the cause of the problem is found.

Detoxification with fasting, juice diets and elimination of substances such as sugar and caffeine, cause the body to release toxins, allowing it to heal itself.

There are lots of techniques and practices that help us regain health and vitality and they have many things in common — cleaning the body, revitalising the body and facilitating the movement of energy through the body. Stress Defusion works most effectively with people who have done lots of work to build health and increase energy flows through the body because Stress Defusion requires energy to clear the blocks and eliminate toxins held in the body.

The reason bodywork techniques help is because our bodies and minds work as a hologram such that the effects of blocked emotions, and the programs that we have written for ourselves, show up in every aspect of our physiology. It is possible to identify problems by studying eyes. This practice is called iridology. Painful areas in the feet correspond to organs in the body that are not working effectively. Sacro-cranial massage uses gentle pressure on the head, neck, and back to relieve the stress and pain caused by compression. Muscles reflect tension which can be relieved by massage, rolfing and shiatsu. Heal one part by releasing blocked energy, and the whole body and mind will heal. Change one cell, and all the cells of the body change because every cell is a hologram of the whole mind/body system. It is not possible to change one area without changing the whole.

§

Stress Defusion, as a healing modality, aims to rectify split brain function, which is a by-product of stress. Having left and right sides of the brain operate separately or having one side of the brain excessively dominant, shows up in facial structure and body development. You can see your own degree of split-brain operation by taking a photograph and drawing a line down the centre of your face then placing the two right sides together and the two left sides together. One of the photos must be mirror reversed of course. It is likely that the face, comprising just the right-side photos, will be very different from the photo of two left sides. The degree of difference indicates the extent of one-sided brain domination. Perhaps one side of the face is fuller than the other. Maybe one eye will be more open, or one will be slightly dropped compared with the other. If the face is centred and balanced, and both sides are the same, then your brain is also working as a whole, rather than functioning as two separate entities. Stress Defusion allows for reinstatement of whole brain operation and when this happens, facial imbalance corrects itself.

Split brain function isn't an all or nothing concept. We switch off the connection between left and right brain depending on our thought patterns. Under stress we tend towards ipsilateral brain function.

Perhaps even more unexpected than facial and physical changes, many people experience changes in food preferences when brain reconnection occurs. Since food is often used as a form of solace in painful situations, people seek consolation in certain foods. Too often these are the foods that taste great but aren't good for us. Once the stressor situation is released, an integration period occurs during which time food cravings are activated. This shows that the body is remembering what it used to crave as a form of comfort. Often the foods we crave are the foods to which we are allergic. A side effect of the Stress Defusion process is that toxins are released, after which allergic reactions to certain foods diminish as does our craving for the comfort foods that keep us overweight.

The Stress Defusion process has always fascinated me because it facilitates bringing forgotten memories to conscious awareness. It provides a way to investigate the contents of the subconscious minds of people, allowing me to identify patterns of behaviour that are common to different problems.

Chapter 15   Mind/Body Connection

Few have had as much public acceptance as Deepak Chopra for his work on the mind/body connection. Being a medical doctor, Chopra's interest has been in the mind/body connection as it relates to health. To quote Chopra, 'To think is to practise brain chemistry, promoting a cascade of responses throughout the body.'[36]

If, as Chopra claims, thought can create a flow of chemicals through every part of the body, it is logical that negative thoughts arising from decisions made in times of trauma will create a flow of chemicals that affect the body negatively. The long-term effect of this will be disease.

Betty had skin cancers on the backs of her hands, which were disfigured with scaly patches and discolouration. After a particularly traumatic Stress Defusion session, Betty cried for several hours. Almost immediately, several physical changes manifested. First the lesions on the backs of her hand became red and inflamed and the indentations became puffy and sore. Two weeks later, the cancerous indentations had filled in and disappeared. All but two of the scaly patches disappeared.

The day following her session, Betty's legs were swollen, bruised in patches to the knee and the skin was covered in bright red areas of discolouration, some as large as half a centimetre in diameter. Her skin was sore to touch, and the soreness extended deep into the muscles of her legs. Betty's varicose veins were swollen and inflamed. After two or three weeks, the varicose veins became less visible than they had

---

36   Chopra, Deepak *Quantum Healing*, Bantam Books, 1988, p.58

been in years. The red discolouration faded and the swelling subsided. Soreness in Betty's legs lasted a couple of days.

Although there appeared to be no direct relationship between the issue that had been investigated during her Stress Defusion session and the healing that subsequently occurred, her body had created physical problems that were clearly connected to decisions she had made years earlier.

When the situation causing stress is removed, the body can heal itself, but the speed and extent of the healing depends to a large extent on the energy available. If the body is weakened by disease, poor diet, inactivity and toxic overload, there is little energy available to do the work required to restore health. Sometimes the effects are quite dramatic and uncomfortable when the body starts to heal.

A particularly traumatic session for Lynnette resulted in her leg being bruised from knee to ankle the following day. She had done nothing that could explain this. She could not remember anything in the past that could have led to this response. Fortunately, the bruising was not painful and cleared within a couple of weeks.

§

Fred's anger was so intense that his leg became extremely hot as I worked to release the tension. The following day a deep ulcer the size of a 20-cent coin appeared. It healed quickly and painlessly.

§

Robyn's eyes wept pus following her session.

§

I was fortunate to have a client who was able to describe for me what happened to the blood when the body processed and released negative thought patterns.

Lyn was a naturopath and had access to a blood testing laboratory at the time of her first Stress Defusion session. Unbeknownst to me, she decided to give herself a live blood analysis test before coming for her first session. Her blood was fine. She was a very healthy 30-year-old woman.

Having been warned that some kind of physical or emotional reaction was possible following a Stress Defusion session, Lyn wasn't surprised that she needed to spend three days in bed to recover. On her return to work, she tested her blood and expected to see positive results. She was shocked by what she saw: blood typical of someone with chronic, degenerative disease. Two weeks later, she tested it again. This time, her blood was better than it had ever been before.

Lyn felt that what had happened with her tests provided confirmation that a direct link existed between mind and body and that the Stress Defusion process caused the release of toxins and/or the restoration of chemical balance within the cells.

For me, her experiment provided wonderful confirmation

that the changes I saw happening could be confirmed scientifically.

Laurie was a student of natural therapies, who was very aware of the likelihood of detoxification symptoms following her session. What she was not prepared for was the speed and intensity of their onset. Within half an hour of the session's completion, Laurie had severe diarrhoea. Less than an hour later she found herself sobbing intensely without any understanding of the reason for her anguish. This lasted for several hours. When she recovered her composure, she started looking through some of her childhood photographs and painful memories came flooding back.

Whilst the period of integration was not pleasant, the benefit for Laurie was that her marks at college immediately started to improve and her fear of exams decreased. Overall, she was much less fearful than she had been.

§

In the Stress Defusion model, chronic pain has its origins in specific life events. When we repress the emotion but do not eliminate it, because we are unable to cope with the emotional pain relating to what is going on, the repressed emotion ends up creating a corresponding physical symptom. Thus, living life from the attitude that *everything is a pain in the gut*, we create pain perhaps in the form of colon cancer. When *we can't stomach things*, we might develop stomach ulcers. If things *piss us off*, then we can expect kidney stones or some sort of kidney infection. This seems farfetched, but our thoughts literally create our physical problems and our bodies are a very vivid demonstration of the contents of our subconscious mind.

Julie worked with Stress Defusion over the course of a year, with the intention of gaining help to remember scientific information that her homeopathy studies demanded. She had been motivated to study homeopathy to help find solutions to intense and chronic pain that she had suffered for over 20 years.

Her body pain was the result of a series of accidents. She injured her coccyx as a child at boarding school. Many years later she crushed her thorax and broke a bone in her spine in a car crash. Shoulder pain and twisted arthritic finger joints combined to create a life of pain and misery.

Over a 12-month period, specific sites of pain were addressed and the pain disappeared immediately. With the relief from pain came the realisation that each painful area was linked to a specific emotional trauma. Damage to her coccyx was connected to her separation from her family. At the time of the car accident, Julie was experiencing infidelity in her marriage. When she accepted the pain, and understood its connection to the events in her life at those times, both the physical pain and the emotional pain were felt and released to be replaced by vitality and freedom of expression.

You wouldn't try to fix a ruptured tendon with Stress Defusion, but you might find it useful to try and find out why the tendon was susceptible to rupture after having standard medical treatment to fix it. Blaming external events as the explanation for physical pain, probably means we are looking in the wrong direction. The exceptions are, of course, pain that is caused by accidental damage or as a consequence of trauma. Even so, sometimes the trauma is something that needs to be experienced because trauma inflicted pain provides the motivation for investigation of the underlying cause.

Born a 500-gram premature baby, Madeleine was not expected to survive. In the unlikely event that she was to live, doctors predicted that she would be a vegetable. Surprisingly, Madeleine survived and thrived.

Now in her late 20s, Madeleine's passion is building with hemp. When I met her, she had just completed building the walls of a hemp house, working with the assistance of the 60-year-old, untrained, home owner. The work was completed in less than two weeks during which time the two of them had mixed a slurry of hemp and lime, bucketed it up to the house, climbed up ladders with the 30kg buckets of slurry and formed the walls within the framework erected. It was hard work. Not surprisingly Madeleine was exhausted when she came for her session.

When I asked her what she wanted to work with, she surprised me by telling me that she was terrified that she was too weak to accomplish the task she has set for herself: establishing a viable hemp house business. Questioned further, I discovered that Madeleine had a leg that was weak and inflexible, a weak right arm and eye. This was ongoing weakness that stemmed from her premature birth. She decided that she wanted to investigate the idea that she was too weak to be successful.

Most people respond to Stress Defusion sessions by recalling past events in their lives. Madeleine's response was different. Rather than going into the story of times when she had suffered because of her weakness, she accessed and released huge levels of emotional energy associated with her birth, the problems of her childhood and her struggles to become strong. Whilst she had processed the events intellectually, she had held onto the emotional response to the difficulties she had experienced because of her reluctance to appear weak. What she needed to do was to feel the emotions associated with her difficulties rather than intellectualise her response.

At the completion of the session, Madeleine realised that she had been born weak, but she had worked really hard to become strong and had been successful in doing this. Becoming strong had been an obsession with her but she had never looked at the idea that, as a baby, she had rightly decided that she was weak, and she had held onto judgements relating to weakness. Now she was being asked to look at the idea that her weakness had actually given her the motivation to work hard to become strong. Refusal to acknowledge the emotional impact of this journey, by holding onto the emotional pain rather than allowing herself to feel it, meant that she was unable to let go the decision that she had made about herself, that she was weak. Judging her weakness meant she couldn't let go those aspects of herself that remained weak.

Two weeks after the session, Madeleine phoned me and

was very excited with the news that she had received, in her terms, a 'VIP upgrade'. The intervening weeks had been very difficult. Now that the emotional dam had been breached, Madeleine had allowed herself to feel miserable, which was what she needed to do. She described what happened after that:

'I was lying in bed at midnight, on the cusp of consciousness between awake and asleep. I was born with muscle tension and wastage that has made physical exercise very difficult and painful. I was using the sheets trying to stretch my Achilles tendon when I felt a sharp pain in my thigh and something popped in my foot. I felt a strong electrical current start at the top of my hip and the current was sustained for at least two to three minutes. When it stopped, I had full a range of movement in not just my leg but also my right hand and arm. It was as if someone had switched the circuit back on.

Ever the cynic, I waited for it to revert back to the twisted mess that it was, kept flexing it, amazed that I could feel every nerve pull and stretch like never before. I cried myself to sleep dreaming of all the exercise I could finally participate in without pain.

I'm still in awe at what has happened. I can't say that any particular memory, emotion or sensation occurred but there is definitely a huge sense of relief. Somehow everything is OK now and I know it will just get better. Even as I write this, I can feel my right eye slowly start to become stronger and focus better.

I do not understand how this has happened. Ever the sceptic after our session, I had minimal sense of what was supposed to change. I felt like it was an impossible ask but even with a cynical mind it has happened; and is here to stay.'

Pain, physical inflexibility, weight problems, and/or illness can all be physical manifestations of unresolved issues we hold within our unconscious mind. Unfortunately, the typical response to physical pain is to try to reduce the pain level, and then believe that the problem has gone away. In my opinion, a far better approach would be to investigate the pain's cause by going within. When pain is present, it is easy to find its origin.

Chapter 16
Energy and Health

Healing takes energy, and when the human body is exhausted by disease, artificial light, inadequate exercise, food that lacks nutrients, poisons and polluted air and water, people wonder why they cannot heal. It is only when energy levels are depleted and people become lethargic and sick that they start to ask questions about energy and why they don't have enough.

The truth is that there is ample energy available. It comes from the sun, the earth and from the food grown on the Earth. A more complete explanation is that the energy that comes from the sun, the earth and from food grown on Earth is available to us depending on the effective operation of our physical systems and on the quality of the environment in which we live. Not understanding the fact that energy has to be filtered through physical processes to make it available to us, is where the problem of having insufficient energy arises. Not understanding that abundant energy is available from natural sources, some people take it from others.

I studied energy on a practical level as a mature-age farmer. I didn't plan to be a farmer. I never even wanted to be a farmer but the years that I spent farming, as a full-time occupation, provided many answers about food as a source of energy and about the health benefits that come from living close to nature.

I became a farmer at an age when most people are planning their retirement. I bought a property on Mt Tamborine, which is a plateau behind the Gold Coast in Queensland. The property was called Castelen, which means many castles. As with the decision to go back into the school system, I was given very firm instructions by the *Elohim* that I needed to leave the city and move to a rural area. I was even given instructions as to what I was to look for when choosing the property that I was to move to. The house was to be in the shape of a cross and the property had a connection with castles. I was told I would find hares and pheasants living there and lots of water. I was even given the date of my departure from Sydney.

The house, when I found it, was in the shape of a cross. As I mentioned earlier, the property was called Castelen. Underneath the land were huge natural water reservoirs caused by the geology of the plateau. There were many hares and cougar pheasants, and I left Sydney on the date that I was told.

When people asked me what I did for a living I told them I worked as a farm labourer: pruning, planting, weeding, harvesting, trenching, mowing, mulching and composting. Every day I worked outdoors in the sun and the rain. I grew fruit: avocados, limes, tamarillos and blueberries, and many vegetables: carrots, beetroot, parsnips, broccoli, cauliflowers, kale, silver beet, lettuce, beans, peas and specialty crops such as turmeric, garlic, ginger and rhubarb. I sold my produce to wholesale distributors of organically produced food, and at a weekly market. It was hard, physically demanding work. The hours were long and for the first five years the financial rewards were minimal.

In retrospect this was one of the more beneficial, challenging and intellectually stimulating periods of my life. During the years I worked as a farmer I wondered why I had to spend so much time learning about growing food. It wasn't until I realised that it is not possible to help people who are energy depleted that I understood the need for me to learn about the sources of energy that are available to us.

§

I find that the universe has an interesting way of backing us into corners where only one choice is available to us, forcing us to do something that we would never otherwise dream of doing. We do what we do because it is the only option available. That is what happened for me. I moved to Queensland expecting to establish a healing centre. That didn't happen. At least it didn't happen in the manner I had envisaged. Needing to earn money, I resorted to growing vegetables. Then I planted fruit trees. It was a case of learning by doing, and I acquired the skills and knowledge I needed in order to become successful. Prior to making the decision to do this, I had minimal experience in growing food and only a basic understanding of what would be involved in becoming a successful farmer.

At the beginning of my farm labouring adventure I

wondered why my life had gone in a direction that I had no desire to follow. In response to guidance from the *Elohim*, I had moved to an idyllic rural setting. My intention was to establish a healing centre so that people could spend time getting their lives back on track. Everything conspired against me. Since all the efforts that were directed to establishing a residential healing centre were thwarted by Council regulations and escalating building costs, managing a healing centre was obviously not supposed to be part of my life plan. Without having the goal of building a healing centre to provide the motivation for my rational mind to do what I did, it is unlikely that I would ever have moved from Sydney.

I found myself the owner of a beautiful property with awe inspiring views, lots of water, good soil. It was reasonably close to Brisbane and the Gold Coast so that it was easily accessible. I had a large house, and clients came for help with their physical and emotional problems. Many stayed for months. Several stayed for a year or more. In addition, I hosted over three hundred young people from Europe and Asia who spent time on the farm as part of the Willing Workers on Organic Farms (WWOOF) program. Whilst Castelen was not officially a healing centre, that is, in essence, what it became.

§

What happened was that I spent twenty years investigating the energies that are vital to life and seeing the benefits that living in a pure energy field has on health and wellbeing. What

I discovered by doing that was that physical health is not dependent just on what goes on inside our bodies and minds. It is also dependent on, and interconnected with, other non-physical levels of energy, such as the energy surrounding the body which is known as the biophoton field, and the energy that is available from Earth itself.

Scientists have decided that the biophoton has a profound impact on health and possibly rules life itself as I explained in chapter 12. My findings were of a practical nature as a result of living in a pure energy and sunshine filled environment, in constant contact with the earth and eating nutrient-rich, organically grown food. I needed to have this experience in order to discover that:

1. Earth is a source of energy,
2. Sunshine is a source of energy,
3 Food is a source of energy,
4. Rural environments are generally the least polluted of all the environments on Earth and the healthiest places to live,
5. Exercise and movement are required to gain and maintain fitness and stamina,
6. Energy is naturally available and does not have to be taken from other people.

1. Earth is a source of energy

When I arrived at what became my farm, it was a beautiful but unproductive park on the edge of an escarpment that overlooked Mt Warning, an ancient volcano. I established everything from scratch and having done so, worked in the garden and orchards for many hours every day and for five or six days of each week. Initially, it was exhausting. Having lived a sedentary life in the city, I needed to work hard to regain physical fitness. My first year was spent growing lavender because being immersed for hours every day in the perfume of the lavender was what I needed in order to heal my own body. This was not something that I worked out for myself. I was given very firm instructions by the *Elohim* that this was what I needed to do as a first step.

Around the time I was spending hours each day in the lavender field, I consulted an Indian reader of Akashic records which are believed to be records of all human events, thoughts and emotions, ever to have occurred encoded in a non-physical plane of existence known as the etheric. He told me that I had come to Earth with a 99.5% chance of dying at the age of sixty. This, he told me, was what had happened for lifetime after lifetime. My challenge in this lifetime was to live beyond sixty years because I would not be able to fulfil my higher purpose unless I had a long lifespan. When I visited the Indian psychic, he told me I had done a lot of work, but there was still more to do if I were to live beyond sixty years of age.

Following the consultation with the Indian Akashic records reader I realised that the healing centre that I planned for others was actually for me. It served its purpose as I have lived far beyond my allotted sixty years, although his prediction that I would die at 60 came close when I had a serious accident just after my sixtieth birthday. Physical work in a clean environment, eating a diet of predominantly organically-grown fruit and vegetables, drinking clean, chemical-free water and doing physical work for 8 hours or more every day was what I did to regain fitness and strength. What I discovered was that being in direct contact with the earth was massively beneficial and calming. For much of the time, I worked in bare feet. I spent many hours on my hands and knees weeding. In doing this I was in constant contact with the soil.

Getting fit and healthy wasn't something that happened quickly, but I did gain strength and stamina. The young people who came to work on the farm as Woofers were amazed that I was so much stronger than they expected someone of my age to be: able to pick or dig composting trenches for hours at a time.

I now know that direct contact with the limitless supply of free electrons on Earth's surface creates a stable bio-electrical environment for the normal functioning of all body systems. Direct contact with the earth allows electrons from antioxidant molecules, found on the Earth's surface, to neutralise free radicals and reduce acute and chronic inflammation.[37] To receive these benefits, contact must be by direct contact with skin, or through leather. Plastic shoe soles or artificial foot coverings don't allow the transfer of electrons.

When the body is in direct contact with the earth its electrical potential comes nearer that of Earth's, so that

---

37 WWW.NIM.NIH.GOV/PMCPARTICLES/PM3265072

the body becomes an extension of Earth's electrical system causing a reduction in overall stress levels and tension. As I have already discussed in Chapter eleven, Earth's vibrational frequency is increasing at this time and it is important to synchronise the body's energy levels with that of Earth. Grounding is a good way to do this.

2. Sunshine is a source of energy

Without sunlight, it is virtually impossible for most life forms to exist. My challenge was not in getting enough sun, but in avoiding sunburn. I settled on a work day that started at daybreak and continued until it was too hot to be outside without a hat. Work resumed in the afternoon when the sun's rays were weaker.

By researching the benefits of sunlight for health, I discovered that without appropriate sun exposure, we become deficient in vitamin D which is critical for overall health. UVB rays cause production by the skin of a precursor of vitamin D, which is then activated by the liver and kidneys. Vitamin D allows us to think more clearly. It helps lower inflammation and is beneficial in controlling diabetes. Most people will be surprised to realise that it also protects against cancer, because this is not what we have been led to believe by slip/slop/slap advertisements which give the impression that sunlight is bad for us.

Sunlight is composed of different parts of the light spectrum, each of which offers crucial benefits. The effect of sunlight is more complicated than just the fact that it is good for you. Sunlight induces co-ordinated endocrine adaptation and activates the body clock. Both eyes and skin detect the colours of light in the environment, causing adaptation of the hormonal system to the specific needs dictated by time and place. Serotonin is released in response to sunlight and this helps elevate mood and energy levels. When it is dark, melatonin levels increase, and this makes us all feel tired. Additionally, UVA stimulates blood flow to skin capillaries where they absorb energy and infrared radiation. It also helps to kill infections in the blood while the infrared spectrum of sunlight re-charges cellular batteries. Infrared primes the cells in the retina so that they can repair and regenerate.

3. Food is a source of energy

Nature is really clever. Not only do plants produce seeds and fruit that are beneficial to our health and provide energy, but they also tell us which foods are specifically designed to help different organs stay healthy. Plants and nuts are designed to replicate in appearance the organ of the body that they benefit.

The indentations and swirls of a walnut look exactly like the surface of the brain and what this tells us is that walnuts are brain food. Walnuts help build more than 30 neurotransmitters within the brain as well as extracting and breaking down protein-based plaque that is associated with Alzheimer's disease. Beans are in the shape of kidneys and this is because beans contain minerals that are beneficial in maintaining kidney health. Onions look like human cells and they help to clear waste materials from cells. Sweet potatoes look like the pancreas and help balance the glycaemic index of diabetes.

These aren't the only foods that are beneficial for health. Some of the others are red grapes, olives, and citrus fruits each of which is designed to tell us which part of the body they are good for.

Until I started farming, I quite happily accepted statements like *broccoli is good for you* and *oranges are high in Vitamin C*. That was before I understood about brix levels. Brix measures the level of nutrients present in food. The nutrient level of food is determined by the population of microbes including bacteria and fungi that live in the soil as well as the balance of mineral content of the soil in which the food is grown. Food grown in nutrient-deficient, microbe-deficient, humus-deficient soil will also be nutrient-deficient. This is self-evident if you take time to think about it, but we don't think about it until we see the connection between good soil, nutrient-rich food and healthy bodies.

Another consideration in relation to the health-giving properties of food is that the time between when the food is picked and when it is eaten is vital. Food value decreases depending on the length of time between harvesting and eating. Food picked and eaten on the same day is far more nutritious than food that is picked, packed, transported, stored, alternatively cooled and/or exposed to sunlight over a period of a few days.

All living organisms emit bio-photons or low-level luminescence. In plants, the higher the biophoton level, the more energy plants provide to the individual who eats them. Live foods act as high-powered electron donors and solar resonance fields in our bodies in order to attract, store, and conduct the sun's energy.

Cooking is another factor that negatively affects the nutrient level of food which is why it is important to have a diet consisting of mainly raw food. The rule is: raw food = live food = healthy light particles.

The greater our store of light energy, the greater the power of our overall electromagnetic field, and consequently the more energy is available for healing and maintenance of optimal health. The more light that a food is able to store, the more nutritious it is. Naturally grown, fresh vegetables and sun-ripened fruits are rich in light energy.

4. Rural Environments

Rural environments have not been as badly affected by man's activities as intensively populated urban areas have been. This is a generalisation of course. Some rural areas where monocultural farming, intensive irrigation farming and such things as factory farming of animals are carried out, are totally dominated by man's activities and are scarcely recognisable in terms of natural vegetation and soil. In such areas, people have chosen to believe that Earth must be changed, enhanced and organised differently from its original state in order to satisfy human greed. People seek to control the land and, in doing so, become separate from it and live in artificial environments of steel, bricks and concrete or in rural areas which are a source of agricultural poisons and pesticides. The *Elohim* explained:

Few people realise the significance of their relationship with

> the Earth. The Earth and people on Earth are one. Both have the same outcome. For Earth, the outcome is to regain the pristine conditions of its origin. Only by doing this can the Earth survive. Only under such conditions can the interacting Earth systems flow. Man is creating blocks within these systems by the over-use of water, air, soil, vegetation and minerals. As despoilers, the human race is destroying the very vehicle that it needs to support itself.

Wherever people dominate the landscape they degrade the Earth's environment which encompasses the interaction of all living and non-living things occurring naturally. They change the Earth's atmosphere with their industrial activities. They change the Earth's shape by reclamation of land and levelling of slopes. They change the Earth's water flow by damming and redirecting rivers and they change the Earth's vegetation and deplete natural resources by over-fishing or mining and by cutting down trees and importing exotic plants to replace those that grow naturally in an area. The longer-term consequence of doing this is to jeopardise the future for mankind. I am hopeful that, in the not too far distant future, people will come to realise the truth of what the *Elohim* told me:

> Man is happiest living in an environment where trees are supreme. Such an environment looks good, feels good, is good. Within a vista of trees man feels at peace because the trees not only balance the gases but they also act as energy transmitters and conductors. You have only to see a tree at the beginning of the day to realise that the energy field that surrounds it is part of the same energy field that man has.

Remove the trees and universal energy becomes unavailable to Earth. Trees are a vital part of earth's life support system which is also man's life support system.

Trees are nature's breathing apparatus. They help maintain optimal balance of all the gases that surround the Earth, and are present within the Earth's crust. Such balance is the optimal balance also for man. Destroy the trees and both suffer.

The soil retains its balance and its ability to bear fruit when it remains unpolluted. Poison the soil with chemicals and insecticides and mankind becomes poisoned. What exists in the soil ultimately exists in man, and when the spirit leaves the body and the body returns to Earth, it adds to the poison level. There are ways of feeding man without the poisons and without the need to employ vast armies of machinery. The Earth in its pure state is prolific. It is capable of producing far more than is required by the population. Poisoning the soil and removing the trees, gradually decreases the Earth's ability to produce and starvation follows. Food, although it may look good, does not contain the nutritional elements essential for man's well-being.

Poison the soil and you poison the water upon which everything depends. Poisons in the soil ultimately end up in the rivers and oceans. They destroy the balance in the seas causing a depletion of the apparently never-ending abundance of fish. As poisoning occurs of the soil, water and air, man will die. He will suffer the consequences of his own actions and he will learn from his mistakes, because, *deep down, he knows that he has chosen to do this to learn the lesson.*

This is what I needed to understand by working the farm. I had been given the intellectual understanding of the importance of the natural world through the messages that I had been given by the *Elohim* prior to my arrival at the place where I built my farm. Many years earlier I had trained as a geographer, and had taught geography, so I had a basic understanding of how natural systems operated. I needed to put this theoretical knowledge into practice to understand it fully. This is the process of what I call whole-body learning: learning by applying intellectual information to the solving of a need or in pursuit of some objective and discovering what happens when you do this. I grew a variety of food crops, both fruit and vegetables. Over time, working with the soil, I increased production levels using natural processes. I studied soil biology and bio-chemistry and gradually developed a system to enhance soil micro-organisms and organic content so that I was able to grow nutrient dense food that was sought after by organic food distributors.

It was challenging and immensely rewarding and as part of this experience I realised that in order for man to return to his origins, all the blocks must be removed and the poisons released from the body, the mind and also from the land. Doing this takes energy; massive levels of energy and the best natural source of energy is from the universe. I had forgotten this and needed to be reminded that unless we validate the Earth's role as a life support mechanism, we place it in limbo, apparently separate from us and without a role to play.

Before I moved to Castelen I was also given the following information by the Elohim:

A balanced yield from the soil creates balance in the soil. Soil regeneration and growth depends on balance. Balance is the key for people. Balance for the land is also the key. Grow some crops, some trees, some herbs and flowers. Flowers represent the spiritual aspect of Earth's productivity. Flowers lift the soul, please the eyes, enhance our whole level of being. A balanced yield from the soil creates balance in the soil. The micro-organisms and creatures within the soil are dependent on balance. Kill them and the soil, which is also a living system, dies.

When I was given this information, I had no knowledge of soil microorganisms and the role they play in developing and maintaining soil health. This is what I needed to understand by working the farm. Over time, working with the soil, I increased production levels using natural processes.

5. Exercise and movement are required to gain fitness and stamina.

Having a high-level energy source is useless if we don't have the physical apparatus which enables that energy to be put to use to maintain the human body. For this to happen, regular exercise is necessary to build lung capacity for efficient exchange of oxygen and carbon dioxide, enhance blood circulation, and build strong muscles.

6. Energy from other people

Abundant energy exists for those who know how to get it from others. Unfortunately, when people live in an artificial environment, cut off from natural energy, other people become their major source of energy.

When people are in close contact their energy fields overlap and interact. This makes it possible for someone to hijack energy from others and use it for themselves. This is why people abuse and get angry with others. It is why they belittle and demean others. These strategies allow them to use the energy of those who feel vulnerable in their presence. Being angry and demeaning of others makes some people feel good because it energises them. It makes them feel powerful. Because of their aggression and anger, they feel in control.

Another version of energy hijacking involves doing good. In the guise of helping others who are weaker than themselves, helpers actually sap the energy of those who they appear to be helping.

When people use energy hijacking strategies and get their energy from others, they discover that the strategy they use is only effective for a relatively short period of time. Those who allow energy to be taken from them become progressively weaker. They become sick and they have insufficient energy for themselves and none for anyone else. Unable to survive in a relationship where their energy is constantly being used by others, they eventually leave, or die. This is what Gwenda needed to understand.

As a consequence of a series of Stress Defusion sessions,

Chapter 16 Energy and Health

Gwenda understood that her father was a very strong and upright man who married a woman who was extremely dependent. She bore him two daughters. Gwenda remembered that even when she was small, her mother was sickly and dependent on her husband. She always relied on him when it came to making decisions and overseeing the day-to-day events of family life.

After years of illness, Gwenda's mother died at a relatively young age. When this happened, Gwenda recognised that if she had shown any sign of weakness, she would suffer the same fate as her mother. As a consequence of this understanding, she modelled herself on her father and became successful in everything she undertook, as her father had done. What she came to realise during the Stress Defusion sessions was that, in the guise of providing support, her father was actually using strategies to sap the energy of his daughters as he had done with his wife. Gwenda instinctively understood this after her mother died. Her sister had not understood what was happening and she took on the energy provider role as her mother had done. From then on, Gwenda's sister's life was disastrous. She committed suicide.

Gwenda recognised that she had adopted her father's strategies. She married a man who was weaker than herself and used his energy for her own purposes. She despised him for his increasing weakness. She did the same with her children. By being a pillar of strength, she developed co-dependent relationships with them in which they relied on her for every need, even as adults.

She recognised what her father had done. She despised him for it and didn't want to be despised by her children for doing to them what her father had done to her mother and sister. In what appeared to be in the spirit of self-sacrifice, she had repeated her father's pattern and this hadn't given her what she wanted. Stress Defusion provided her with the tools to break this pattern.

All of us have, at some time or another, felt ourselves sag when we hear others complain about us or criticise us. When this happens, we feel our energy going because we have allowed others to make us feel like a victim. At an individual and group level this is what conflict is all about: a technique for taking energy from others.

Co-dependency is a struggle for available energy. Sometimes one partner wins, at other times the other wins and the winner takes the energy. On a global level this is what war is. It is a fight for energy. Sometimes the energy is of a commercial variety such as oil and mineral resources. Sometimes it is a fight for land.

§

Energy is vital for health and wellbeing. There is ample energy available from Earth, the sun and from the food that is produced in poison-free, natural environments. Unfortunately, we live in a society where food production methods are geared more to quantity than quality, where poison is an accepted agricultural input, and where methods such as genetic engineering produce food that is suspect in terms of its value to life sustaining processes. More and more frequently people are persuaded to rely on processed fast food which is of low nutrient value.

A large percentage of the world's population live in urban environments of steel, concrete and artificial light. More and more distanced from natural environments, they cannot access energy from the Earth and from sunshine to sustain themselves.

I know now that moving from the centre of a large city was important if I was going to regain my health and live a long life. It was not something that I thought about as a resident of a densely populated city. As a city dweller I expected to be healthy, but I had no real understanding of what I needed to do in order to achieve that goal. Had I not trusted the guidance that I was given almost 30 years ago, I would not be writing this book today.

Chapter 17
Past Lives

At some time in the late 1980s I was sitting on the balcony of a very beautiful hotel on Big Island, Hawaii. I had just arrived from Sydney, for a workshop that was to be attended by people from all over the world. I was eavesdropping on a conversation between two young men sitting at a nearby table. They were discussing their past lives.

My reaction to overhearing this conversation was that they were crazy. How could what they were discussing be true?

At the time, past lives were not something I was familiar with and I had no inclination to become familiar with this strange concept. That attitude changed a few days later, in part because one of the participants at the workshop was a lady who did portraits of what people looked like in past lives. I thought that a past life portrait would be a great souvenir to take home with me, but I didn't expect my strong emotional response on seeing the portrait. It was as if I recognised the person in the portrait and knew all about her. Even more intriguing was that the artist told me the date when I looked as I did in the portrait and where I had lived in that lifetime. The date was 1897. The place she named was only a few miles from where my mother's family had farmed for three generations. She had no way of knowing this. Several years after this episode, I was working with clients by assisting them to access past lives.

The *Elohim* confirmed the significance of past lives.

Life is like an act in a play repeated over and over again changing the characters, the dialogue, the background, the period. Sometimes we play the heroine, sometimes the victim, sometimes the villain, in an investigation of a theme — a theme common to all humanity. There are various themes being investigated all over the world: greed, domination, brutality, separation, abuse of power, annihilation, mayhem, control, irresponsibility, worthlessness, poverty of mind and spirit.

For each negative theme there is a positive side. Sometimes our lives are dominated by the negative aspect of a theme. When we understand every aspect and integrate the learnings of one theme, we proceed to another one. There is logic and order in this but too often we get so caught up in the application of the negative aspect that we fail to see beyond the condition in which such negative aspects of existence place us. Lives illustrate themes and the choice one makes of one's family provides the data needed for our investigation.

§

Since the 1990s, I have become really well acquainted with past lives — my own and the past lives of others. This was not something I planned to do. My initial experience of past lives came from accessing my own vivid memories. Following this,

I found that clients sometimes accessed past life memories for the first time and, like Peter, were in a state of wonderment and disbelief because of their experience.

'Where are you Peter?'

'I don't know. When I look down, I know I've got really hairy feet. No, it's not just my feet that are covered in hair. I'm hairy all over. I'm a cave man. My family are cold and starving and I am injured. I can do nothing to save them and I feel very sad.'

I have mentioned previously that I am not clairvoyant. I cannot access the memories of others. I simply documented the stories they told me and added these to the library of past life memories I have accessed in relation to my own soul's journey.

Working with past lives was never my intention. As with the discovery of the Stress Defusion technique, this was not something I anticipated. It just happened. When I used the same techniques that I used with clients to bring past memories from this lifetime to conscious awareness, some of them chose to go back to times prior to this lifetime. Sometimes they went back much further than I expected, to what seemed to be the beginning of time. I hypothesised that, for them, it was appropriate to do this in order to understand the origins of the programs that their lives played out in this lifetime. What they saw, in many cases, was that the problems they were experiencing in this lifetime were the same, or a variation, of problems they had experienced in previous lifetimes. Realising this, helped to explain events in this lifetime. Sometimes, however, it was not possible to establish a link, but the fact that there was one was demonstrated by the changes that occurred subsequently. This was the case for Lance.

Lance was a nineteen-year-old who had dropped out of school in Year 11, spent a couple of years involved with drugs and alcohol, and was, at the time he came to see me, attempting to rebuild his life. He was enrolled in a computer training course and was having great difficulty passing the assessment tasks. The training course was run by a division of the company I had developed the personal development training programs for. They had referred Lance to me.

At the end of the third session, Lance said: 'Do you know that while you were working with that leg, I had some really vivid memories of riding a white horse. I was dressed in armour. It seemed to be at the Court of King Arthur back in mediaeval times. What was that all about? Weird heh?'

I told him that I didn't know what it was all about and agreed that it was very weird. During the following session, I was again working to relieve the pain in Lance's legs when he said, 'I'm back in King Arthur's Court again. This time it's a jousting competition. I'm riding the white horse again. I've just killed someone. It's my best friend. I feel really guilty.' I agreed that what he had remembered and felt was extraordinary and left him to work it out for himself.

Whatever the relevance of these memories was to Lance's ability to pass his computer assignments, I'll never know, but there definitely was a connection. Weird or not, Lance's *marks in his assignments improved and six months later he graduated.*

§

I have never thought of myself as a past life therapist because I have no idea how to deliberately provide people with the opportunity to investigate their past lives. If this is what happens, I assume that it needs to happen rather than as a conscious facilitation on my part. I certainly didn't expect Sam to share past life information with me.

Sam had great difficulties in school. He could barely read and was dyslexic. Sam's problems were made worse as his classmates bullied him unmercifully because he couldn't play sport and he was frequently sick with allergic reactions. The final straw came when he was refused enrolment by the local Catholic high school because of his dismal academic record.

Sam demonstrated characteristics that are typical of some children with severe learning difficulties: sensitivity and acute perception including awareness of energies and entities and awareness of information that is not generally known. During his second session, Sam opened up a little and started talking about his friend, an old man, who told him things. The old man wasn't really present. Sam knew this.

This was the first time Sam had ever spoken to anyone about the old man. He also talked about the times he had visits at night from extra-terrestrial beings who spoke to him. When they first came, he had been very scared, but he was accustomed to their visits by the time he spoke to me about them.

Sam also shared some of the experiences he had gone through during his earlier Stress Defusion session which he hadn't been prepared to talk about at that time. He spoke about Atlantis and the crystal technology available in Atlantis. He described the way the Atlantans travelled in space cars powered by the energy of crystals.

'Have you read about Atlantis?' I asked.

'No. I just remember it.' When I questioned him, Sam described another past life in Egypt. He talked about the pyramids.

'We just looked carefully at the blocks of stone and saw the arrangements of the particles. Then we mentally moved the blocks to where they were needed and, using the power of our minds, we re-assembled the stone blocks. This is how the pyramids were built.'

Sam was labelled as intellectually handicapped with severe learning difficulties. There was absolutely no way he could have read about these things. Unfortunately, after our sessions, Sam went into a state of denial about the things he spoke of.

When clients slip into past life recollection without any preparation, they can be quite shocked. Such was the case with Brendan who came to me for help with difficulties in Year 11. His history classes were causing him real problems. Brendan was antagonistic towards the teacher and hated his World War II studies.

Working with the issue, I hate history, Brendan started shivering violently. He asked 'Why is it so cold, suddenly?' On a hot summer's day his arms were covered in goose bumps.

'What can you see?' I asked.

'There's a boy walking in wet grass. He has no shoes. It's cold. It's very cold. He's with someone else. A girl. She's his sister. I can see the city behind them. It's on fire. Ruined burning buildings. Now they're running.'

Suddenly Brendan began talking about what he was seeing as if he were there. 'I feel very scared. Everyone has been killed. I'm going to die too. There's no oxygen. Bombs are falling.'

It was not surprising that Brendan hated his World War II history classes. From the memories he had tapped into, it was obvious that he had been a child during World War II and had been killed. Studying this period in history had caused him to access subconscious memories of events in Germany, which was why he had become so antagonistic towards his teacher and to his history lessons. To overcome this problem all that he needed to do was to re-experience the terror of that time. This is what the Stress Defusion session allowed him to do and his problems with history faded after the sessions.

Intrigued by stories of the successes that some of her astrology clients had experienced as a consequence of Stress Defusion sessions, Narelle decided to investigate whether it would help her to resolve her problem of lack of money. No matter how hard she worked, she was unable to earn a sufficient amount to live on. It wasn't that her skills were deficient. She was well known as one of Sydney's top astrologers.

During her session, Narelle accessed childhood memories of living in a temporary home with a dirt floor and insufficient space. She was able to access and resolve her resentment about her childhood.

Her next memory was not so easy to explain. When she accessed a different area of her peripheral vision, Narelle described a scene very different from her memories of her childhood. The memory was of a young woman walking through thick snow. It was late afternoon and the snow was still falling. Dressed in a thick fur coat and hat, the young woman was about seventeen years of age and was accompanied by her parents, brothers and sisters. Walking behind the family were two young soldiers. They, too, wore thick overcoats, blue in colour with fur collars. They were carrying guns.

Narelle saw the young girl look back over her shoulder at the palatial home they were walking away from. The lights of the house were glowing through the dim afternoon light. She recalled the decision she made at that moment: *I'll never have such wealth or such a lovely home ever again.* At that moment, the young woman and the rest of her family were killed by the young soldiers.

Rarely are the consequences of past life recollections and the identification of a point of death decision as instantaneous or as dramatic as they were for Narelle. Her first action on returning home following her session was to clear out boxes of junk she had accumulated for years: books, old clothes, broken and obsolete appliances and pieces of equipment. Her home had also been a repository for all her friends' and family's unwanted possessions. She phoned them and told them to take whatever belonged to them as she was not going to store it any longer. As she was doing this, the phone rang constantly with clients wanting her to do their astrology charts. They were happy to pay. The next day cheques started arriving from people who Narelle had done work for previously and who hadn't paid.

For the next few days Narelle was extremely ill. She phoned the clinic where she worked on Saturdays to tell them that she wouldn't be coming in. To her surprise, she learned that she was booked solid for the following Saturday. Normally, she would expect to have one or two clients for the day.

Narelle's income during the next month quadrupled — and that was only the start. Several weeks later, I was present when Narelle met with a group of friends and found herself angrily confronting a young man, whom she had not met previously. To my absolute astonishment, he turned on her and said, 'You're just angry because I shot you in a past life. You were a member of the Jewish aristocracy in Poland and I killed you and your whole family.' This was not something that had been discussed in the conversation so there was no way that he could have known of this event because of something that Narelle had told him.

Past life stories are unimaginable to someone who hasn't accessed memories of times other than the present, however, reincarnation and the laws of Karma form a fundamental part of Eastern religions such as Buddhism and Hinduism. Jesus is reported to have accepted reincarnation as true but references to this were removed in 553 CE in the Second Council of Constantinople. Reincarnation is touched upon in the writings of St Augustine, St Gregory and St Francis of Assisi.

§

In chapter 13, I discussed Garry's story. Even though he was a patient in a psychiatric hospital the staff allowed me to work with him. Narelle, the astrologer whose story I told earlier in this chapter, suggested I might be able to help him. Garry's mother was one of Narelle's clients. In addition to her abilities as an astrologer, Narelle was psychically aware. She recognised that Garry spoke many different languages, some of which were ancient languages that are not easy to identify. She knew that he was psychically aware. Although he denied it, his memories of past lives were so vivid that many of his problems were due to the fact that he could not distinguish between when he was living in this life and when he was accessing past life memories. He had no sense of time. Everything was in the now. Narelle warned me that there was a past life connection between myself and Garry, and that we had been together in Tibet in a past life.

> *On one occasion, while looking at a book that I had brought for him, Garry saw a photograph of a fountain in Hobart and enthusiastically said: 'I helped to make that. I worked*

on the bottom section and my friend Claudio did the top half. That was when I lived in France.' When I read the caption under the photograph, it was of little surprise to find that the fountain had indeed been imported from France.

Questioning him one day about his childhood experiences, he told me about a small girl who was run over by a truck and in an offhand manner he said: 'She was run over before too. That was in France. She was run over by a cart. She was very young then. About 15. She didn't die but she was crippled. I was married to her when she was run over.'

Curious about my past life connection with him, I asked Garry if we had been together in an earlier lifetime.

'Yes. In Tibet. You were in charge of the monastery and I was a novice.'

'What happened?'

'I did something very stupid and you expelled me from the monastery. I committed suicide.'

I wondered whether I had carried guilt about this episode which was why I chose to help him in this lifetime but if that was the case, I had no conscious knowledge of it.

§

Assuming that past life memories exist, and that we can access the universal library of past lives, the question remains: what purpose do they serve?

I don't know whether past life memories are accessible on an individual basis, or if there is a collective library from which we can borrow to understand a given situation in this lifetime. If, as I believe, Earth is a hologram, this idea makes sense and each of us have the ability to tap into all memories of the Earth's, and possibly even the universes's, history, as well as into our own personal past lives. I tend to think this is the most likely case. These thoughts were confirmed by the *Elohim:*

Memories aren't necessarily individual to us. We can tap into any universal memory if it serves us in helping us to understand a concept or learn a lesson. This is why so many people experience similar past lives. They are tapping into just one aspect of universal memory. Someone, somewhere, actually had the experience that we are re-living. That is true. When we understand that we are in fact, all one, their experience becomes our experience. There is no distinguishing one from the other.

§

My understanding of Karma is that each lifetime is presented to us as a learning experience designed to allow us to understand something we have not yet understood. I believe that the people who we are in contact with in this life are the same people we connected with in previous lifetimes. When we fail to learn what a specific lifetime is intended to teach us, we repeat experiences with slight variations, until we understand what the experiences that result from our actions are designed to teach us.

Consider the possibility that we are not our bodies or the

people we believe ourselves to be. If we are much more than that and we are spiritual beings having an earthly experience, we have the ability to know All That Is. If we are on Earth to provide us with all the knowledge that being human entails, then each past life memory allows us to tap into an experience that provides us with a greater depth of understanding and a grasp of relationships we would not have otherwise. Each lifetime, and each memory, investigates some aspect of life from a different perspective: an aspect that we have chosen to understand. When we do not gain the understanding required within one lifetime, we repeat our experiences investigating the issue, from a variety of different perspectives.

Clients who had the ability to slip easily into past life memories, recalled how they experienced specific themes for lifetime after lifetime. To understand, for example, the meaning of power, each lifetime is designed to investigate some aspect of power and powerlessness. Some lifetimes are designed in order to know what happens when power is exercised unwisely and unjustly. Some lives may be designed to experience how it feels to be a victim of someone who exercises power unwisely and unjustly. In other lives, the use of power for the wrong purpose may be the focus.

Over time, this aspect of human motivation has been experienced often so that there is a lot of information in the universal bank of knowledge about use and misuse of power. Being able to tap into this universal library of knowledge enables us to really understand power and ultimately, to come up with the realisation that the only true power is that which is within and that we don't have to exert power over others to achieve true power.

§

My experience is that re-activation of past life patterns occurs only after re-experiencing, in this lifetime, people associated with, or events similar to those from past life experiences. Experiences in this life bring to our awareness patterns from the past, together with the physical and emotional responses that are appropriate to these experiences. I had no memories of past lives relating to Indian civilisations in the USA until I drove from Sedona, Arizona through the land now occupied by the Hopi, to Denver, Colorado. When I accessed those past life memories, it seemed that the route I took in making that journey was the same route taken annually by Indian tribes in former times. The time of my memory was when the Indians knew that they were being dispossessed by white people. The great sadness that I felt was due to knowing that the disruption to the Indian way of life that I had foreseen, would soon happen. Before I accessed these past life memories, I recall standing on the main road that winds through Sedona, looking at the red cliffs and mesas that surround Oak Creek Canyon, and weeping, without having any idea what had triggered my sadness.

At the time of birth, children have no past life memories. As experiences occur, cellular memories that are in some way associated with particular events are activated. Understanding the issue and feeling emotions which are and were connected, allows the clearing of emotional energy that has been blocked over many lifetimes. Unexplained fears and reactions to things which logically do not justify extreme reactions, come to the surface. This provides the motivation to do what is necessary to discover the cause.

For me, the importance of past lives is in seeing them as a tool to analyse themes that mankind has investigated for lifetime after lifetime and seeing how decisions made in previous lifetimes are repeated lifetime after lifetime and then are subtly changed so that the issue can be looked at from a slightly different perspective.

Lewis came to see me because he was facing a dilemma. He was unhappy in his marriage, but he knew that divorcing his wife was going to place him in a position of financial hardship. If he were to choose to stay in the marriage, he felt he had no hope for future happiness. By working through many past lives where he had to choose between doing nothing or acting in a way that involved risk, Lewis realised that his unwillingness to act was a pattern of behaviour that he had repeated for lifetime after lifetime where he had avoided responsibility for his decisions. His lifetimes included some that he recalled as being far, far earlier than it is believed that man has been on Earth.

In 264,000 BCE in what is now part of Russia, Lewis had psychic abilities and belonged to a family of priestly class. He sensed that someone was subtly poisoning his child using some sort of vibrational frequency. The reason they were doing this was something to do with power in the priesthood.

He took the easy way out and didn't confront them because he didn't trust his ability to make the right decision regarding what to do. His child died.

As an Australian aboriginal who had responsibility for his tribe, Lewis decided that the tribe should move on. They left a child behind and he drowned. This was in 3235 BC. He decided to blame others rather than feel the sadness of his own irresponsibility.

In the 1100s in China he worked with ginseng. He knew some varieties of ginseng were dangerous but as they aged, they were difficult to distinguish. He ate one that was poisonous and hovered between life and death for a long time and made the decision to avoid risk in a future life.

In 1907 he again decided to avoid the risk and act as if there was no problem. In that lifetime, he had gone broke because of gambling but he decided to fight his way out of it.

His reluctance to take risks started to change later in that lifetime when in 1917 as a lawyer he accepted legal cases that involved risking his reputation.

Again in 1940, as a young girl in the Ukraine during World War II he decided that it was better to take the risk of trying to escape from captivity even though it was dangerous. In that lifetime he deferred to the wishes of his parents who wanted to take what seemed to be the safer option, and they were all killed.

As a consequence of an incident in his current lifetime when, as a three-year-old he was pulled away from danger by his father, he decided that taking risks made his father *very angry so it was better to avoid taking risks. It was this incident that gave Lewis the ability to access past lives where he had investigated avoiding responsibility for the consequences of his decisions.*

By accessing numerous past lives where Lewis had been reluctant to act in situations that involved risk, he understood why he was prevaricating over his decision whether or not to divorce his wife. He came to the conclusion that he needed to take what seemed to be the more difficult option, which was to ask for a divorce.

By seeing his behaviour pattern over many lifetimes, when difficult decisions had been faced, Lewis understood what these life experiences were designed to teach him: that sometimes when a choice is needed, the better option may appear to be the more difficult one. In the earlier lifetimes that Lewis accessed, he was unable to make important decisions. In more recent lifetimes he was unable to accept responsibility for the consequences of his decisions. He began to make progress when he learned to see the consequences of not taking risks. Moving on from there, he started to accept that, whilst risk might be involved, taking the more difficult option available was probably the best choice.

I believe that Lewis' story indicates the process by which spiritual evolution occurs. Each decision we make triggers a particular set of actions. By seeing the consequences of our actions, we learn to make wiser decisions.

Chapter 18
Ending Separation

Stories told to me by my clients confirmed the idea that pain and struggle are last resort tools for learning and spiritual evolvement. In general, clients came to me wanting help to fix a problem that was causing them difficulties in their lives. They blamed people who were causing the difficulties that they were experiencing and identified these people as their problem. Some blamed the situations in their lives as the problem. My intention was always to help them learn that the negative situations and people that have featured in their lives were valuable tools that could be used to help them heal. Rather than being something to fear or be angry about, their anguish and discomfort were actually showing them something that they needed to investigate in more depth. I attempted to show clients that the means by which the pain and struggle was inflicted, was irrelevant. I helped them to move out of the stories that had governed their attitudes to life to a position where they could approach an understanding of what the stories that they had told me during our sessions were designed to teach them. What these clients also realised was that pain and struggle decreased when they understood that all they had to do was to feel appropriately in response to the situations of their lives, to let go of the judgements that they had made about what had happened, and about how they felt in relation to what had happened.

Letting go of judgement brings us to a state of unconditional love, which involves ending of separation and total acceptance of All That Is. Judgement of pain causes separation. The form that separation takes is different for each person. Separation can occur between the two hemispheres of someone's brain so that neither the left nor the right hemisphere is able to communicate with the other. Some people experience separation of the mind from the body or separation of the mind from their emotions. For many, the separation is from their families, or indeed from themselves, a condition that is called disassociation. Disassociation happens when people go into a state of extreme pain avoidance by stepping outside themselves and living life from the perspective of total non-involvement as if the things that happen are happening to someone else. In such situations, it is possible to look on oneself going through the routine of daily life as if it is someone else who is involved. I knew this state well. It was how I experienced life from the time I was twelve years old until I did the work that was needed for me to heal.

The Elohim explained the purpose of separation in the following way:

> *By creating separation, we make it possible for us to keep parts of ourselves locked away. We even put the old, the infirm and the sick into institutions so we don't have to deal with their problems, which are only a reflection of our own*

problems. We punish the guilty to avoid our guilt. We sedate those in pain so we don't feel our pain.

Separation can be observed in someone forgetting that they have a life purpose and that they possess unique gifts which will enable them to do what they have come to Earth to do. Whilst they are separated from their purpose, they find little true meaning in life.

Clients would say to me, 'I don't know my purpose'. My response would be that it wasn't important for them to know so much as to realise that whatever path they were on, was the right path. Even doing nothing could be part of a person's life purpose if their purpose was to learn patience.

I explained to clients that their situation could be compared to a rocket that is launched to head towards a particular target. As it moves towards its target, the percentage of time it is on course is very small. Even so, it will hit the target. This is because it is programmed so that each time the rocket heads off course, it self corrects and in doing so, heads towards its target in a zigzag fashion. This also happens in life. Each person has a purpose, even if they are not consciously aware that they do and for many, the time that is spent in heading directly towards achieving the purpose is small in terms of total time spent. Even so, the purpose will be achieved as long as the person has sufficient energy available to keep going. Their purpose will be achieved because their unconscious mind and intuition guide them.

§

Another aspect of separation shows up in over-reliance on intelligence, a function of the left brain, to solve problems. There is nothing wrong with intellectual thought. It is the outcome of left brain processes. But when someone relies too much on thinking as the only tool they have to solve problems, they can easily get into trouble. Over reliance on thinking means they lose touch with how they feel about something. Feeling is just as valuable a tool as thinking is. When someone operates in a manner that is totally left brain dominant, their right brain, emotions, body and spirit have to take a back seat. If some situation evokes a strong emotional response, they ignore their feelings or choose to avoid the situation. Life is similarly difficult for the person who relies totally on their emotional response to what is happening without referring to logical thinking.

Daniel's life illustrated what happened when two conflicting strategies existed side by side with him having the ability to switch between the two. His life also illustrated that people are capable of extraordinarily complex strategies to reconcile the paradox that exists when contradictory opposites exist side by side at a subconscious level.

Daniel needed to reconcile two different lifestyles to be able to function effectively. In one, he thought of himself as a monk, and he behaved in a monk-like fashion. He liked to spend hours in contemplation and meditation and he was a trained psychologist. Daniel's other personality was that of a warrior. As a warrior he was adept at making business deals and he was a very successful senior executive working for a multi-national clothing company. He was highly motivated and he enjoyed a successful career.

Neither aspect of his personality was totally satisfying and Daniel found it confusing when he switched between the two personalities. He didn't understand the mechanism that caused this to happen, or what triggered the switch. By testing for ipsilaterity at the beginning of his session, I could see that Daniel operated with a split brain and he switched between left and right brain operation. What he discovered during his session was that the monk came from one past life and the decisions made in that lifetime controlled his right brain responses. The warrior came from another lifetime and controlled his left brain responses. Daniel functioned quite well regardless of which personality pattern was dominant. Neither mode gave him what he suspected was possible if he could combine the two in order to synthesise the positive aspects of both. That happened when he was able to end the left/right brain separation by identifying two irreconcilable decisions that caused him to go into split brain function. His decisions about who he was in the world had not been the problem. Confusion arose from periodically switching from one to the other.

§

Many of mankind's problems stem from separation in some form. For the individual, separation occurs when one aspect is ignored, undervalued or deliberately hidden because acknowledgement of this aspect causes distress. Family breakdown occurs when individuals feel unaccepted within the family because some aspect of their personality or behaviour is unacceptable within the family. Within a society, categorisation of individuals by race, religion, colour, class and/or economic status causes separation, particularly when specific groups are judged as unacceptable. Community breakdown occurs when specific groups feel alienated.

Separation, in one form or another, appeared to be central to many of the problems experienced by the people I saw as clients. It appeared that different issues created different separation effects. The list of issues that created separation was long: co-operation vs competition, honesty vs dishonesty, creation vs destruction, courage vs cowardice, acceptance vs alienation. When the negative aspect of one of these concepts was addressed by a client, that person's life became more balanced. Addressing the causes of disharmony allowed someone to move towards harmony in their life. When they were in harmony they were in balance. When a person investigated the reasons for their refusal to look at the truth about themselves, or in relation to others, they discovered the reason for the disharmony. They understood that their fear of facing the truth stemmed from a desire to cover something up because they felt ashamed. Once the shame was addressed, they were able to acknowledge the truth about themselves and their journey.

§

Chapter 18   Ending Separation

To identify issues that were the cause of separation, I suggested that clients looked to their families because families provide many clues as to where the causes of separations lie. Dysfunctional family situations indicated the existence of issues that needed to be resolved for each individual within the family. Surprisingly, when one family member resolved their problems, the whole family benefitted by becoming more united. Clients told me that they experienced greater evidence of compassion within their family unit. I understood that as each individual worked to heal themselves, it helped others to do the same.

I saw that when families had a strong and dominating member who was dictatorial, the needs of other members of the family became secondary to the needs of the dominant member. Where a situation like this occurred, it was likely that each family member would also have a dominant aspect and other aspects would be ignored. It might have been that one family member became immersed in their emotional response to what was happening around them and that they were reluctant to engage in any form of physical activity. Another member might have been strongly intellectual and their emotional and spiritual aspects were ignored. In such situations, each family member was likely to display dominance in a different aspect of themselves so that, overall, the family was balanced.

In this chapter, Julie and Suzanne tell their own stories. Whilst the Stress Defusion process has helped many people who have suffered from a variety of mental health conditions as a consequence of separation issues as both Julie and Suzanne did, I did not work with these women in order to *fix* them. I didn't think they had anything wrong that needed fixing. I suspected that their responses to terrifying, depressing or incomprehensible life events were perfectly understandable and I thought that if I could help them see this, they would have the ability to heal themselves. For the most part I did not even realise the extent of their trauma until much of the work was completed and they were prepared to share the stories of their experiences with me. I worked with them, to help them understand the relationship between the events of their life and the long-term effect these events had on both their physical and their mental wellbeing. I was astounded by their willingness to share their stories so that others could understand that severe mental health issues can be resolved.

Suzanne and Julie's stories were typical of situations where their physical survival and/or mental stability were at stake. Julie's story of growing up in a family where one parent's need to dominate in conjunction with the need to be recognised within society destroyed the mental stability of all members of that family. Julie allowed me to tell her story in the hope that others would find hope within situations when they appeared to have none.

This is her story.

My father was an ex-Army physical education instructor who had achieved celebrity status as a young man for his athletics prowess. When I was growing up, he taught athletics at the high school I attended and believed corporal punishment was the way to achieve excellence.

I knew my father as a vicious psychopath. He terrified me. He terrified the kids at my school. He would cane an entire class when one member of the class forgot their sandshoes. That was his strategy for turning everyone against the offender. The other teachers probably knew that what he was doing was wrong, but the students didn't dare be anything less than outstanding and the school achieved amazing sporting achievements. In a perverted sort of way, the kids were proud because he pushed them to levels that they would never have achieved otherwise.

My father developed humiliation as an art form and he took great delight in making me an object of ridicule in front of my school friends. He physically abused me on a regular basis. He was also a rapist. I tried to tell the teachers at school that he had raped me continuously from the time I was three years old. They didn't believe me. My mother didn't believe me.

My mother left when I was nine and took my youngest sister with her. My older sister and I chose to stay with my father because we didn't want to be a burden on our mother. I knew that her life was going to be very difficult and I didn't want to make things any worse for her than it needed to be. After a Stress Defusion session, I realised that mine was a totally irrational decision but at the time I didn't believe I had any other choice. After Mum left, Dad told us she didn't want to have anything to do with us. I didn't find out the truth until I was almost seventeen years old.

My father remarried and his new wife treated my sister and I really badly. If we told Dad about the things she did, he would explode and punish us for telling lies. I became depressed and started seeing a counsellor. It was an easy step from counselling to being admitted to a psychiatric hospital, and the times I spent in the hospital always seemed to coincide with school holidays. In hospital they put me on to medication for my depression. When I told the psychiatrists about my father raping me, they told him what I had said. He punished me. When I stopped talking to the counsellors, they assumed I needed more medication. When I returned to school my father made sure everyone knew where I had been. Not understanding the real situation, the teaching staff at the school were very supportive of his efforts to help me.

I left home when I was sixteen. By then I was totally dependent on anti-depressant drugs and convinced that there was something wrong with me. I was suicidal until my mid 30s. I finally got off anti-depression medication when I decided it was OK to be depressed. Until then I had assumed that depression was the first phase of a downward spiral into manic depression rather than the appropriate response to what was happening in my life. Once I decided that being depressed was a valid response to what was happening in my life, I gave myself permission to feel miserable, and then put it aside. Once I made that decision my life changed. I had a successful career and did years of volunteer work with various refuges, gaols and juvenile justice departments. This helped me to understand that what I had experienced was part of a journey designed to allow me to let go of judgements around injustice, and specifically the injustice I had suffered as a child.

Needing to understand the purpose behind what had happened drew me to Stress Defusion. Understanding the need to let go the judgements was one thing. Actually doing it was a lot more challenging. An intensive period of Stress Defusion allowed me to gain insights into the purpose for my journey.

Mine was a particularly brutal and lonely youth. My situation was made worse by my determination to stand up to my father. Had I given in, he would have destroyed me as he destroyed my mother. I wouldn't let him win. No matter how far I was pulled into the depths of despair I retained a sense of dignity and self-respect and the willpower to keep going.

If members of a family are judgemental of themselves and others and are fearful of being heard, or of telling the truth, it follows that no one will be prepared to express their thoughts or their feelings. Over time they become more and more repressed out of fear of what others will think.

§

As I discussed in chapter 16, when decisions are made at the time of a particularly traumatic event involving intense fear, anger and/or sadness and judgements are made about the cruelty, unfairness and/or horror of the experience, we attempt to avoid accessing these emotions and judgements by locking them away in some part of our body. Giving the body the task of holding onto the energy of these emotions and associated judgements blocks energy flow and becomes a source of chronic fatigue.

Locking the emotions and judgements away does not always happen by accident. When someone makes a decision such as I don't want to feel the pain, the body has a variety of responses available to it that ensure we do not feel the pain of that event, or indeed of any subsequent event of a similar nature. Someone who doesn't want to feel pain shuts down that part of their body that is storing the pain. Alternatively, they might separate that part of their body from their head in order to disconnect from the pain. Similarly, they might shut down their hearing or their sight because they decide they don't want to see or hear things that make them feel bad. They reduce their mental functions so that they cannot remember.

It is often surprising how literal people are in giving themselves instructions which the brain interprets and puts into action. For example, someone may decide that they have no option but to shoulder the blame or carry the load on their shoulders. The body translates this instruction literally and shoulder pain and/or tension develops. The rest of that person's body doesn't want the shoulders to release what they are carrying because that would mean the whole body would have to carry the load.

Having shut off various parts of themselves as a pain avoidance strategy, people then judge the part of them they have shut down. They get angry because they can't remember. They become frustrated because their life doesn't seem to have a purpose. Over time, they become upset because they are in pain and do not understand why.

§

Since the universe operates on an all or nothing basis, shutting down is not selective in its application. Intending only to shut out what they don't want to remember, people also shut down what they do want to remember. In choosing not to feel fear, people choose also not to feel love and joy. In choosing not to see or hear something that is distressing, they also lose the ability to see and hear those things that give them pleasure. It is not possible to selectively feel, selectively see or selectively hear. Shutting down is what Suzanne did. In response to experiences that were both terrifying and horrifying, and in her reluctance to remember the events involved, Suzanne shut down so many aspects of herself that life became extremely difficult. The energy required to keep her fear under control left her very little energy to manage the daily tasks of day to day living. This is Suzanne's story.

I have been in fear most of my life but over the past fifteen years, my life has been dominated by fear. It caused me to leave my family, my friends and my country and go into hiding. My story is about the lasting effects of extreme trauma. Counselling and therapy did not cure it. My mother was a Jungian analyst and neither she nor her colleagues could help me. I tried many different forms of counselling and alternative therapies. They just made me more and more frustrated because they didn't have the answers. Transcendental Meditation helped me keep the lid on my problems and provided wonderful coping mechanisms, but no solutions. I needed very powerful strategies to avoid remembering the experiences life handed me but these strategies took so much time and energy I had nothing left for living.

As a three-year-old, I was kidnapped for ransom. I never forgot the event but had persuaded myself that it was unimportant. My first Stress Defusion session allowed me to see the truth, which was very different from what I had thought was the truth. The session brought to the fore the terror I had felt while I was in captivity and I thought I had been abandoned by my family.

After my first session I knew I had found something that was capable of shifting my intense anxiety and I realised why the strategies I had used to that point had not worked. It took me several months before I could handle the idea of confronting fears relating to various traumatic episodes, but I knew it was what was needed. Other therapies had wandered around the events in my life that were the origin of my fear or helped me to suppress or avoid what I feared. By contrast, Stress Defusion put me right into my fear. By confronting my fear I was able to understand and accept that fear was a totally acceptable response to what had happened and I no longer needed to resist these feelings. Even so, my resistance to going back into fear was very strong. I hoped the problem would go away but it didn't. It got worse and it was this that persuaded me to continue.

I had been able to dismiss being kidnapped but I was never able to repress the feelings or memories associated with seeing a friend and workmate deliberately burnt to death. Her fellow countrymen poured petrol down her throat and put a tyre over her head and set her alight. As they did this they guffawed with laughter and made obscene comments. I still feel the guilt because I knew that they chose to do to her what they wanted to do to me but didn't dare. They wanted to punish me for having the power, money and position that they lacked. I still can't cope with loud, hysterical laughter that arises in the guilty. Neither can I forget the baby my friend had gagged and bound and strapped to the underside of her bed to keep her safe because she knew what was planned. I've been rescuing babies ever since.

I learned to live with phone taps and being under surveillance by members of the Special Branch. It was what I expected as the daughter of rich, famous and politically active parents who worked against the apartheid system in South Africa. I was not able to forget the terror and sense of utter powerlessness I felt when I was put into gaol for politically motivated activities. I had a mental breakdown that left me with impaired brain function and dyslexia. I was unable to write coherently or to learn for years after that. I know now that these are symptoms of mental shut down that occurred as a means of avoiding total stress overload.

The despair of total powerlessness remained with me. My strategy was to create my own powerlessness out of fear that others would make me powerless. I made sure I was never noticed. I would do anything to avoid conflict. I became agoraphobic, unable to open the door to friends or strangers. I kept my distance from everyone with a facade of smiles and good nature.

I knew things were changing when I no longer needed to sleep with my head under the pillow. Shortly after, following several Stress Defusion sessions, I accepted a job where I spent my days dealing with the aftermath of situations involving staff who had been injured and/or abused by the mentally and physically disabled people they dealt with as clients. I travelled. My work involved meeting new people all the time. This was not something I could have done six months earlier. Stress Defusion allowed me to come out of hiding.

§

Separation between people ends when people end the separation within themselves. The stories that clients have allowed me to tell show that it is possible, but not easy, to heal separation that results from situations of extreme violence and trauma.

§

It is my conclusion that problems arise because people attempt to find happiness by doing the things that others expect them to do, rather than what they really want to do.

Problems become bigger because they allow themselves to rely on the judgements of others, rather than on their own knowing. Their intuitive knowing can be invalidated by those who find meaning in their lives through the manipulation of others. Since children are easily manipulated, they often suffer because they are powerless to resist. Through this manipulation and denial of what is real, the child finds that others invalidate their knowing, causing them to substitute the values and belief of others, for their own. This leads to a great void of feeling. The child, as he grows to adulthood, attempts to fill the vacuum with things that will not provide satisfaction for more than a short period.

Problems arise when our expectation of who we should be differs from who we are. Because of our perceived failure to live up to the expectation of others, we feel that there is something wrong with us and we feel ashamed of who we are. When this happens, we separate who we think we are from who we really are. Separation, as I have explained, can take many different forms and be at many different levels: physical, emotional, mental, spiritual or environmental.

When we end all separation within, we discover that within each of us there is a blueprint for individual excellence and an internal set of goals. Furthermore, my experience is that we are guided by a higher force, or perhaps by our own internal knowing, which assists us to make appropriate choices so that we learn what it is we have come to Earth to learn. Often, the choices that we make are motivated by an inner knowing, and these are choices that others do not deem appropriate.

Making choices within the context of our life purpose allows events and people to come into our lives to assist us but, until we are validated in this way, we question whether the choices we make are the right ones. I still remember the absolute incredulity expressed by family members when I told them of my plans to return to a high school environment and give up the successful career I was forging in adult education.

'How can you throw away everything you've achieved?' they said. 'You're crazy to think that you can solve the problem of children being unable to learn.' These were typical of the comments made. From the perspective of someone who didn't know my life purpose, they were absolutely correct. Fortunately, I knew it was the right course of action, although I didn't have any understanding where it would lead. And having done it once, it became easier to follow intuition rather than logic the next time around.

Judgement of how assistance is provided short-circuits the process. I was certainly unhappy about the circumstances around my son's birth, but had it not been for the problems associated with his learning difficulties I would never have started on the path that has taken me so far.

Giving up, shutting down or succumbing to addictions or worldly pleasures, takes us off course and it is so easy to allow this to happen. However, once we learn to trust that things that are presented appropriately it becomes easier to stay on target, rather than to be tempted by time-filling activities that have no real purpose. However, even when we go off course, in terms of our life purpose, something happens that causes us to change direction and continue the journey that we are destined to travel.

Following the herd is unlikely to lead us to where we need to go so, oftentimes, we need to travel alone on a journey of discovery. Much of that journey will present challenges, as I have discovered.

Chapter 19
Fake News

For individuals, we feel that our lives are chaotic when we have no explanation for what is happening. When we don't see the cause and effect connection, we continue to behave as we have always done, not realising that chaos is the consequence of decisions we have made. Many of the clients I saw over a period of many years had lives that were chaotic. On a world scale, I could also see that world chaos seemed to be accelerating and there seemed to be no apparent reason why things would not continue to deteriorate, rather than get better. Solutions seemed to be available, but the problems that were creating the greatest chaos weren't being addressed. On a world scale things were happening that replicated what was happening in the lives of individuals: chaos was getting progressively worse. Unfortunately, little has changed during the intervening years.

Having received information about chaos from the *Elohim* I felt drawn to investigate the cause of chaos on a world scale. This is the information I received:

Mankind is evolving, though many doubt the truth of this at a time where disharmony, violence and destruction reign supreme. The shift from one level of being involves chaos as the structures of the old are torn down and new ones erected. You are living at such a time. There is chaos on all fronts but underneath there are signs of massive shifts occurring. The evidence is all around.

Politicians no longer work in secrecy as they have done in the past. Politics is no longer a secure platform from which to launch into games with the intention of personal gain. Politicians and leaders of all kinds are being exposed for what they are. It is almost to the stage where they have only to think of wrongdoing and they are exposed. It is a very brave being, or a very foolish one, who steps into the political arena these days, believing that their secrets will be respected. Even the most secure bastions of power are being torn apart and subjected to ridicule.

Of course, this breaking down of secrecy has a destabilising effect. It is a confusing time. In chaos there will be suffering.

Imbalance on Earth is putting great strain on Earth. The climatic extremes are a symptom of imbalance and it is likely that these climatic extremes and abnormalities will become the norm for a period: destructive hurricanes where no hurricanes have ever occurred before, extreme variations in temperature, hail and tempests of ever-increasing violence, extended droughts and flooding. For those of you who have eyes to see, the evidence of this already exists.

The answer is in speeding up the learning, seeing the connections, remembering the decisions. As each person remembers, they facilitate others in doing the same. The effect is cumulative and exponential. Change starts slowly at first and then accelerates. Change is now accelerating at an ever-increasing rate.

You can choose to understand the causes or you can choose to resist. You have that choice. The more you resist, the more control you will need to exert. Some groups are doing this already. They are digging their heels in and saying, 'We're in control. We like things the way they were. Let's return to the old values.' They are becoming more aggressive in their marketing. The growth in fundamentalist church organisations is a prime example of this type of stance. They are aggressively marketing their beliefs and many are buying them because a return to church control seems to be the only answer in a world of uncertainty.

Don't judge. Just accept that what is happening is what is needed for this time. The experiences are what you need in order to learn.

§

I took the statement 'you can choose to understand the causes or you can choose to resist' as an instruction to discover why things were happening around the world in the way they were, but for years I ignored the message that I should start to investigate the causes of imbalance on Earth. Up until 2010 I accepted what I was told nightly on the TV news, and I didn't pay a lot of attention to what was going on beyond my areas of immediate interest: working with clients, learning about organic farming, establishing an organic market and attending to the day-to-day activities of running a farm.

My perspective changed when I gained access to the internet

and I started investigating alternative news sites. My curiosity was initially aroused when I came across information that led me to question the disparity between what I was hearing on mainstream news, and what I was learning from a variety of internet websites. These sources have since been called fake news, but after investigating a variety of topics I started to question which source of news was fake and which was closer to the truth. I discovered that the mainstream media omitted and manipulated significant details concerning world events in order to influence public attitudes. Significantly, when a particular point of view was being fostered, the same message was reinforced over and over again on television, internet and radio so that whatever was being told became the truth, apparently with the intention for it to be accepted without question.

§

When working with clients, resolution of problems occurred as a consequence of delving deeply to discover the 'truth' about what had happened in someone's life, as opposed to the 'truth' that made the clients feel comfortable. Much of the time the truth about past events was hidden, deliberately or as an unintended effect of reluctance to feel the appropriate response to behaviours that were totally unacceptable. Only when the truth was fully exposed did it become possible to resolve problems.

In the same way that individuals had covered up the truth, I suspected that the truth about both historic and current events had been and was being hidden or deliberately changed to make the account fit an agenda that we don't yet fully comprehend. Until this is understood, and the truth about such things as the invasion of Libya which I discuss in some detail, is exposed, little can be done to fix world problems.

§

Whilst I started delving into a variety of issues that were making world headlines, one event caught my attention early in 2011. An award was to be given by the United Nations General Assembly Human Rights Council in March, 2011 to Libya for its progress in human rights issues. What I read was supporting evidence collected by an investigative team from Senegal, Norway and Argentina which had been in Libya to verify information provided by Libya in support of the award. I found the information fascinating because I had not realised that Libya was a country that was making a great progress in areas of education, health and human rights.

I was aware that Gaddafi was a very contentious character and claims had been made that he used Libyan oil revenues for himself and his family. These claims may have been true but whether or not they were, they did not change the information relating to the award which was to be conferred on Libya only a few weeks prior to the planned invasion by NATO forces.

The information I read prior to the Libyan invasion totally contradicted what I was then hearing every day on the news. The invasion and destruction of Libya was justified in terms of Libya being under the control of an irrational and despotic dictator who was unpopular with the people of Libya and was treating them despicably.

From the assessment reports I read, I learnt that education in Libya was free and universal. Not only did children receive free primary and secondary schooling, but anyone who had the ability to pursue higher studies, was given the opportunity to study anywhere in the world. Higher education tuition fees were covered by the State as were living expenses, not just for the student, but for the student's family. At the time of the report 25% of school graduates were going on to university level study.

I learned that people were encouraged to own their own homes in Libya and that newlyweds were given $50,000 to help them establish their own home. Electricity was free for everyone and the price of petrol was extremely low. Loans were available at zero interest from the state-owned bank.

Health care was provided free and when babies were born, their mothers were given $5000 to cover the cost of caring for the infant.

Huge underground water resources had been discovered inland, and an industry had been established so that pipes could be manufactured to transport water to areas that were being developed to grow food. This was one of the largest irrigation projects in the world and people wanting to start farming were given free land and housing.

The reason why the people of Libya were being given so much was because Libya was rich in oil and the oil revenues were being used for the benefit of the Libyan people. The country had the highest standard of living of any country in Africa and it had no state debt. Decisions as to how the money was to be distributed was decided by the Libyan Arab Jamahiriya, or peoples' government, which included members from the different ethnic and cultural groups of Libya, who were selected by these groups to represent them. It seems that Gaddafi's major objective was to increase popular participation in local government and in 1988 he began to curb the power of the revolutionary committee and pursue an anti-fundamentalist Islamic policy.

§

The official report, given at the 16th Session of the United Nations General Assembly Human Rights Council contained impressive information and was subsequently published in the Universal Periodic Review under the title: Report of the Working Group on the Libyan Arab Jamahiriya (Document A/HRC/16/15). It highlighted such things as:
1) A legal framework that ensured promotion and protection of human rights including political, economic, social and cultural rights.
2) Women's rights guaranteed by legislation such that Libyan women occupied prominent positions in the public sector, the judicial system, the legal system, the police and the military.
3) Freedom of expression.
4) Programs to distribute wealth to low income families including monthly allowances, free services including

electricity, water and transport, domestic help and home services to people with special needs.

The information contained in the Human Rights Council Report, just weeks before Libya was invaded was in stark contrast to the stories that were being told in the mainstream media about Gaddafi. It did not support the United Nations suspension of Libya from the United Nations General Assembly following the invasion.

When I spoke to friends about what I had learnt, they didn't believe me. Seeking to substantiate what I was telling them, I returned to the internet to retrieve the information I had read a few months earlier. The assessment reports had been removed but the official documents could still be found. I could not find the original newspaper articles that had been written about the award, including one from the New York Times but a later, disparaging article, was still available. The *Sign of the Times*,[38] an alternative news website was the only non-United Nations reference I could find that substantiated what I had read.

Not surprisingly the award was not presented in March 2011. Fortunately, the story did not end there.

Returning to obtain information relating to the Libya invasion in 2019, I found that others had noticed the conflicting evidence regarding the invasion and had investigated the issue in great detail during the years that followed. Their research confirmed the details I discovered in relation to education

---

38 sott.net/article/236961-UN-Report-Offers-Smoking-Gun-Proof0of-NATO-and US-Lies-about Libya

benefits and health care that were provided prior to 2011, but they provided even more compelling evidence to support the suggestion that the stories told against Mummer Gaddafi being a despotic dictator who deserved to be killed, were lies.

At the time of the NATO invasion of Libya, Dr Udo Ulfkotte, a political scientist and journalist, was editor of a large circulation German Newspaper Frankfurter Allgemeine Zeitung. in 2014, Dr Ulfkotte testified on television that the Central Intelligence Agency ordered major Western newspapers and agencies to spread lies about Mummer Gaddafi in 2011 to justify foreign intervention in Libya under the pretext of protecting democracy and the Libyan people. Dr Ulfkotte personally received and then published an article written for the CIA against Gaddafi[39] and stated that *all German news agencies received orders from the CIA to write and publish articles and even report the news from the CIA.* In case of refusal to publish, Ulfkotte testified *they will leave their jobs or worse, will be threatened.* He went on public television in 2014 and stated that he was forced to publish the works of intelligence agents under his own name and said:[40]

'I've been a journalist for twenty-five years and I was educated to lie, to betray, and not to tell the truth to the public. But right now, within the last months, now the German and American media tries to bring war to the people in Europe, to bring war to Russia — this is a point of no return and I'm

39 katehon.com/articles/libya-2011-revolt-or-revolution
40 globalresearch.ca/world-class-journalist-spills-the-beans-admits-mainstream-media-is-completely-fake/5516749

going to stand up and say it is not right what I have done in the past to manipulate people, to make propaganda against Russia, and it is not right what my colleagues do and have done in the past because they are bribed to betray the people, not only in Germany, all over Europe.'

The Katehon website provided further details relating to the insurrection that was used as the excuse to invade. According to this website, on February 15, 2011 a program of propaganda was started on the internet with calls to oppose the Gaddafi regime. On the same day a human rights activist was detained for criticising the authorities. He was later released.

On February 16, thousands of Libyan demonstrators waving green State flags swept across the Jamahiriya in support of Gaddafi. These demonstrations were shown on Libyan TV. Western agencies reported that a popular uprising had occurred and argued that the people were protesting against the dictator. Numerous Western politicians, as well as the media, spoke of numerous protests against the Gaddafi regime and referring to Gaddafi as a 'bloody tyrant'.

On February 17, bloody attacks began against individual Libyan police officers, police stations and military barracks. At the same time the Western media began to assert that Gaddafi himself had started the insurrection by shooting at the people but it was the mercenaries that were shooting at unarmed policemen.[41]

---

41 globalresearch.ca/libya-10-things-about-Gaddafi-they-don't-want-you-to know/5414289

Chapter 19   Fake News

§

I have provided an account of what I discovered about events immediately prior to the Libyan invasion and of research that was done in the years that followed, in order to illustrate what I understand to be the methods that are being used to misinform the general populace about what is really happening around the world. I have supported this with evidence from the testimony of a well-regarded German reporter. Dr Ulfkotte died or was killed shortly after he gave his testimony.

Clearly some form of intimidation exists if countries can be persuaded to do a 90 degree turn, as Italy and Norway did when, after having commended Mummer Gaddafi for his achievement one week, they were prepared to label him a brutal dictator a few weeks later, and to be willing to kill him and those of his countrymen who supported him.

Having seen information manipulated in this way in one situation, I wondered whether this was something that was far more commonplace than I had realised. What I learnt about the way misinformation was being used to substantiate actions that, in this case, involved waging war, destroying cities and infrastructure and killing thousands of people, concerned me. I saw that information was removed from the internet if it contradicted the mainstream narrative, and I saw what I interpreted to be major misuse of power justified by lies.

Libya is not an isolated example of chaos inflicted by war, which has been justified by information that has later been shown to be untrue. Iraq was invaded because of a fabricated story about weapons of mass destruction, which were never found. Syria was invaded to overthrow a supposedly malevolent dictator who was reported to have poisoned his people but was subsequently re-elected as President by a large majority. President Trump has been vilified because of allegations of collusion with Russia and many have sought to impeach him for something that the comprehensive Mueller investigation has shown to be untrue. When misinformation is repeated over and over again via mainstream media outlets, people absorb the lies and become convinced that what they are being told is true. These lies are used to justify actions that lead to chaos.

There has to be a purpose for these sorts of things to be happening but before that purpose can be identified, it is necessary to look beyond the superficial reports that are published in mainstream newspapers and on television and discover the truth.

Chapter 20
Every Experience is for a Purpose

I have always believed that the Elohim's words that, 'every experience we have is for a purpose' were true and, once I understood this, I realised that even the worst events of our lives can be viewed in a positive way when we understand what these things are designed to teach us. Because of the holographic principle, I am convinced that the same holds true for world events. Understanding this, it is possible to believe that perhaps there is a reason that events, such as the invasion of Libya and the cover-up of the true reasons for that invasion, are occurring. Perhaps there is also a reason for destruction of the natural environment of Earth, for the transfer of Earth's wealth and resources into the hands of a very small group of people and for the constant waging of war. Perhaps events like this are happening for reasons that we don't yet understand. In saying this, I am not seeking to excuse the situation on Earth at present. I am contemplating that the purpose might be for us to learn from what is happening, to understand something *very* important and to provide us with the incentive to do something about it.

For individuals, the purpose for having even very unpleasant experiences might be so that they can learn something important that they have not previously understood. Alternately the events of their lives might bring to conscious awareness past life experiences that help explain current life situations. Experiences might awaken within them skills or knowledge that they have acquired in previous lifetimes or allow them to feel emotions that they have not allowed themselves to feel. Perhaps, on occasion, the purpose of the experience is to direct them to go in a direction that they would otherwise prefer not to go or to back them so far into a corner that they have no option but to do the things they would not consider doing otherwise.

Perhaps what is true for one, is true for all.

§

Because of what happened in my life I came to the conclusion that my life had a definite purpose and that the things that happened were not accidental. I realised that the experiences of my life were part of a plan, which would prepare me to fulfil my purpose by allowing me to understand things that I had not understood in previous lifetimes. Having done this, I would then be able to fulfil my higher purpose: contributing in a way that would allow people to understand things they had not understood previously.

I felt the information I channelled from the *Elohim*, some of which is referred to in *Everything in Its Place* was significant and as time passed I became convinced of the truth of the information I had received. The things that I was told would happen, actually did happen. Additionally, my life had unfolded in a way that suggested that the information I tapped into, during the meditation session I described in the Introduction to *Everything in Its Place*, actually foretold the direction my life was to take.

I found myself being directed along a path I felt destined to follow and I learned to trust that I was being guided in the direction that would allow me to achieve the purpose for which I was on Earth at this time. I met people who told me things that I needed to know. After a while, I expected things to happen in a synchronistic manner so that I would be guided in the steps I needed to take. When I needed knowledge to progress my understanding, it became available. When I needed to meet people that would assist me, they appeared. This is a fundamental premise of spiritual growth as outlined by Buddha: 'When the student is ready, the teacher will appear' and it is what I experienced and continue to experience in every aspect of my life.

One incident stands out. I had come across books written by Joseph Chiltern Pearce and I was fascinated by the philosophy that was expounded by this author. Chiltern Pearce's book that really caught my attention was *Evolutions End* published in 1992. It provided insight into how children should be raised. Joseph Chiltern Pearce was someone I really wanted to meet.

At the time I was living about two kilometres from the local shopping centre and I invariably chose to drive the car rather than walk to the shops. It was uphill and I was lazy. One Saturday morning I decided to walk to the shopping centre. On the way up the hill to the shops, my attention was drawn to a poster attached to an electricity pole. To my astonishment, the poster announced that Joseph Chiltern Pearce was giving a lecture in a neighbouring suburb that same night. I remember thinking that I must have been guided to walk to the shops that day and I was so fascinated by the fact that the poster had been placed near my house where I could see it that I paid particular attention from then on to see how many others I could find. The one that caught my attention was the only one I saw in the whole street.

That night I went to hear what Joseph Chiltern Pearce had to say and the room where he gave the lecture was full. I subsequently used *Evolutions End* as reference material for the practitioner training courses I ran.

§

I have been told that, from a very young age, I drove my parents to distraction because I always wanted to know *why*. Why are the stars up in the sky? Why do I have to wear the striped dress? Why is that person in a wheelchair? The tendency to ask *why* has continued throughout my entire life. No one seemed to have a satisfactory answer to the question: Why do some children have learning difficulties for no apparent reason? I had to work out that one for myself and the answer, when I found it, was not something I expected.

In view of my need to find out *why*, it is perhaps not surprising that I also wanted an explanation for why Earth's history is full of stories of war, destruction of people and land, greed and dishonesty. The answer 'It is the nature of Man' did not satisfy me because that explanation just led to my next question. 'Why is it the nature of man?'

Discovering answers to questions I posed for myself occupied much of my thinking time and I spent much of my life pondering on impossible to answer issues including why Earth's history focuses so often on the negative aspects of humanity. The following information from the Elohim provided a few clues.

There is an increasing awareness that life isn't all that we have been taught. Life is not an end in itself. Rather, it is the means by which we grow and develop spiritual awareness, which links us with each other, the Earth and the universe. As a learning tool it is unparalleled.

Experience allows us to tap into the cellular memories not only of our life histories, but also of the history of the world and indeed the whole universe. As we expand our own consciousness and awareness, we provide an opening for others to do the same. It is a cumulative process.

Memories are accessible to us as we develop and open up because by doing this, the range of frequencies available to us is expanded. Not only can we tap into an awareness of what is happening now, the past and the future are also available to us if we are prepared to tune in. All this is available to us. What stops us having the capability to tune in is our own disregard of the possibility that this is so, and our fear of the consequences of having such capabilities.

Memories are the means by which we retrieve information

in a way we can understand, from the vast storehouse of information available to us. Akashic records contain the knowledge of the universe. Our vibrational level permits us to access those parts of the akashic records that we are able to decipher and interpret in the light of our experience in this lifetime. It is for this reason that experience is such a valuable tool. Not only does it enable us to draw conclusions based on what we have experienced personally, it also enables us to tap into the vast libraries of humanity's experience relating to a specific issue. Again, the availability of this information depends on the individual's willingness to let go of their own ego and become one with universe, and their willingness to allow the knowledge of the universe to become their knowledge. Knowledge is not a static commodity. Through experience we build knowledge of the universe so that universe is ever expanding.

Imagine that knowledge is floating in a vast celestial library. It is contained as energy vibration. Just as television taps into the energy frequencies being transmitted by the TV station, our personal memory receiver is tuned into a particular band of frequencies, depending on our life experiences. If these experiences are of rape, incest and violence we will be allowed access to the universal knowledge relating to these issues. Our dreams will tune into this knowledge so we can experience these things and by doing so, process information. The fluttering of the eyes during REM sleep indicates that the frequencies are being accessed. This is what nightmares are all about: the integrating of our own *personal experience with the universal knowledge relating to our experiences. By feeling the terror, outrage and fear again and again, we gradually release the need to feel these particular emotional frequencies.*

Often the sense of outrage we feel at the actions of others allows us to tap into our own personal memories of outrage. Sensational journalism has a purpose beyond the selling of newspapers and TV time. Its usefulness is as a clearing mechanism.

§

When I started using the Stress Defusion process, my intention was to help people overcome problems that were making their lives difficult. By working with this process, I came to the conclusion that evolution occurs through learning and there is a brilliantly designed, logical plan in place to ensure that learning is maximised for each individual within each lifetime. It seems that the plan is that people come to Earth fully aware of why they are here, what they need to learn and what they need to do. They are aware that everything is in place to ensure that the purpose for each incarnation will be accomplished.

For all but a few, within a few years, because of the circumstances within the family and community they choose to be born into, they make decisions that are a denial of everything they have learnt and achieved up to this point in their soul's journey. Decisions such as, 'I'm stupid', 'I can't have what I want', 'Nobody loves me', or, 'Nobody listens to me,' work to frame their experiences from then on.

In consequence of making such decisions they separate themselves from who they are at the soul level, and their decisions represent a denial of what they know and what they can do. The purpose for doing this is put aside the skills and knowledge that have been acquired during their soul's journey up until that point. The reason that this happens is because if they were to retain the skills that they have already honed and the knowledge that they have acquired, their preference would be to use those skills and that knowledge, because by doing so they would obtain maximum benefit for least effort. By eliminating those things that they have already perfected, only areas in which there are deficiencies remain. Thus, their life purpose is to rectify one or more of those deficiencies, but people would not willingly make the effort to hone new skills or develop knowledge in areas that are unfamiliar, if they already have perfectly adequate skills and knowledge to use.

By denying the skills and knowledge that they have already developed, they must rely on what remains: poorly developed skills and a poorly developed knowledge base. Feeling inadequate and incompetent initially, in the same way that someone feels whenever he or she accepts the challenge of learning something new or doing something they've not done before, some people persevere and practise to acquire new skills and different knowledge in areas where they had none before. Unfortunately, many choose to accept the labels they have given themselves and make no effort to overcome them.

For many people, the initial experience of life is through being and feeling inadequate. If, for example, they deny their ability to communicate as I did, they are left with no option but to spend their time as observers of others. In this role they hone their ability to watch and analyse. Perhaps they learn to listen to what others say and perfect the skill of knowing who is telling the truth and who is talking nonsense. Over time, they become skilled in observation, an attribute that they did not previously possess. Gaining the skill or knowledge that they acquire by working in the area of greatest deficiency is their life purpose.

§

The situation continues for longer than it needs to when, having developed the skill that their life's experiences have been designed to teach them, many people retain the labels that they gave themselves when they were young: labels that correctly identified that they did not have the ability to do what they have come to Earth to do. If they decide, as a small child, that they are *not good enough*, no matter how well they perform, nothing they achieve, no matter how good it is, will ever be *good enough*. To change their perception of themselves as being someone who is not good enough, they need to revisit the original decision, realise that the decision was an accurate assessment of the situation at the time it was made and realise also that since that time, they have changed and become *good enough*. The decision that they originally made no longer applies.

The process that I have described is a generalisation. Some people have amazing skills and abilities from a very early age; skills that cannot have been learnt in this lifetime. They are gifted musicians, artists, philosophers, physicists and mathematicians from an early age. Some have psychic abilities or specific knowledge that goes far beyond what is normally expected. The difference between these children and most others is that, as a consequence of their upbringing, they retain some of the special gifts they had acquired in previous lifetimes, rather than denying them as most do. They retain their gifts and they are described as geniuses.

They are exceptions to the norm and their learning will be of a different nature from those who deny their skills and abilities. Perhaps their learning will be about humility verses arrogance, or about being accepted in spite of being different. Perhaps it will be about being scorned and ostracised for knowing things that others are unaware of, or their gifts are labelled as being a mark of the devil.

§

The plan that I have described is complicated by the fact that the family into which people are born provides them with a framework for their learning, and guarantees that background information they have available to them from past lives comes on-stream as a result of incidents and attitudes within the family. For many people, families provide them with the things they really don't want to experience: invalidation, judgement, ignorance, trauma, rivalry, jealousy, neglect, over-indulgence, or greed. Additional past life memories and responses will be triggered as they move through life.

As people grow, they learn through experience. For many people learning initially comes from experiencing the things that don't work. Gradually they build their knowledge or understanding in the areas they have designed this lifetime to teach them. Eventually, they reach a point where they are accomplished in whatever they have come to learn. The time it takes to do this will depend on the contribution that individuals have come to Earth to make, and on their willingness to trust that the path they need to follow is the right one for them.

Once they have completed their learning phase, they must release all judgements regarding the difficulty of the journey that has led them to this point. The reason for this is that when judgement is released, the skills and abilities that they had available to them when they were born, but which they denied as children, become available to them once again. Combining the skills and understandings that they have acquired in this lifetime with what they already knew or could do when they were born, causes an exponential shift in their abilities. From that point their challenge is to use their higher-level skills and understanding for the benefit of humanity.

The process I have outlined has been in place for a very long time. I suspect that relatively few have completed their mission but many will do so in this lifetime. We know the stories of some that have: Gandhi, Jesus, Buddha, Tesla, and Mandela for example. The good news is that, provided someone does the work that they need to do to develop the skills and understandings they have chosen to develop in this lifetime, they can move on to achieve their higher purpose.

As long as someone can reach a state of non-judgement about the challenges that they have chosen for themselves, and the way these challenges were set up for them, they have the opportunity, at some point, to regain the skills and knowledge that they have developed over lifetimes. The key is to accept their deficiencies and work within the limits that they provide until such time as they conquer the challenges that they have set for themselves. By doing this, they attract into their lives, experiences that will, eventually, allow them to learn whatever it is that they have come into this lifetime, to learn. At times they will have experiences that they would prefer not to have and these are the experiences from which they gain the most. When they do not learn, the experiences repeat, becoming more and more difficult each time and more and more painful. Eventually they learn what the experiences have been designed to teach them.

The process I have described may seem far-fetched, but I have personally experienced it and have seen it happen for others. I have used the Stress Defusion process to facilitate people make the transition from achieving their life purpose to working with their higher purpose.

The process is logical. Over many lifetimes people have worked hard to develop skills and understandings, and the work that they have done would have no value unless they have the ability to regain the skills and knowledge they have acquired in previous lifetimes — and to use them. It is my belief that this is what will enable the shift to a higher frequency for each individual. When the constraints that have been in place are removed, many will have the opportunity and ability to apply the knowledge and skills that they have gained but have not yet applied for the benefit of all.

§

If the process I have described is the plan that fosters individual growth and spiritual awareness for individuals, then it follows, applying the holographic principle, that this is also the plan for Earth. Dramatic shifts occur for individuals when they gain the insights that their experiences have been designed to teach them, let go judgement of the manner in which those insights have been gained and re-connect with past learnings. This may be similar to what is in store for Earth and its people.

The first step for people who are engaged in this process is to remember the experiences of their lives that have been forgotten. The process described provides an explanation for the frequency shift that is anticipated for Earth: a shift that has been foretold by many religions and cultures. It is also important, therefore, to uncover the truth about the history of Earth.

Chapter 21
Ancient History

The Stress Defusion process was significant for my own journey. It was valuable as a healing tool for myself and in using it, I helped many people. For me, the greater significance was that it gave me insights into the patterns of peoples' lives. I saw that life circumstances changed for my clients when they learned what the experiences their lives offered were designed to teach them. Stress Defusion also gave me the opportunity to access past life information, which provided me with a view of the history of Earth that was very different from what I had believed previously. Clients told me detailed stories of events as far back as the beginning of time. They were as surprised as I was when they accessed detailed information about events that were not included in Ancient History textbooks.

§

If, as I believe, Earth operates as a hologram, and we have experiences in order to develop our spiritual awareness, it follows that every experience of Earth is also for a purpose. My hypothesis is that the purpose is to enable the people on Earth to make the shift from 3rd to 5th dimensional frequency: a shift in spiritual awareness. This shift has been foretold by many cultures. Wanting to understand more, I looked at the history of Earth to find out as much as I could. In doing this, I didn't look to the sources that are commonly accepted. Instead, I looked at my own and my clients' past life memories, I looked at the revelations from well-known clairvoyants such as Edgar Cayce and I looked at alternative media sources, the ones that are labelled fake media. I researched archaeology discoveries.

Clients were able to see more clearly when they remembered the events of their past and understood that, by their thoughts and experiences, they had created the pathway to their present. Understanding how this had happened for individuals, I wondered whether the discoveries that are being made about civilisations that are far more ancient than anyone thought possible until recently, will provide the information the people of Earth need in order to understand that Earth's history is far longer and more complex than we have been led to believe.

As with individuals, whose memories of the past are buried deep within the subconscious, much of the information about Earth's past has been hidden, ignored and possibly distorted. This is changing. Awakening will occur when we understand who we were before the destruction of humanity which occurred as a consequence of the Younger Dryas Impact event that put an end to the last ice age but also wiped out advanced civilisations. A series of catastrophic floods due to the melting of ice caused sea levels to rise by 400 feet and forced scattered survivors to resettle in different areas of the world. It is this scenario that makes sense of the similarities of artefacts and building designs from a variety of different areas. Rulers or leaders, including Osiris, the Egyptian god and Quetzalcoatl, the legendary ruler of Toltec and Aztec cultures, are depicted as large beings with bird-like heads who carried what appear to be handbags but which might have had a variety of uses including one that has been suggested: communications devices much like our cell phones.

We have been taught that humans are descended from ape-like creatures. This may be true, but it is not the complete story.

§

Information is available from a variety of alternative sources, including:
1. Archaeological excavations and research studies
2. Clairvoyant Information
3. Past life Information
4. Manuscripts and ancient scrolls

The points I make below are not meant to be exhaustive. They are simply examples of the sort of things I discovered and thought were interesting.

1. Archaeological Excavations and Research

Recently developed technology has enabled the identification of past civilisations including:

a. Amazon cities and community networks

Remnants of large community networks that once existed in

the area that is now covered by the Amazon rainforest have been identified. What is now being discovered suggests that Earth's history goes back much further than the 6,000 years of recorded history.

b. Easter Island Statues

Easter Island statues that were thought to be the body and head of people have been excavated. It has been found that the statues are over 72ft tall and have been buried by natural sediments that took thousands of years to form. This indicates that the statues have been in place for far longer than was previously thought.

c. Water Erosion near the Sphinx

The walls around the Sphinx in Egypt, which reveal weathering caused by heavy rain over thousands of years indicates that the Sphinx is at least 10,500 years old, which contradicts the information we have been given about the age of this monument.

d. Gobekli Tepe

Excavations at Gobekli Tepe in Turkey are generating great interest because this site is thought to be 12,000 years old. The site contains massive pillars weighing 20 – 60 tons topped with stone blocks that weigh 10 tons. The site is thought to have been, among other things, an ancient observatory for monitoring the night sky. Some pillars are decorated with animal drawings and one, called the Vulture Stone, has animal carvings that correspond to astronomical constellations.

Curiously, this pillar pre-dates the buildings at Gobekli Tepe and was thought to be built in 11,000 BCE. Carvings on pillars also show a swarm of comet fragments hitting Earth. Called the Younger Dryas Impact event this is thought to have been the cause of a mini ice age that changed civilisation. Interestingly, iconography found at Gobekli Tepe is also found at megalithic sites around the world.

The Gobekli Tepe site pre-dates the Younger Dryas impact event and there is evidence that it was the site of an advanced civilisation for nearly 3,000 years. The site was backfilled and covered before being abandoned.

e. South African Stone Circles

In southern Africa, thousands of stone circles are thought to provide archaeological proof of ancient civilisations who possessed knowledge relating to harmonic frequencies. Adam's Calendar is a place where stone walls amplify the quartz/silica components of stone walls to become powerful energy generators. This amplification creates moving sound frequencies and magnetic anomalies that in turn create electro-magnetic fields in the same way that sound creates visible patterns within iron filings spread over a smooth surface. This indicates that ancient people knew how to take the subtle sound frequencies of the surface of earth and amplify them to resonate with the Prime Resonance Frequency of Earth.

In an interview with *Gaia* on January 8th, 2016, Michael Tellinger, who realised the significance of the stone circles, said:

'It is possible and probable that the smaller elongated stones were most likely used in activating a standing wave when placed in a circle, where they were activated somehow: possibly by the stones being placed in a torus in the middle and emitting a powerful frequency into the smaller surrounding stones. These resonating stones, placed in a circle, are then activated by the ash placed in the centre, like sand on a metal plate, which create the cymatic patterns to show the shape of the flow of the sound energy coming out of the earth. The walls were then packed along the lines of the cymatic pattern to amplify the subtle frequencies in the walls – and to create powerful electromagnetic fields and frequencies in very high decibels. The stone circles give off frequencies in the gigahertz range and as high as 30,000 decibels. This is a very powerful energy source that we cannot fathom yet.'

Michael Tellinger's conclusions confirm thinking that the chambers within the Egyptian pyramids also acted as acoustic devices designed to amplify sound.

f. Bosnian Pyramids

I read about pyramids near Sarajevo in Bosnia, and then had the opportunity to listen to a lecture by Sam Osmanagic, who recognised that landforms that were familiar to him were, in fact, pyramids. Because I was in Europe at the time, I was able to visit the pyramids and see for myself whether or not they were natural landforms as has been claimed by sceptics. Many academics dispute Sam Osmanagic's claims that they are pyramids designed to generate energy in much the same way that the stone circles of Africa were designed to do, but scientific testing has proven that energy is being emitted from within the pyramids.

I saw that the sides of the pyramid were covered in huge slabs of rocks that had been fitted together precisely in order to maintain the angle of the slopes. I meditated for hours in the tunnels that are under the pyramids, and saw the work being done to excavate the gravel that was used to fill the tunnels in the same way the site at Gobekli Tepe had been covered. What I saw led me to conclude that, at the very least, the pyramids were natural hills that had been modified to exactly replicate the pyramid shape.

g. Pyramids in the Antarctic

On the internet I have seen photographs of pyramids that have emerged from the ice in Antarctica and have read about some of the strange underground cavities and artefacts that have been discovered there. Having read of many well-known people including 86 year-old astronaut Buzz Aldrin, the American politician, John Kerry, Prince Harry of England, Russian Orthodox Church leader Patriarch Kirill and Australian Governor General Sir Peter Cosgrove visiting Antarctica in late 2016 and during 2017, I suspected that something very interesting had been found there. John Kerry visited Antarctica on the day of the 2016 US Presidential election. Patriarch Krill visited in February, 2017. It is obvious that discoveries such as the ones I have outlined above indicate that evidence relating to the history of ancient Earth is not yet fully documented or understood.

2. Clairvoyant Information

American clairvoyant Edgar Cayce became well known because of his predictions relating to the U.S stock market crash, the date of the start of World War II, the return of the Jewish people to Israel and the discovery of the Dead Sea Scrolls. For forty years he did daily readings until he died in 1945. He spoke at length about Atlantis.

Amongst the detailed records of Cayce's predictions and information about historical events and future predictions, there are several references to the use of crystals and sound waves for healing, and to the amplification power of crystals. Cayce referred to 'the entity' in several descriptions of past civilisations, and it seems that when he talks about 'the entity' he is referring to himself in a past incarnation, and the information he provided is what he remembered from having lived during those times:

> *And the entity aided in establishing the temple through which there was hoped to be the appearance again of the children of the Law of One, as they listened to the oracles that came through the stone, the crystals that were prepared for communication in what we know now as radio.*[42]

Cayce spoke of energy being harnessed from the sun with

---

42 Reading 3253 — 2 (25) bibliotecapleyades.net/esp-cayce-3.htm#contents

crystals, and it was misuse of the power of crystal energy that caused a catastrophic disaster, the result of which was that the land that was called Atlantis became submerged,

> '...the first destructive influences used by the Sons of Belial, when the influences of the sun were crystallised through the crystal that then controlled the motivational forces in the experiences.'[43]

I don't doubt the connection Cayce makes between harnessing the sun's energy with crystals and the destruction of Atlantis. The danger of abusing advanced crystal technology was the focus of my past life memories of Atlantis.

According to Cayce, two rival groups fought for control of Atlantis. One group, the Sons of Belial, wanted to exploit Earth's natural resources for material gain. The other group, called the Children of the Law of One, wanted to return to a stewardship of the land that was based on spiritual laws.[44] I have no confirmation that Laws that Cayce refers to are the same as those I channelled from the Elohim, and which are the subject of my first book *Final Days of Judgement*, but I suspect that they are. The focus of the conflict in Atlantis was the half-awake sub-humans, who were used as slave labour and in sacrifice. The Sons of Belial wanted to use those from other lands as slaves and keep those who were not of their own kind, in ignorance.

> There were those places where there came eventually the

---

43 Reading 877-26 bibliotecapleyades.net/esp-cayce-3.htm#contents

44 historicmysteries.com/edgar-cayce-atlantis/

necessity of offering human sacrifices which when put into fires became the ashes that we cast upon the waters for the drinking of the same by those who were made prisoners from portions of other lands.[45]

Patterns repeat in terms of peoples' lives, but they also repeat on a much broader scale. What Earth is presently working through seems to parallel what happened in Atlantis, twelve thousand years ago. The story of Atlantis and information relating to Poseida, a city of Atlantis, including a detailed description of its layout and physical appearance, was outlined in two Socratic dialogues called [46]Timaeus and Critias written at around 360 BCE written by Plato.[47] Plato also wrote of the destruction of a highly evolved civilisation by tidal waves, volcanic eruption and then submersion.

3. Past Life Information

I have personally accessed a variety of past life memories of times far back in history. One vivid past life memory is of Atlantis at a time prior to its destruction. My memory is of rebelling against the use of crystals by the leaders who intended to use them to avert some impending disaster. I lost the argument and was cast into dungeons and subsequently I drowned. During a session when I went back to the time of

---

45 Reading 364 bibliotecapleyades .net/esp-cayce-3. htm#contents
46 https://sarahwestall.com/alien-elohim-created-and-still-control-modern-humans-w-maur
47 thoughtco.com/plato-atlantis-from-the-timaeus-119667

Atlantis, I accessed my extreme anguish because I knew that the arrogance of the Atlantean hierarchy and their extremely left brain emphasis on technical solutions involving crystals to correct an impending disaster was doomed to failure. The information available to me wasn't clear but the sensation of impending catastrophe involving flooding was very strong.

On another occasion, when I was training someone to use the Stress Defusion technique, my student inadvertently enabled me to go into another very vivid past life memory. The information I accessed was that as a mixed-race slave. I chose to help extra-terrestrial beings who were mining the gold. I did this because I was impressed by their knowledge and I wanted to learn what they knew. I didn't know who these beings were at the time I accessed these memories but subsequently identified them as the Annunaki. The location was in the Middle East, in the area that was the location of the ancient cities of Sumer, Babylon and Ur, which became technologically advanced within a short period of time.

Because I chose to help these beings, I was regarded as a betrayer of the Earth people. I have no memories of what the Annunaki looked like, but when I accessed memories of that time, I recognised them as very powerful and a great source of information about things that were not known about on Earth back then. Having acquired as much knowledge as I could gain from them, I chose to use my newly acquired knowledge in an attempt to free the mixed extra-terrestrial/human slaves. I failed. The rebellion failed. The people who worked as gold miners all had their eyes put out. Additionally, I had both my hands chopped off. I was told that one hand was chopped off for betraying the humans. The other was chopped off for betraying the extra-terrestrial beings to whom I had sworn allegiance. For days after the session that gave me access to this story, I had no use of my arms. It was as if they didn't exist. Loss of feeling and movement in my arms provided me with confirmation that the story, as far-fetched as it seemed to be, was probably true. Losing the use of my arms also provided me with confirmation that trauma is held in the body for lifetime after lifetime.

Later, to my surprise, stories similar to the one I had accessed were told to me by several clients who had no knowledge that I had possessed similar information and told their stories from a different perspective to my own. Years later, I read of accounts of the Annunaki which gave me confirmation that they had existed and were not figments of my imagination.

Because I had accessed this information, and because it had been confirmed by clients and by my own physical reaction to releasing the trauma associated with my own personal story, I accepted that there might be some basis to it. It seemed possible that there have been times during Earth's history when people of Earth handed control of their lives to extra-terrestrial beings that they thought of as gods, because they were in awe of them.

§

Author Zecharia Sitchin translated the Sumerian Cuneiform tablets, and his 1976 book *Twelfth Planet* confirms this story. Although there is much controversy about whether Sitchin's translations are accurate, what is true is that the tablets do exist. Many are in the British Museum. According to Sitchin, the stories in the texts, written on clay tablets, are of extra-terrestrial beings from the planet Niburu who came to Earth to mine gold because their planet was dying, and gold was needed to seed the atmosphere. This confirmed the information I accessed; mixed origin humans, and I was one of them, were mining gold for extra-terrestrial beings. That is what I learned when I went back into that past life experience, prior to which I had no knowledge that gold had been mined by extra-terrestrials or even that they had come to Earth. In fact, prior to this experience, I scoffed at the idea and judged it as preposterous. Now, I'm not so sure.

4. Manuscripts and Ancient Scrolls

Because I regarded the idea that the Annunaki came to Earth to control it for a considerable period of time as being very strange, I was surprised to discover that there is evidence from a variety of different sources to support the idea that this may actually have happened.

In 1945, sealed earthen jars containing a collection of 13 ancient manuscripts were discovered at a place called Nag Hammadi in Upper Egypt. Archaeologists discovered that the jars had been hidden around 400 CE by people called Gnostics. Presumably this had been done to preserve the information contained in the manuscripts for fear that the information would be destroyed. Their fear was justified. The great library of Alexandria, believed to be a storehouse of immensely valuable historical information, was destroyed by fire sometime between 385 and 412 BCE. The story is that manuscripts from the library were burnt to provide fuel for the bathhouses and the library buildings themselves were also burned. Roman leaders were not interested in information that did not support their ambitions.

The manuscripts found at Nag Hammadi refer to rulers of immense power who were manipulating human society. The name given to these rulers was Annunaki. These beings were also referred to as Archons, a term that means *rulers* in Subakhmimic and Sahidic languages. According to the writings in the manuscripts, the Annunaki saw themselves as all-powerful, and the rightful rulers of Earth. Coptic and Sahidic translations of one of the documents, the Hypostasis of the Archons 93.22, the title of which means The Reality of the Rulers says: 'I have sent this to you because you enquire about the reality of the authorities.'

This statement led me to realise that the source of some or all of the information contained in these manuscripts must have come as a channelled message, in much the same way that information was given to me. The manuscript continues:

'The chief is blind; because of his power and his arrogance he said, with his power 'It is I who am God; there is none apart from me.' When he said this, he sinned against the entirety.'

By allowing others to think of them as gods, the rulers, who may well have been extra-terrestrial beings, distorted reality and hid the truth of who they really were, from humanity.

The Nag Hammadi scrolls pre-date the version of the Bible that was authorised by the Emperor Constantine in 325 CE. The scrolls have been studied exhaustively. In 2018, Donald M Blackwell published a book called the *Annunaki Bible*. Blackwell asserts that the current version of the Bible, agreed upon at the Council of Nicaea is a version of the *Code for Life* that is of Annunaki origin. In his book, Blackwell overlays the texts contained in the Bible with the texts found at Nag Hammadi, revealing that both sources are identical in content. However, the Nag Hammadi scrolls pre-date the Bible. Blackwell states:

'What you will find, in our opinion, without question, is that the vast majority of the Bible is, empirically speaking the plagiarised words of the ancient texts and other ancient writings.'

If this is true, as Blackwell asserts, this information could undermine the basis of all Judeo-Christian and Muslim belief systems.

The work of Mauro Biglino, Italian scholar of religious studies who researched the 'sacred texts' for the Vatican Publishing House for over thirty years, suggests that Blackwell's assertions may well be true. Biglino, who worked on translating 17 volumes of the Old Testament until 2018, asserts that the original Hebrew Bible and old testament was not a religious document, but rather a historic text on the origins of homo sapiens. Biglino states that the documents were all about creation but were not the word of

God. According to Biglino, God is never mentioned in the original documents. The documents refer to one person called Yahweh, one of the Elohim who are men of flesh and blood beings from somewhere other than Earth. He claims that the original texts explain that human beings were genetically modified and created by an advanced race using genes from advanced alien races and primates. Cloning was referred to in the original documents that Biglino translated and it was explained in these documents that the purpose for cloning of mixed origin beings was to create slaves who could be controlled. Biglino understood that the story in the Bible was about the area in the Middle East but that on all continents there are stories of children born with and possibly created from extra-terrestrial and adamite (human) DNA.

§

Surprisingly, clients have revealed past life memories which substantiate this hypothesis. Their stories didn't make sense when they described their memories to me originally, but now they do.

'Where are you Lucy?'

'I'm not sure. It's some sort of laboratory.'

'Are you one of the technicians?'

'No. I'm a baby. Or I might not even be a baby. I might still be an embryo. I'm one of many. There are lots of babies in things that look like incubators. I'm very sad.'

'What are you sad about?'

'I'm not good enough to survive.'

'What do you mean, you're not good enough to survive?'

'I'm just not good enough. My body isn't firm enough. It's like jelly. It didn't form properly.'

'So, you really aren't good enough, are you? You can't survive and grow.'

'No. That's why I feel so sad.'

'Perhaps in that lifetime you actually weren't good enough. You've needed time to become perfect and that's what has happened. It might have taken a lot of time, but now you've become good enough. The only problem is that you are still carrying the 'I'm not good enough' label you gave yourself way back then and you've held onto the sadness of that time. It was true then but is it still true?'

'No. I've become good enough to survive and grow. I've even been good enough to have children of my own.'

'Where are you holding the sadness connected to the idea that you're not good enough?'

'In my heart.'

'Can you thank your heart for holding onto that sadness for many, many lifetimes and tell your heart that you are now prepared to feel the sadness. It doesn't have to hold onto it any longer.'

'Yes. I can do that.'

'How do you feel now that you've let the sadness go?'

'I feel different. Lighter, somehow.'

Mauro Biglino left the Vatican publishing house in 2018 and

started speaking publicly about the conclusions he reached from working on translating the original documents. In interviews, he claims that he didn't discover anything new, rather he just deciphered what was written. In interviews he has also stated his belief that senior Jewish rabbis are aware of the information he uncovered explaining that rabbis choose to claim that the Bible is a translation of the word of God, because by convincing people that this is true, they gain power. Shortly after going public about his findings Mauro Biglino died, or possibly was killed to silence him but not before many of his interviews and lectures were published on the internet.[48]

§

Recently uncovered ancient history information suggests that:
1. Earth's history spans a period far longer than we have been led to believe.
2. Earth's history is complex and evidence exists that civilisations existed thousands of years ago that were, in some respects, more technologically advanced and the people were more spiritually aware than we are now.
3. The human population of Earth may be of mixed extra-terrestrial and human origin and the problems we are experiencing now, might have their origins in events that took place a long time ago.

---

48 https://sarahwestall.com/alien-elohim-created-and-still-control-modern-humans-w-maur

4. Cataclysmic events forced advanced civilisations to backtrack and disperse so that evolution has not been the gradual process that Darwin's Theory of Evolution suggests.

Chapter 22
Holographic Patterns

I have mentioned that patterns repeat over time and over every level of generality as in a hologram. The Elohim refer to patterns in the following way:

There is a pattern to everything. To identify the pattern, you have first to remember the bits: the infinite variety of tiny pieces of information that weave together. Being able to see the pattern requires the abilities of right brain processing. Fitting the little bits together within the right brain framework requires left-brain processing. It only gets put together as a whole when integration occurs. First remember. Then identify the learnings. Then see the application through space and time.

Over and over again, I have seen that life patterns repeat until whatever lessons can be learnt from the experiences that are part of the pattern, are learnt. That was something that was clearly demonstrated by individual clients. If the principle of the hologram is valid in terms of the organisation on Earth, this idea applies to Earth and the universe as a whole.

Wanting to understand the patterns of the Earth, I looked at the patterns within individual lives to see whether these provided clues regarding the patterns for Earth as a whole. In summary, the patterns seem to be that we are born with total understanding of our soul's journey, but soon after birth we forget what we have learnt. We are born into a family which provides the understanding we need to identify and complete our life purpose, because our purpose is signposted by patterns within our family of origin and in particular the patterns demonstrated by our parents. When, at some time in our life, we gain understanding of something that we have not understood previously, the 'something' that constitutes our life purpose, we can then proceed to fulfil our higher purpose. Problems occur when we 'forget' important information which provides clues as to the purpose for our experiences in this lifetime.

In chapter 21, I presented evidence from a variety of sources that the humans may be the mixed heritage offspring of a powerful, spiritually aware and intellectually advanced extra-terrestrial people called the Annunaki and native beings who evolved on Earth. It is the only conclusion that makes sense of archaeologic discoveries indicating that highly evolved civilisations existed on Earth far earlier than was possible if people on Earth developed according to the timeline that has been generally accepted. It is the only explanation for the ancient written accounts that are in existence. It explains past life memories.

If this is true, then our 'parents' were hugely different in terms of their life skills and understandings. Our job, as descendants of these two groups has been to reconcile their totally different aspects.

It appears that one group, the Annunaki, might have been highly skilled technically, highly evolved spiritually, but lacking in compassion for others or for their environment. Their skills and abilities are typical of people who are left brain dominant and who take leadership roles in today's society. The other group, who I call the aborigines, or original people, were attuned to the needs of the planet and able to live without exploiting and destroying available resources. They would have lived in close community groups and cared for members of their community in the same way that they do today. They were also evolved spiritually in that they had the ability to communicate telepathically and tune in to 'the dreamtime'. These attributes are evident today in the native peoples of Earth who live in remote environments. People of Australian aboriginal, African and South American cultures have a spiritual awareness far beyond the average westerner. They also have a very close association and respect for the natural world that the rest of us have little understanding of. Their skills and abilities are typical of people who are right brain dominant.

It is my hypothesis that each group represented the attributes of people who are either right or left brain dominant and a society of mixed race heritage will only reach full potential when the attributes of each are integrated in the same way that individuals who are left or right brain dominant are only capable of reaching their potential when both hemispheres are integrated. I believe the people of Earth, descendants of both groups, have access to information from both ancestor groups but are unable to access and integrate this information while they remain separate.

If an extra-terrestrial race inhabited Earth for a long period of time, as the evidence suggests, it was because Earth was perceived as a source of raw materials needed to sustain a planet that was endangered. It would appear that the inhabitants of this planet were not good caretakers. Patterns repeat. We, their descendants, are not good planetary caretakers either. This is one of the important lessons that we have needed to learn, but haven't yet done so.

If humans were bred as a source of slave labour, it explains why humans continue to have an issue with slave labour, because we haven't learnt the lesson that slavery is an abomination.

If the Annunaki came to Earth to take what they wanted, it explains why some groups of people on Earth still believe that they can take what they want from others. The pattern of greed and theft still operates. The lessons have not yet been learnt.

As a race, we do not have the intellectual capabilities of the Annunaki or the technical know-how. We cannot move huge weights by thought as they must have done in order to build some of the structures that still stand. Neither do we have the spiritual awareness that is a feature of the indigenous cultures that have evolved from the original Earth beings or the connection with the natural world. In forgetting what our forebears knew we have given ourselves a major challenge and the pathway we have chosen to meet that challenge has been a very demanding one.

§

Working with clients, one of the patterns that I observed over and over again was that people frequently gave their power to others for a variety of reasons. I told the story of Alice in chapter 10. For years, she worked to provide for the needs of others who were dependent on her: her partners, her children, other peoples' children and her partners' children. What can be learned from stories like the one Alice tells is that when someone works primarily for the benefit of others, they develop strength, perseverance and resilience. Those who rely on the efforts of others to provide them with the things in life that they believe will make them happy, become progressively weaker. The beneficiary of these types of situations is actually the one who starts out in a subservient role and through hard work over a period of time gains attributes they desire for themselves.

It would be nice to think that people are sufficiently motivated to work hard without some incentive, but that isn't the case. Some form of incentive generally needs to apply. The incentive for some is money: the means to purchase security and/or prestige. For others the incentive is power and control. The motivation for many is survival: the need to create or purchase the essentials for life. For others, it takes a different form: subjugation to the will of others. Another group work to help those who have fallen by the wayside and need help.

The motivators I have listed are what keep most people working. The problem is that the work many people do contributes to the power and prestige of those who are already powerful. By contributing their skills and knowledge to those who already own and control so much, people perpetuate an unfair system. This does not seem to be a good idea but perhaps there is a purpose for this to happen as it does. I believe that the situation will continue in the same way it has in the past, until it becomes totally obvious that the pathway the people of Earth are following at present is leading to total destruction. Only when the destruction that is becoming increasingly obvious starts to have a devastating impact will things really change. The time has not yet come for this to happen but it is getting closer.

If there is purpose for everything that happens, as I believe there is, then the pattern I have described must be in place to enable us to learn something significant. If, as I also believe, the purpose for life is to grow intellectually, physically, emotionally and spiritually then it follows that these things don't happen by sitting back and waiting for them. Growth comes from hard work over a long time. The motivation for doing the work might be the motivation that comes from being powerless, but the form the motivation takes is irrelevant. However, whilst we hold onto judgement about the situation that motivates us, or even forces us to do the work needed to move us from weakness to a position of strength, we stay stuck in blame and resentment.

§

Applying this idea to what has happened on Earth, we can see that for most if not all of Earth's history certain groups of people have dominated, enslaved and controlled others so that those in positions of power benefit disproportionately from the work of others. This is the situation on Earth now. There is a small group of people who have control over the majority of the population and most of Earth's resources. To a large degree, they are the descendants of people who have held positions of control and authority for a very long time.

The small number of powerful groups that control governments, the media, the military machine and most, if not all, of the world major international corporations, are fighting to stay in control. Whilst in the past, brutality has been the main tool of control, now much more subtle advanced technologies are available to use against the general population: mind control, media control, directed energy weapons, chemtrails, HAARP energies, thermonuclear devices, 5D communications technology, surveillance technology, bio-engineering, genetic modification and agricultural pesticides and herbicides. Whilst these technologies are promoted in terms of being helpful, they have significant negative downside and many are being used to the detriment of the general population. Advanced technology, and the willingness to use it against those who oppose them is why people are frightened to confront the powerful elite, but a growing number of people are doing it regardless of the danger.

§

What is happening on Earth today starts to make sense when we realise that there are a number of global issues that are coming to peoples' awareness and as each is healed, the population is shifting in terms of energy frequency. In the same way that people need to feel the emotion associated with particular life events, so too, does the population of the world need to feel emotions that are associated with these issues. This is happening as world events are brought to public awareness through news programs, films, documentaries or as a consequence of being involved in real life and death dramas. As the truth of appalling events, strategies designed to control and manipulate humanity are exposed, people are feeling confused, shocked, even traumatised as they comprehend the evil that has been perpetrated. Only when the truth is finally exposed do they see the level to which people have been prepared to sink in order to maintain control and dominance. But it will take this level of evil and horror for us to feel the enormity of the sins of the world and this is something we are being prepared for. Only when we truly comprehend this, can we let go the need for the evil in the world to continue.

I believe it is important to understand why this is happening and what the events of today's world are designed to teach us. Subjugation to the will of others is never a good place to be in but subjugation is a wonderful motivator for action. Forced into conditions of poverty and virtual servitude by a group that are now being identified as greedy and self-serving, people are resisting and, in some cases, they are fighting back. Resistance and appropriately expressed anger by the many, if it goes on for long enough, will bring down governments who act to preserve the power of the elite but fighting back is probably not the best course of action. Exposure to the truth of what has led to this situation, should be sufficient to bring down the ruling elite. This is already happening. The secrets that have allowed the elite to hold onto their positions of power are being disclosed, and the truth is being revealed. Dealing with information that is undermining the authority of the churches, legal and government institutions, is challenging and unsettling.

Bringing down those who now have control will not take Earth to the next level unless we also learn why the strategies that they have used, are inappropriate. Fighting back is an example of exerting pressure, which is only appropriate in a society where service to self outweighs other considerations. The shift must be created, not from a victim/saviour mentality, but from a viewpoint that encompasses acceptance, release of resistance, allowing and compassion rather than force and manipulation.

Today's elite do not represent themselves as gods, but they create an illusion of personal power that is false. They manipulate information and they use threat and intimidation to keep people from standing in their own power. Fear has been one of the tools used to ensure a compliant population. The irony is that use of fear is a double-edged sword. To escape the burden of fear and the guilt that people feel as a result of things they have done at the behest of the elite, they are now taking steps that allow them to release the fear. This is happening for many and the number is growing. These are the whistle-blowers who are coming forward to tell the truth of what they have done, what has been done to them and what they know.

§

The important question is: What is all this meant to teach us?

My observation of clients is that people who take a subservient role either submit and become weaker or they gain in strength and start to assert their own authority. Those who use adverse situations to their advantage, eventually become stronger than those they previously thought of as being superior or who thought of themselves as being superior. Doing the work that is required of them allows them to grow physically, emotionally, intellectually and spiritually. The incentives used to enforce the learning that has occurred, is immaterial in the greater scheme of things.

The journey that provides them with the opportunity to learn is important because, having undertaken this journey, they know what it is like to be enslaved or subjected to the humiliation of being perceived as inferior. By having this experience, they can recognise that subjecting others to the sort of experiences that they have had to suffer is unfair. Eventually they realise that they are equally important as those who have perceived them as slaves, or as 'inferior' beings.

The *Elohim* describe the imperative of equality in the following passage:

Everything in the universe is of equal value. No one is more or less important. Nothing is more or less important.

Equality brings into play the idea that everything has a purpose and shall be looked at in this way without judgement. Judgement causes us to label things and people and put them into boxes thereby causing separation. Sometimes the judgements are harsh enough to cause us to build physical boxes in the institutions where high walls and security systems enforce the separation.

Could what has happened during the course of Earth's history have been designed with the purpose of ensuring spiritual growth for all mankind I wondered? Will we awaken when we realise that everyone and everything is of equal value and that the 'Earth parent' and the 'extra-terrestrial parent' races both had important contributions to make — and that neither group was inferior or superior, just different? Will the people of Earth shift to 5th dimensional reality when the attributes of both sets of 'parents' are integrated in the same way that for individuals, a huge shift occurs when left and right brain hemispheres are integrated? I wondered whether the shift in human evolution would be of the same magnitude of mental competence that happens when both left and right sides of the brain are integrated: from being able to process 2,560,000 bits of information compared with 40 which is 'normal' for many people.

To discover if there was any merit in these thoughts, I investigated a variety of sources in order to discover what conclusions others had come to regarding significant events of Earth's history and to see whether the conclusions I had reached were confirmed by the findings of others.

One source that supported my ideas was the Nag Hammadi scrolls that I referred to in chapter 21 and to make my next point, I need to digress a little and explain what happened for clients when they looked at judgements that they had held about themselves. When they recalled a decision such as *I'm not clever enough* that they had made when they were young, they also realised that the decision they had made at that time was an accurate assessment of their abilities at the time. They were not clever enough to do what they wanted to do, or what others required of them. They needed time to acquire the knowledge, skills and expertise, which would make them clever enough, or good enough. That is what many did in the years following the event when they made original decision. They worked hard to develop the skills and knowledge that they lacked when they were younger.

Years later, because they hadn't reviewed their original decision, they still held onto the idea that they were not clever enough to do what they wanted to do, even though, by that time, they were definitely capable of doing what they were unable to do when they were young. They still held onto the shame that they had felt when they acknowledged, as a small child, that they were inadequate, even though the reasons for feeling inadequate no longer applied. It was this judgement and shame that stopped them from achieving their goals once they acquired the skills and knowledge that they originally lacked. The decision they made as a small child was still operating but the reasons for it to do so no longer applied.

Applying the logic of this scenario to a much larger scale,

it is possible to understand that the original mixed-race population of Earth beings controlled by the Annunaki may not have been evolved beings. Possibly, the mixed-race humans were not as intellectual or as spiritually aware as the rulers who were of extra-terrestrial origin. They needed time to evolve so that they could reach a level of awareness and assume responsibility for their own wellbeing. It may have taken thousands of years, but I suspect that this is what has happened in the intervening period. Humanity has evolved to a sufficient level of spiritual awareness to make the transition to 5th dimension reality, but it is stuck because the negative programs that were put in place thousands of years ago, are still operating in the same way that they do for individuals who do not go back and review the origins of their negative thought patterns.

This idea led me to look at some excerpts from the Nag Hammadi scrolls:

This the spirit ordained when he first planned that man should experience the great evil, which is death, and that he should experience all the evils that come from this and, after the deprivation and cares which are in these, that he should receive of the greatest good, which is life eternal. That is, firm knowledge of the Totalities and the reception of all good things.

And also, the following passage from the Tripartite Trachtate.

Those who will be brought forth from the lust for power which is given to them for a time and for certain periods, and who will give glory to the Lord of glory, and who will relinquish their wrath, they will receive the reward for their humility, which is to remain forever. Those, however, who are proud because of the desire of ambition, and who love temporary glory, and who forget that it was only for certain periods and times which they have that they were entrusted with power, and for this reason did not acknowledge that the Son of God is the Lord of all and Saviour, and were not brought out of wrath and the resemblance to the evil ones, they will receive judgment for their ignorance and their senselessness, which is suffering, along with those who went astray, anyone of them who turned away; and even more [for] wickedness in doing to the Lord things which were not fitting, which the powers of the left did to him, even including his death.

They persevered saying, 'We shall become rulers of the universe, if the one who has been proclaimed king of the universe is slain,' [they said this] when they laboured to do this, namely the men and angels who are not from the good disposition of the right ones but from the mixture. And they first chose for themselves honour, though it was only a temporary wish and desire, while the path to eternal rest is by way of humility for salvation of those who will be saved, those of the right ones.

What is suggested in the Nag Hammadi scripts is that spiritual evolution comes from a position of humility, rather than from a position of lust for power. The scripts state that, *'the path to eternal rest is by way of humility'* will only become an option when the lessons that can be learnt by experiencing

Chapter 22 Holographic Patterns

being controlled by greedy, power hungry individuals have been learnt. If others rise up to positions of power and control before the lessons are learnt, mankind will need to go back and re-do this episode of the journey towards enlightenment. Repetition of similar experiences, in different ways, is how Karma works for an individual, until that individual understands what those experiences were designed to teach. The principle for the people of Earth has to be the same.

Whilst people sit in judgement of those who operate from greed, from needing to be powerful, from selfishness and from ego they do not stop and consider that these attributes exist within almost everyone. Those who live on Earth demonstrate elements of these characteristics and that is where change needs to start: with the individual. Resolution will come from understanding that the problems on Earth are a reflection of the imbalances that exist within each person.

There is only one solution, and that is to heal the greed, the need to be in control and the addictions within each of us. Each person must heal the need to be better than others, specifically they must confront the feelings of superiority or inferiority within themselves that cause them to exert power over others or allow others to take power away from them. Each person must heal themselves and regain balance. Only then will they realise that as they heal the separation of aspects of themselves, they will return to balance within their own lives.

As each person does this, it will be easier for others to do the same. When each person returns to balance, they will realise that the power that they seek is within, it is not found by exerting power over another. Only then will they know that they cannot be controlled by outside events and people or be kept in a state of subservience, and they will seek to implement strategies that are of benefit to all.

People are waking up and seeing that greed and need for control, which benefits the few, is leading to a situation that is untenable. Lies that have been told to maintain the secrecy about what is really happening, are being exposed.

Those who are in control do not welcome changes in awareness.

Whilst Earth's situation looks grim, the fact that the elite are now choosing to use the weapons of destruction listed earlier in this chapter, rather than much more subtle strategies like mind control and perception manipulation as they have done in the immediate past, indicates that they are losing power. Whilst most identify the elite few as being the problem, the real problem is that the lessons that the situation on Earth at present is designed to teach, have not yet been understood by the many.

It is important to realise that the controlling elite who appear to be the problem are not the problem. Their role is simply to be a catalyst for understanding and growth. I suspect that they will push harder and harder in an effort to maintain control until such time that the people of Earth learn what they have not previously understood. I don't know what that is for certain, but I suspect it is something like: 'everyone and everything is equally important and all have a contribution to make' and that 'Earth and its inhabitants are inter-dependent.

Neither can exist without the other.' When whatever it is that needs to be understood, is understood, the shift that has been expected will occur.

As this is happening the universe seems to be co-operating. Earth's prime resonance vibrational frequency is increasing as the increased Schumann Resonance frequency shows. High frequency energy is being directed to Earth, and Earth is responding in ways that are unpredictable in terms of extreme weather conditions, volcanic eruptions and earthquakes.

§

Energy frequency increases as people release the low frequency emotional energies of fear, anger, rage, hate, envy and guilt that they have held onto. The reason for the shift that is happening may not be understood, but it is being felt because anything and everything that goes against the prime resonance frequency is being destroyed by its own dissonance. When there is dissonance or disharmony, things break and fall apart. This is what is happening for the elite and for those who operate at a low frequency. As Earth's resonance increases, because of release of negative energies by more and more people, the structures of control that have been put in place by the elite are crumbling. It is for this reason that individuals must make the effort to increase their own personal resonance in alignment with Earth.

Exposure of the truth is needed at this time because we are shifting into a different dimension, a world very different from what we have experienced up until now. It will be a world of co-operation not domination, a world of love, not hate, a world that demonstrates heaven on Earth: the translation of all that is good, in material form.

Chapter 23
The Plan

My purpose in writing *Everything in Its Place* has been to provide evidence that within each of us we have the capacity to overcome the conditioning of past traumatic experiences. Once we do this, we move into a state where we perceive the world as it really is: a perception that is different from how we have learnt to perceive it. Seeing things as they really are, rather than through negative filters that we have created, allows us to understand why we have behaved in the way we have in the past. When filters are removed, different and better choices are available to us: choices which involve acceptance, patience, compassion and allowing. When this happens, the sense of separation between ourselves and the rest of the world also vanishes.

The plan as it applies for individuals, must also apply to Earth if the principle of the hologram holds true.

It is important that people understand this because the world is at a point where the imperative to make a choice is crucial. We can choose to evolve by releasing the conditioning that has caused humanity to adopt destructive, aggressive, violent, and self-centred attitudes of personal gain, or we can continue along the path on which the people of Earth are now travelling; a pathway to annihilation. This really is an evolve or die moment in Earth's history.

Collaboration with, rather than separation from, each other and with our ecosystem is required. But for as long as people are susceptible to manipulation by powerful people who control the narrative, this cannot happen. As with individuals, when the collective is open to seeing the truth, which is that they are capable of taking control of their lives rather than being controlled by others, change happens.

I am optimistic that a choice has been made and that the people of Earth are actually doing the work that needs to be done. Some, like those I have referred to in *Everything in Its Place*, have shed light on repressed childhood traumas and in doing so they have enabled the expression of their emotions. Unhindered by the weight of negative programs, they have regained the ability to perceive and act upon deep inner guidance, which is leading them to take actions that will benefit both themselves and their communities. My reward has been in seeing lives transformed.

As the Elohim have told me, this is a cumulative process. For Earth to shift, the process needs to be applied collectively. This is happening as more people become aware of the reality of situations, as opposed to a false narrative presented by those who contrive situations and the explanation of those situations, for their own benefit. What is needed is for situations to be presented truthfully rather than as false narratives.

At an individual level I have described how people enslave and are enslaved by others in personal relationships. I have shown how racism, sexism, social ostracism and other forms of bigotry prevent wholesome relationships. With intense inner

Chapter 23 The Plan

work it is possible to learn the truth about ourselves and this is required before we can begin to resolve the problems that have been obscured by disinformation.

§

More than thirty years ago I received a channelled message from the Elohim that I didn't initially understand. I now realise that this is what quantum scientists have come to realise. It is how life operates but more importantly it provides a framework for thinking of how we will solve the problems that lie ahead.

Matter manifests when the mind chooses that it manifest. Universe is everything — and nothing. It contains all the thoughts that have ever existed and since there is nothing other than thought that is all there is. At the same time, it is nothing because thought is nothing but vibration.

We trick ourselves into believing that what we see is real. For each of us, reality is different because we create our own reality on the basis of our past experiences. Everything that we create is a hallucination because, in truth, the only thing that is, is energy. Thought is energy. We have the power to manipulate this energy from flowing waves, to static particles or to solid crystal by thought. Energy in motion is created by thought and contains all the information of the universe.

Until we start to accept responsibility for things being the way we design them, we will continue to experience those things which will provide us with understanding both of our own power and of the way things are. This is the main purpose of experience for each of us.

We tap into this information at the level of our own vibrational frequency. When our frequency is at a high level, we tap into the knowledge which corresponds to it: knowledge of how the universe operates and the structures of the material, ethereal and angelic realms. Working with such vibration, we understand the meaning of the universe, the meaning of life itself.

It is an exciting yet challenging journey, moving upwards in vibrational frequency. We are given examples of such journeys in the stories of the 'enlightened ones'. Such journeys are undertaken because of the need to satisfy an inner yearning, an inner direction, which propels us to cast aside the misconceptions of the material world, and to seek something else. It is not a matter of better or worse, it is just different.

The journey to understanding of the material world is just as worthwhile as the journey to understanding of the higher realms. They differ only in terms of frequency. It is like preferring to tune into radio band 1164 rather than 1248. What you get from each is different in quality but not in substance. The messages are essentially the same, or rather, are based on the same formulae or rules.

The problem with being in tune with the energy pattern of the material world is that we pick up information which is not always pleasant. The sordid details of life on Earth don't make us feel very good. To let go all that is sordid and squalid we have to let go all that is sordid and squalid in our

Chapter 23 The Plan

own being. These events are merely reflections of our cellular encoding and the blocks we retain in place of our inability to remember.

Remembering, including the memories of feeling, is all that is needed to change the vibrational level at which we operate. The events of our lives are designed as the tools we require to spark off the process of memory. Whilst we do almost everything in our power to keep these memories hidden, because of shame, guilt, fear and confusion that is associated with each memory, the design of human life is so brilliant that total blocking is impossible. Resistance is possible for just so long.

You have the Laws of Universe and you have everything you need to move into balance, to be at one with All That Is. Life can be lived with ease when the Laws of Universe are taken into consideration. Understanding of the Laws provides guidelines for the future. When one lives at variance with the Laws, problems arise.

First you need to become aware that the imbalance exists. Then become aware of the messages of your body and the messages that the universe is providing you. Things don't happen by accident. They occur by design. The design is magnificent. Understand that you are far greater than you have ever dreamed — as great as the universe. As great as All That Is. From the holographic principle, you are All That Is. It cannot be any other way.

Understand this and you understand All That Is and you know that everything is in its place. You know it all already.

This book is simply a tool to help you remember that it is time. Trust what you know to be true.

In order to understand the meaning of this message I had to:
1. Discover what was true as opposed to that which was an illusion. Things that felt true, generally were true.
2. Take responsibility for what happened in my life.
3. Work to increase my own vibrational frequency by identifying the negative programs I had written for my life. This is an on-going process.
4. Release the blocked energy of low vibration emotions. This was my most difficult task and it too, is on-going.
5. Become aware of the messages I was being given. I was fortunate that some of the more profound messages came from the Elohim but others came from people I met, from my experiences and by looking at the consequences of the actions I took.
6. Learn to trust the process and accept that everything happens by design.
7. Incorporate the Universal Laws of Nature within my daily life.

§

Mine has been a fascinating and totally enthralling journey of discovery and it has taught me much.

What have I gained from the journey I have undertaken?

Chapter 23   The Plan

The most important thing I have learnt, is that life is not random. There is a purpose for each individual and for everything as a whole. I am not sure that I really know where this purpose originates, or where it is taking us, but I am confident that there is a higher intelligence at work, somehow or somewhere. That higher intelligence and everything that emanates from that higher intelligence is how I define All That Is.

I have come a long way towards letting go judgement of confrontational events, people associated with those events, and of myself for having had to experience them. Letting go judgement has involved acceptance of everything and everyone. I have realised that whilst I hold onto judgement, I create separation and unconditional love cannot exist where there is separation. I don't have to like everything or everyone. I just have to accept even those things I don't like and don't want as aspects of All That Is. Where I haven't liked my experiences, I have learnt to accept them as tools of learning.

I have learnt that for learning to be meaningful it must be grounded in practical experience.

I have learnt to trust that what I have been given, was what I needed to experience even when I didn't like it. When I have learnt what the experience was designed to teach me, I moved on. It has been that simple. When I resisted the experience, I stayed stuck until I stopped fighting. What I resisted, persisted.

I have learnt that my journey through life has had purpose and the end result is spiritual evolution. It has been my experience that nothing happened accidentally. I strongly feel that there is a universal design in place and when I worked with the design, rather than fought against it, I had a greater chance of happiness and connection with All That Is.

§

For me it has been a long and eventful journey. The essence of what I have discovered was summed up beautifully by artist Tom Bass. In answer to the question: 'What has life taught you?' he replied:

> When I was sixty-eight, I was full of incomprehension still. I was sitting at the table and I got a sudden flash of explanation. Everything that happens has meaning. There's no question of sorting out and saying: 'This is dreadful. God shouldn't have allowed this to happen'.
>
> As I got the thought, I got an image of a water-worn pebble, which began existence as a jagged piece of stone, then had countless encounters with other objects — some could have been catastrophic — which finally shaped it. And everything becomes the essence of the shape it is.
>
> A pebble is always a pebble whether it be rough or smooth, round or uneven in shape. Ultimately, through experience, we understand that being a pebble is what life is all about. The shape, size, texture is irrelevant. We don't judge a pebble because it is slightly worn, or slightly misshapen. That's what makes it an interesting pebble.
>
> When we understand that we are all pebbles and stop judging ourselves and others for being the wrong sort of pebble, we know who we really are. We understand the

relationship between us and the Earth. We understand the meaning and purpose of life in general and the meaning and purpose of our own life specifically. We understand the laws and principles that apply within the universe and how life is to be lived if we are to operate within those laws.

Chapter 24
In the Beginning

'Where are you Carol?'

'I'm back in the 'God space' I went to last session. That was the space of total nothingness where I had nowhere to go. I felt lost and my fear was that in being and having nothing I didn't exist. But in that space I realise that the situation is not one of non-existence but of pure potential because within that space there is energy: the energy of thought. It is by thought that creation happens.

This time, within that space, I don't feel so lost, so directionless. But I still can't be seen or acknowledged and when I am not acknowledged I feel worthless. Again, without acknowledgement, I don't exist.'

'So go to a time when you felt totally worthless.'

'It is a time when I have given birth to a deformed and grotesque baby. I feel bereft, gutted and worthless and I don't want to accept responsibility for being the creator of such an atrocity.'

'What did you decide when you gave birth to a deformed and grotesque baby?'

'If my creation is not acknowledged I don't exist.'

'Go back to the place where you felt as if you did not exist.'

'It is the place of total nothingness. '

'So what happened?'

'First there was the thought 'I don't exist.' It is not possible to know that existence exists without reflection. Duality is created in order to acknowledge existence. The created negative polarity is judged to be abhorrent.'

'What happens then?'

'Over time the negative is more and more prevalent. We are now immersed in the negative polarity: in fear, anger, sadness and all other so-called negative emotions, and we choose to not feel. We push the negative feelings down, hide and judge them. We don't want to acknowledge or experience them'.

'What have you learned from doing this?'

'In retrospect I feel that in that 'god space' there is nothing but unconditional love but it wasn't recognised. This caused the first judgement. The polarity of love was created. Non acceptance of the negative polarity caused it to become more and more significant.'

'So what do you have to do to change that?'

'Just accept that all emotions — so called 'negative and positive' — are part of the whole and we need to experience them because without the experience love wouldn't be recognised.'

'So what have you learned from this?'

'The 'God space' is a place of unconditional love, but I did not recognise it then. If love is all there is, it is not appreciated because there is nothing to compare it with. I have had to understand that I can exist without external *acknowledgment. That's what I have learned that I didn't understand initially. In fact it cannot come from others. It can only be given to me by me. This lesson is profound and is the result of so called 'negative experiences' in my life so far. We seek love from others but until we learn to love ourselves unconditionally we cannot give to or receive it from others.'*

www.ingramcontent.com/pod-product-compliance
Lightning Source LLC
Chambersburg PA
CBHW021050080526

44587CB00010B/200